C0-BPZ-626

3 2711 00104 1767

DATE DUE

Demco, Inc. 38-293

ENTERED OCT 2 5 2006

TRANSNATIONAL MEDIA AND CONTOURED MARKETS

Concerning this book...

"Amos Owen Thomas presents a compelling case that the conditions under which global communications operate are a dynamic intersection between the local and the global. This is a welcome, pioneering addition to the literature on transnational communication."

BRIAN SHOESMITH
ADJUNCT PROFESSOR, EDITH COWAN UNIVERSITY, AUSTRALIA
DIRECTOR, MEDIA STUDIES, UNIVERSITY OF LIBERAL ARTS, DHAKA

"The author makes his unique contribution to knowledge by critically examining the strengths and limitations of different lines of scholarship.... His survey of the very extensive literature relevant to the issue is comprehensive, systematic and perceptive."

WILLIAM MELODY
MANAGING DIRECTOR, LIRNE.NET
VISITING PROFESSOR, TECHNICAL UNIVERSITY OF DENMARK

"Robust and coherent.... Will constitute a significant contribution to our understanding of transnational broadcasting in Asia."

INDRAJIT BANERJEE
SECRETARY-GENERAL, ASIAN MEDIA INFORMATION
AND COMMUNICATION CENTRE (AMIC), SINGAPORE

"This book is unique because it does not pretend to prescribe a solution; rather it offers bountiful information on wide ranges of subjects surrounding the debate on international advertising (mass media, culture, government policies, economic status and financing) that marketers would find useful as they embark on a particular campaign. Thus, Amos may be redirecting the future debate on the subject by telling marketers what to think about, but not to do."

EMMANUEL C. ALOZIE
UNIVERSITY PROFESSOR OF MEDIA COMMUNICATIONS
GOVERNORS STATE UNIVERSITY, ILLINOIS
CO-EDITOR OF *TOWARD THE COMMON GOOD* (2004)

COLUMBIA COLLEGE LIBRARY
600 S. MICHIGAN AVENUE
CHICAGO, IL 60605

TRANSNATIONAL MEDIA AND CONTOURED MARKETS

Redefining Asian Television and Advertising

AMOS OWEN THOMAS

SAGE Publications
New Delhi / Thousand Oaks / London

COLUMBIA COLLEGE LIBRARY
600 S. MICHIGAN AVENUE
CHICAGO, IL 60605

Copyright © Amos Owen Thomas, 2006

All rights reserved. No part of this book may be reproduced or utilised in any form or by any means, electronic or mechanical, including photocopying, recording or by any information storage or retrieval system, without permission in writing from the publisher.

First published in 2006 by

Sage Publications India Pvt Ltd
B-42, Panchsheel Enclave
New Delhi 110 017
www.indiasage.com

Sage Publications Inc
2455 Teller Road
Thousand Oaks, California 91320

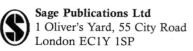

Sage Publications Ltd
1 Oliver's Yard, 55 City Road
London EC1Y 1SP

Published by Tejeshwar Singh for Sage Publications India Pvt Ltd, photo-typeset in 10/12 Calisto MT by Star Compugraphics Private Limited, Delhi and printed at Chaman Enterprises, New Delhi.

Library of Congress Cataloging-in-Publication Data

Thomas, Amos Owen, 1954–
    Transnational media and contoured markets: redefining asian television and advertising/Amos Owen Thomas.
        p. cm.
    Includes bibliographical references and index.
    1. Television—Asia. 2. Digital media. 3. Globalization. I. Title.

| HE8700.9.A78T49 | 384.55095—dc22 | 2006 | 2006008454 |

ISBN: 0–7619–3483–9 (Hb)   81–7829–630–6 (India–Hb)
        0–7619–3484–7 (Pb)   81–7829–631–4 (India–Pb)

Sage Production Team: Malathi Ramamoorthy, Rrishi Raote, Girish Sharma, Sanjeev Sharma and Santosh Rawat

CONTENTS

LIST OF TABLES

LIST OF FIGURES

This book and its companion volume, *Imagi-Nations and Borderless Television*, have their roots in two distinct experiences of mine in the Asia-Pacific region decades ago. The first was that of adapting global advertising campaigns for East Asia or creating campaigns for multinational marketers which could be utilised in one or more countries in the region, as copywriter in international advertising agencies based in Singapore. The other was encountering transnational television from Australia, the US and Indonesia available quasi-illegally via satellite and cable in Papua New Guinea, a developing country in the South Pacific, while resident there as an expatriate academic. Both of these experiences raised the issues of the globalisation of media, advertising, economy and culture. Yet when first seeking to research this in the late 1980s, transnational television was not yet a reality across much of Asia and my interest in it seemed somewhat esoteric. But in the early 1990s it was to take the continent and its media industries by storm, stimulating much premature speculation about its consequences, both good and bad.

Over the past decade or so, my views on the issue of globalisation and approach to researching the media industry have metamorphosed somewhat. The varied schools of thought on globalisation across multiple academic disciplines—sociology, political science, literary studies, communications, marketing—were far more than I had realised or initially thought relevant. On empirical aspects I was soon finding that some of my earlier hunches about the impact of the new medium were not quite borne out in many of the countries I visited and so new analysis was needed. As such this book is both a chronicle and creative outcome of a professional journey of discovery of over a decade within the television and advertising industries in Asia, not to mention the increasingly convergent media, communications, telephony and information industries. I trust that its insights are helpful to others who, like me, are fascinated by transnational television via satellite/cable, and eager to understand how these media are shaping and being shaped by our world, at least from an Asia-Pacific vantage point.

Amos Owen Thomas
Maastricht, the Netherlands

ACKNOWLEDGEMENTS

A work of the magnitude of this book and its predecessor owes many a debt to more people than it is possible to list comprehensively. Unfortunately, there is neither space nor time to acknowledge exactly how they helped over the long gestation of these books. Those mentioned here, from academia, industry, government and elsewhere, were particularly supportive of my research in varied ways and to whom I am deeply grateful.

Australasia: John Sinclair, Lynda Berends, Robin Jeffrey, Steve Crook, Albert Moran, Tom O'Regan, Tim Scrase, James Gray, Andrew Gibson.

Southeast Asia: Jonathan Parapak, Naswil Idris, Hinca Panjaitan, Lotte Mohammad, Milton Oh, Yusca Ismail, Ishadi S.K., Gunadi Sugiharso, Rosni Jaafar, Samsudin Rahim, Tan Sio Chian, O.M. Khushu, Jeyasingham.

Northeast Asia: André Nair, Keith Taylor, Robert Wilson, Joseph Man Chan, Tim Foley, Samuel Liu, Katie Fung, Georgette Wang.

South Asia: Keval Kumar, Katy Merchant, Radha Iyer, Anil Wanwari, M.R. Dua, Jayasree Lengade, P.R.P. Nair, Roop Sharma.

There are more yet, particularly the over 200 interviewees and others who have provided me with data or helped in various practical ways over almost a decade, without which this book might not have been possible. Many would actually prefer to remain anonymous. Still I would like to record my appreciation to them for the time and energy they put into cooperating with me, and hope that if they should read this book, they might discern their tangible contribution to knowledge.

To the many others who as colleagues, family and friends played a supportive role, I am deeply grateful. This book is dedicated to the memory of my late mother, Mabel Selima Owen Thomas, from whom I inherited a love of reading and learning.

Fieldwork for this book was mostly conducted between 1994 and 2002, and some work-in-progress was presented at various academic and policy conferences. Later versions of some papers were subsequently published as journal articles or invited as chapters for edited books, in both communications and business disciplines. My own thinking on the subject has matured and been radicalised over the decade. Thus the current book *Transnational Media and Contoured Markets* represents not just a significant updating of data but deviation from earlier partial publications as those familiar with the latter might not help noticing.

References

Thomas, Amos Owen (1998). "Transnational Satellite Television and Advertising in SE Asia", *Journal of Marketing Communications*, 4 (4), pp. 1–17.

——— (1998). "Transnational Satellite Television in Asia: Current Approaches of Marketers", in Gabriel Ogunmukum and Ronald Gabbay (eds), *Classical and Contemporary Issues in Marketing*. Perth: Academic Press International/University of Western Australia, pp. 145–63.

——— (1999). "Broadcast Satellites in Asia: Global Actors on a Continental Stage", *Transnational Broadcasting Studies*, 1 (2), Spring. (www.tbsjournal.com)

——— (1999). "Australia Television in Southeast Asia: Free-to-air yet Scarcely Rebroadcast", *Australian Journal of Communication*, 26 (2), pp. 97–111.

——— (2000). "Transborder Television for Greater China Markets: Hong Kong as Sub-regional Hub?", in David French and Michael Richards (eds), *Television in Contemporary Asia*. London, New Delhi and Thousand Oaks: Sage Publications, pp. 91–110.

——— (2000). "Marketing, Advertising and the New Media: Transnational, Multi-domestic or Postmodern?", in S.B. Dahiya (ed.), *Current State of Business Disciplines: Volume 6*. Rohtak: Spellbound Publishers, pp. 2577–90.

——— (2001). "Transborder Television in Asian Contexts: Towards a Contingency Approach to Strategy", *International Quarterly Journal of Marketing*, 1 (1), January, pp. 73–84.

——— (2001). "The Quiet Transition in Indonesian Television", *InterMedia*, 26 (3), January.

EMERGENCE AND DIVERGENCE

O ver the 1990s, transnational television providers entered the Asian media marketplace in fairly rapid succession. The first Gulf crisis and subsequent war in 1991 was the catalyst for the reception of "live" news via ad hoc downlinking of CNN satellite transmissions. But the pioneer broadcaster to target Asia, StarTV, commenced by beaming its five channels from AsiaSat1 in late 1991 and claimed household penetration figures across the continent which kept increasing by the tens of millions each year. While StarTV was acknowledged as the early market leader, its audience research had the advertising and broadcasting industries expressing some doubts about reliability and validity. The aspiring pan-Asian broadcaster's silence on actual viewership and advertising revenue raised further suspicions. In the mid-1990s the global media conglomerate News Corporation bought first a controlling interest and eventually all of StarTV from its founding Asian owners and altered its strategic direction. Around the same time other global channels like MTV, ESPN, Discovery, TNT and HBO entered the fray, first broadcasting via satellites previously used solely for domestic broadcasting before migrating to more powerful satellite platforms with Asia-wide broadcast footprints. Transnational channels that came later to Asia, often specialised in business, entertainment, movie, news, educational, children's and women's programming, among other niche market segments in search of audiences with which to entice advertisers.

CROWDED SKIES, DIVIDED PIE

With the launching of newer satellites in the mid- to late 1990s, a plethora of channels went on air, many of them clones of the pioneers.

Specialist business services such as Asian Business News and CNBC Asia began to appear, followed by a number of regional channels in Asian languages led by TVB Superchannel and ZeeTV. Some Asian governments took to beaming their domestic quasi-commercial channels via satellite, intentionally directed towards other countries and diasporic communities in their region and beyond. Public broadcasters which decided to go regional, even global, included China's CCTV and India's Doordarshan. Other transnational broadcasters were relative newcomers from associated media industries such as film and music production, such as MGM Gold and Sony Entertainment Television. Soon satellite-broadcast channels were being re-transmitted selectively on domestic terrestrial channels or via cable networks that carried also their competitors. Early transnational channels such as CNN and StarTV might initially have appeared as instruments of western media imperialism, but many soon adapted their global or pan-Asian content for specific regional, national or ethnic markets. This stimulated the creation of channels within and directed at regional markets such as Greater China and the Indian subcontinent, and national markets like Taiwan and India. Even subnational ethnic-language channels like Cantonese and Tamil and diasporic groups across West Asia and Southeast Asia were soon targeted. Thus there has been a blurring of the distinctions between global, regional and domestic broadcasts, as well as between satellite, cable and terrestrial channels.

The ascendancy of global media corporations in Asia, as in Europe, has been predicated on the commercialisation of the television medium. Multinational corporations wishing to market their products nationally or regionally are sought as major sponsors of the growth of commercial television, with their advertising agencies serving as catalysts. The deregulated 1980s and 1990s had seen a more diversified market for communications media and the unimpeded dominance of international advertising agencies in many national markets worldwide. The arrival of transnational television in Asia spawned speculation that viewership of domestic television would decline and hence national advertising might be increasingly consolidated into regional, if not global, advertising. Despite being major players in the media industry, advertising and marketing are oft-neglected fields in media research, a situation which this book will attempt to redress. This book will survey the transnational television channels in South, Southeast and Northeast Asia in the early 1990s to early 2000s, meta-analysing their growth in the context of the politico-economic and sociocultural environments and wider media and advertising industries of the region.

Television was seen as essential to the economic strategies of most countries in the developing world since the 1950s and 1960s, and thus a protected national resource. Among them were India, China and Indonesia, which commissioned domestic satellites early to reach far-flung corners of their nation states with public television broadcasts in support of their nationalistic agendas. Only in the 1990s did governments in Asia face the intrusion into their media-space of trans-national broadcasts via both satellite and cable, over the reception of which by their citizens they had limited control. The television services within each country, including related cultural industries such as film production and cable operations, constitute the unique media ecology that mitigates or accentuates the impact of this new broadcast medium. Any study of transnational television must then take into consideration the historic development of domestic television in specific national markets. By the turn of the century, there were far more trans-national channels operating in Asia, and the rapid entry and exits from the market were quite impossible to keep track of. The Asia-wide scope of this book and its companion volume, *Imagi-Nations and Borderless Television*, seeks to map the television environment as a prelude to analysis of impact in specific regions and countries. Still, given the magnitude and pace of change of the market, no survey can lay claim to being fully comprehensive.

UNDERSTANDING MEDIA IMPACT

The crux of this book is an exploration of the impact the new medium had principally on the television and advertising industries of Asia, secondarily on sociocultural and politico-economic changes in its diverse nation-states, and vice versa. By and large, the evidence cited thus far in support of government policies concerning transnational television has been largely anecdotal and speculative in nature. The other data commonly referenced is proprietary market research commissioned by the broadcasters and advertisers themselves, such as audience ratings which largely remain well-guarded commercial secrets and which in any case are quite deficient in assessing broader societal impact. Adopting an empirical as well as critical approach, and utilising both qualitative and quantitative data gathered from primary and secondary sources, this book aims to understand the growth and development of transnational television in Asia. Few studies of complex phenomena, even if qualitative and phenomenological, begin without a tentative conceptual framework or some orientating ideas, and the present book is no exception. Thus some issues concerning the relationships between various factors have been gleaned from the vast literature on social change, media theory, global communications, international marketing and advertising management to help guide this critical exploration of the historical development of transnational television in Asia.

Media and Communications Globalisation

How have transnational satellite broadcasters differentiated among themselves, and from domestic broadcasters, by their programming strategies? Has advertiser and audience response or non-response to their offerings in Asia affected transnational broadcaster programming strategies subsequently? How have domestic television broadcasters responded to the entry of this new competitor of transnational satellite television? Which of their strategies have proved more effective than others in retaining and/or attracting audiences and advertisers, and why? These questions seek to examine the competitive environment of television broadcasting, including the globalisation and localisation strategies. The situation will be analysed using interview responses, content analysis of programme schedules and taped prime time programmes, in-country observation and inter-media commentary.

Marketing and Advertising Globalisation

Has transnational television stimulated the consolidation of advertising strategy, media buying or creative execution through international advertising agencies? If this has not happened in all or any markets, what are the reasons? What are the types of products and brands advertised on transnational television? What are the target markets of and creative styles used in commercials on this new medium? How different are these from advertising on domestic television in various countries? Has domestic advertising imitated global advertising, thus contributing further to cultural change? These questions seek to discover whether and how the new transnational medium has affected the practice of advertising, and answers will be inferred from secondary data provided by advertising agencies, media owners and market researchers, as well as their interview responses and content analysis of commercials.

The transnationalisation of marketing and advertising has taken place in tandem with the spread of the capitalist world economy, growth of global marketing and the development of new electronic media. Yet, there has been a considerable lag in understanding of the phenomenon, both its managerial and social implications. An increasing body of research in the developing nations of Latin America, Africa and Asia suggests that the impact of new electronic media depends rather on the political ideologies, integration with the world economy, cultural and language affinities, domestic television and film industries, consumer affluence and more. By adopting a mid-range approach of media-market strategy, one that draws from both the macro-perspective of political economy and the micro-perspective of cultural studies, this book addresses an apparent gap in systematic analysis on the diffusion of transnational television across Asia and beyond at the turn of the twenty-first century.

SYNERGY OR AUTONOMY

The concept of globalisation is critical to transnational television, yet it still remains unclear. For both in the academic use of the term across different disciplines and the popular usage of the term in various professional fields it has acquired a plurality of meanings. Hence we begin with a literature review in Chapter 2 that surveys the phenomenon of globalisation, its antecedents, causes and dynamics, as well as its consequences and potentialities. It begins with the media-broadcasting arena and then turns to the specific fields of marketing and advertising, revisiting questions raised by past research. The alternative theoretical perspectives and research paradigms they suggest, as well as reflections on the strengths of the research methodology adopted by this book, are spelt out in Appendix C. Further issues surrounding the impact of satellite and cable television, drawn from the extensive literature on globalisation, are interspersed across the book. Then the pivotal Chapter 3 discusses the metamorphosis of StarTV from a pan-Asian to a regional broadcaster and its impact on audiences in key markets in Asia, anchored by India, Indonesia and China.

Developments in transnational television in Asia over 1992–2002 were documented in greater detail in the preceding book, *Imagi-Nations and Borderless Television*, which identifies and classifies the major players, both channel providers and satellite platforms, as well as their corporate ownership links. Chapter 4 in this book comprises an introduction to the regions of South, Southeast Asia and Northeast Asia, with particular reference to their history, geography, cultural policies and broadcasting development. Chapter 5 investigates the role of the new medium on the globalisation of marketing in the three specific countries, while Chapter 6 provides a comparative study of advertising strategy in relation to transnational television as practised in three major cities. Chapter 7 extends the application of a previously introduced analytical framework to the comparative experience of transnational television and advertising in selected countries and cities. Then the general implications of the research findings for businesses, particularly in the media and cultural industries of the region and beyond are sketched in Chapter 8. Finally the anticipated socio-ethical consequences of media globalisation for rapid political, economic, social and cultural change in the developing countries are touched on from the author's personal standpoint in Chapter 9. In seeking to provide breadth of coverage across Asian regions, some depth of detail about countries and industry players has had to be sacrificed in this book. Furthermore, since the field of transnational media and advertising was progressing at a rapid pace at the turn of the twenty-first century in Asia, it has simply not been possible to report, let alone analyse, all developments in the region up-to-the-minute. Still, in adopting a systematic approach in analysis of media industries, this book, along with its companion volume, *Imagi-Nations and Borderless Media*, focuses on developments during the first decade following the advent of transnational television in Asia.

PUBLIC VERSUS PRIVATE DOMAINS

Adoption of improved communication technologies tends to reduce national control over information, ideas and culture, as governments of developing countries have found to their chagrin. Nonetheless some developing countries have sought to prohibit or at least limit access to transnational broadcasts, with varying degrees of success. Thus the development of the new medium has been far from uniform across Asia, in part because national governments have responded in differing ways to the perceived threat of globalisation to their cultures. But the limited academic research available thus far on transnational television suggests that its impact on national audiences may not be moderated by regulatory policies alone. This research will examine the various factors that explain the varying diffusion of transnational television in the three regions studied, with the intention of being able to generalise some of the findings to other developing countries in Asia, if not further afield. It will also examine the concerns of governments regarding erosion of national culture as well as the claims of transnational broadcasters to deliver sizeable cross-border market segments.

The debate in international marketing over whether to globalise or localise strategies that has raged on for a few decades still remains unresolved. This is despite attempts by some theorists to make a case for middle-road strategies like regionalisation or selective adaptation of marketing elements. As far as advertising is concerned, some international business academics and executives would argue that globalisation is imperative given the increasing international competition with the lowering of trade barriers, homogenisation of consumer markets and convergence of media technologies. The relatively few empirical studies on comparative advertising, based largely on content analysis of advertisements or surveys of decision makers, have failed to provide definitive answers to this debate. This book will endeavour to describe salient factors affecting market response to transnational satellite television such as the character of domestic television alternatives, linguistic and cultural barriers, production costs, consumer affluence and advertising revenues.

On the one hand, transnational satellite television has gone regional, multi-domestic, even subnational, forming symbiotic relationships with domestic and regional partners. On the other hand, broadcasters of domestic and regional origin have developed markets for their media products and services which have crossed borders within their own region, penetrated other regions of Asia and catered to ethnic minorities on other far-flung continents to the detriment of national identity and possibly civil society as well. In an increasingly globalised world, the media have demonstrably been influenced by such diverse factors as national integration with the world-economy, cultural and language affinities, domestic television and film industries, consumer affluence and advertiser sponsorship.

In the context of Asia, where most of the world's population lives, this book investigates how globalisation of the media and advertising has occurred within the larger context of economic, political, social and cultural processes within regions, nation states, transborder ethnic communities, even international diaspora. It will demonstrate that in the case of transnational television, growth was influenced not just by governments and policy makers and regulators but also by the management decisions of media-owners, cable operators, satellite providers, advertising agencies, marketers, software developers and other players, whether proactive or reactive. It will document and examine the responses of domestic and regional marketers as well as their advertising agencies to the new media alternative. Not only might this book explicate the processes of television and advertising globalisation in selected Asian markets, it should also raise some socio-ethical issues that need to be addressed in managing newer electronic media in other emerging markets around the world. It is hoped that this book will prove to be useful to scholar, policy maker and practitioner alike seeking to understand the global media and advertising industries at the turn of the twenty-first century, from a developing world perspective.

2   MEDIATING GLOBALISATION

The widespread use, currently, of the term "globalisation" in media and business circles certainly reflects an acute awareness of the interdependence of economies and societies within a world system. Although advocates of newer communications technologies claim access to information will lead to greater democratisation within societies and equality between nations, critics point out that in reality such technologies perpetuate the status quo of inequity and dependency. Furthermore, the growth of new media may be facilitating global networks of information and political action, yet seriously undermining the role of governments. Significant in the development of such media through commercialisation are global marketing and advertising, though their mediating impact on culture and consumption in Asia has been relatively overlooked.

MEDIA AND COMMUNICATIONS

Geostationary satellites, digital transmission, optical fibre, satellite television, broadband cable, mobile telephony, computer networks, electronic mail and the World Wide Web are among the many forms of technology which have revolutionised global media and communications in recent decades. On a global level development and control of such state-of-the-art technologies lie with developed countries and their multinational corporations, and their services are distributed only selectively to developing countries. Even within the latter countries, control of and access to communications are often largely in the hands of the local elite with transnational cultural affinities and economic links. Just as corporate and government decisions concerning media and communications hardware and software are being made increasingly with the global context in mind, so must transnational television in Asia be analysed and understood.

Media Technologies

The idea of using satellites as a means of global communications has been attributed to the broadcast engineer and science-fiction writer, Arthur C. Clarke, who in 1945 spelt out the technical criteria necessary. Placed in geostationary berths above the equator, satellites orbit the earth at the same speed as the earth rotates and thus stay above the same location. Beams broadcast from their transponders could then cover up to a third of the world's surface at a time that constitutes their footprint. This renders distances on earth immaterial since the distance of one city from the satellite is practically the same as it is from another (Frederick 1993: 91–99). Consequently for a signal to travel from Singapore to nearby Kuala Lumpur via a satellite such as AsiaSat2 takes the same time and cost as for it to travel from Tokyo across the continent to Kuwait. Applied to television, satellite technology has meant that costs of broadcasting become independent of audience distance, while costs of downlinking and redistribution of signals are low. Uplinking is possible from mobile earth stations anywhere within the satellite's footprint or reception zone on the earth's surface, as is downlinking via increasingly smaller satellite dishes by small entrepreneurs and consumers alike, thus making control of access by authorities difficult.

Though a number of developing countries launched satellites for domestic telecommunications purposes, they continued to be dependent on developed countries for technology manufacture and maintenance, and are relatively minor players on the global stage. Hamelink (1983) argued that technologies such as satellite television remained concentrated in the hands of developed or core countries and their services are disseminated to developing or periphery countries, to borrow the terminology of "world-systems" theory. Though he neglected to point out that even within developing countries control over these communications technologies tends to be concentrated in the hands of technocrats in urban centres from which information flows unidirectionally to the rural hinterlands. On the other hand, Hoskins et al. (1997) acknowledged that the newer communications technologies destroy the tyranny of distance, lower costs of information, weaken media monopolies and supersede government regulation with consumer choice. These technologies favour simultaneously the individual and the global community over the nation state, but this view failed to address adequately the role of corporations and consequences for culture. Developing countries such as those researched for this book were more often than not in the footprint of broadcast satellites owned by developed countries and their multinational corporations (MNCs). Which of these scenarios would prove more valid in Asia is worth exploring.

With the availability of these new transnational media technologies, decisions concerning programming software and target audiences were naturally being made on a global basis by commercial entities. Unrepentant about his long-held views on media imperialism, Schiller (1991) highlighted the shift of control from the nation to the multinational corporation that has become evident in television programming, sports, politics, language and other elements of culture even in countries that maintained a strong national culture. The so-called indigenisation of television was to him no more than a copy of US television formats, replete with all the values and behaviour norms necessary for persuading consumption of the goods produced by MNCs. Denigrating "active audience", cultural studies and postmodern viewpoints, Schiller alleged that these MNCs, largely western media conglomerates, were responsible not just for media imperialism but were able to offer a total cultural package via film, printed publications, theme parks, shopping malls and more. In the era of digital and interactive media a decade on, McAllister and Turow (2002) would raise related concerns about corporate influence on editorial content, commodity fetishism through advertising and invasion of privacy. By the same token, transnational television could arguably be just one element of wider media imperialism, set to dominate the cultural landscape of Asian countries.

Broadcast Commercialisation

Claiming research support that media content and thus social consciousness globally were being controlled indirectly by the majority of multinational corporations through advertising, Nordenstreng and

Schiller (1979) promoted the concept of national sovereignty over media. Nonetheless they acknowledged that the developing world then could not be divided into capitalist versus socialist spheres of influence, and that the elite across all nations may already be part of a global economic and informational system. Mattelart (1983) also contended that multinational corporations dominate national culture and in evidence he cited the Nordenstreng and Varis (1974) research on dominant programme flows especially from the US, plus further information on news and programming distribution networks and international advertising agencies. A decade later UNESCO-sponsored research on the international television programme flows in 50 countries by Varis (1988) found that the global average of imported programmes was still approximately one-third of total programme time. However the latter study reported that there was wider variation between nations as to their imports and that much of the imported programming was predominantly from nations in the same politico-economic or geo-linguistic regions rather than from the US.

Nonetheless Schiller (1989: 115–17) himself remained convinced that the reality in television broadcasting is one of increased domination of culture by largely US corporate interests. He saw the US withdrawal from support of UNESCO in the 1980s on the pretext of defending press freedom, as a conspiracy to undermine the prime regulatory body of its cultural industries. Furthermore, the US exercised its deregulatory crusade through the World Bank/IMF stipulation requiring the privatisation of broadcasting before loans were granted to developing countries. Since public broadcasting proves expensive for developing countries and is often not able to gain popular support, commercial broadcasters who are able to attract advertising revenue will be tend to be encouraged instead. Subsequently McChesney (1999) argued that the best antidote for the relentless commercialisation of the media, in the US as throughout the world, is a resurgence of the political left. Capitalist economic systems may appear to grant civil liberties but work primarily for the interests of a wealthy minority who own, among other things, the media and thus control its output. Thus it has been effective in undermining left-wing activism in the media through their propaganda that commercial media is politically neutral. Only through traditional advocacy of left-wing politics for true democratic representation and against social inequality did McChesney see any hope of constraints being placed on unfettered and exploitative capitalism, to bring about media reforms.

Programme Flows

As early as the 1980s, Collins et al. (1988) demonstrated that neither the US nor the UK had a monopoly of programming exports when Japan and Mexico had carved out successful niches globally, and so they ridiculed alarm over imported values as overly conservative. Doubtless, some Third World programming, notably soap operas, have gone on to enjoy almost universal appeal. The Japanese creation *Oshin*, for instance, has been broadcast in over 30 countries ranging from Belgium to Indonesia, often all 297 episodes, because it had achieved iconic status, not to mention precipitated social change (Svenkerud et al. 1995). On the other hand, ardent cultural imperialism theorists like Mattelart (1983: 52–60) remained sceptical of this so-called Third World media development, arguing that it is confined to a minority of unique nations, still represents technological dependence, promotes consumption by extensive advertising and recreates colonial structures of communication. This view may have found some basis, though, in the African context. There the heavy use of imported television fiction programming was attributed to financial constraints of local production, television penetration being largely confined to the urban areas, the difficulty of catering to the diversity of languages of rural and illiterate populations, and the lack of adequate broadcasting planning and policy (Ndumbu 1991).

Yet the prevalence of foreign programming may have to do with the country's differing histories with television. Researching rural communities in Brazil, Kottak (1991) discerned stages in the impact of the medium. The first stage was of novelty and mesmerisation by television, the second of selective acceptance and reworking of the message, the third of community saturation and lack of differentiation among viewers, and the fourth of a national television culture. Research in the Dominican Republic pointed to programme genre being a significant factor in determining country-of-origin of the more popular programmes: for example, local news and variety shows from the republic itself, telenovelas from the Latin American region, feature films, action series, foreign news, children's and scientific programmes from the US and Europe (Straubhaar and Viscasillas 1991). Programmes of local and other Latin American origin enjoyed considerable popularity among locals, particularly among the lower-middle to lower classes and had displaced US imports over the years. In revealing the domination of local television broadcasters Televisa in Mexico and Globo in Brazil, and their successful forays into Hispanic markets worldwide via programme production and satellite television, Sinclair (1992) made the case that the cultural imperialism thesis was in need of re-definition.

International Policies

The call for a New World Information and Communication Order (NWICO) stemmed from a new realisation of the role of the media in the social, cultural, political and economic spheres of developing countries in Asia, Africa and Latin America. These former colonies were disenchanted with the media imperialism they were being sub-jected to, mainly from the US. The desire of developing countries to harness their cultural industries for socio-economic development and to redress imbalances in the worldwide flows of television program-ming was expressed in a number of international forums such as the Non-Aligned Movement, International Telecommunications Union (ITU), the UN and UNESCO in the 1970s. Seeing it as a threat to its own economic interests, the US waged a counter-campaign to discredit the proponents of NWICO by alleging that they were against freedom of the press and were for repressive control of the media by the state (Roach 1987). On the instructions of its member countries UNESCO established an International Commission for the Study of Communi-cation Problems chaired by Sean MacBride. The Commission enlarged on its brief and addressed a whole gamut of global communications issues including government controls on media, information flows, freedom and responsibility of the press, protection of journalists, com-mercialisation of the mass media, media ownership, the revolution in communications technology, and cultural policies (Kleinwachter 1993).

Even prior to the publication of the MacBride Commission report, UNESCO adopted the Mass Media Declaration in 1978 which stressed the responsibility of mass media to promote peace, international under-standing and human rights. The same year the UN General Assembly adopted a similar resolution and the next year it established the UN Committee on Information to promote the NWICO concept. In 1980 the UNESCO conference adopted the MacBride Report and established the International Programme for the Development of Communication

(IPDC), both actions being ratified by the UN that same year. This led to withdrawal of financial support from UNESCO by the US under Reagan and by the UK under Thatcher, in late 1984, alleging plans to restrict press freedoms and human rights (MacBride and Roach 1993). Despite further roundtables, conferences, and resolutions, the NWICO ideal was never achieved, in large part because programmes for its development suffered from UNESCO's financial constraints (Kleinwachter 1993). Over a decade later another UNESCO commission in 1993 on Culture and Development called for recognition of diversity and encouragement of competition in national broadcasting through public, commercial and community sources. On the level of international broadcasting its report broadcasts (Pérez de Cuéllar 1995) recommended the imposition of a form of cultural tax on satellite radio and television services for using the "global commons" of airwaves and outer space, the revenue from which could be utilised for alternative international and regional public broadcasting. But for Vincent (1997), technologies like the Global Information Infrastructure (GII) and the Information Superhighway or Internet will tend to serve narrow interests rather than address the broad social goals of NWICO. Whether these commendable ideas of UNESCO are simply platitudes or will be acted upon by the international community has yet to be seen.

Media Imperialism

At the centre of the NWICO debate in the 1980s was the issue of media imperialism, itself part of the larger phenomenon of cultural imperialism in a post-colonial or neo-colonial world. Cultural imperialism was said to occur when the cultures of developed or core countries were dominant in developing or peripheral countries, a symptom of politico-economic dependency or a similar exploitative relationship. The developed world's ignorance of other countries' cultures and history, and interest in its own political and economic agenda had tragic consequences for the developing world. Said (1994) demonstrated this by tracing the history of imperialism in western culture from nineteenth century colonial literature right down to the mass media of today. Cultural imperialism was illustrated by European colonisation of Asia and Africa in past centuries, as much as by US interventions in the Middle East, Latin America and Central Asia in the late twentieth and early twenty-first centuries. As further evidence of cultural imperialism in the media, Golding (1977: 294–300) observed that models of broadcast systems in many independent Third World nations were remarkably similar to that of their former colonists. If most television programmes were imported from developed countries it was both because of the higher cost of local production and the entertainment tastes of the local elite. So he concluded that there could be no value-free technology either, when the training provided in television production replicated what was done in the First World without regard to the objectives to which the media might be used in the Third World. Whatever programmes are produced locally are often mere clones of foreign programmes because of their low-cost formats, given a veneer of pseudo-indigenisation to satisfy domestic regulatory requirements.

The free-market capitalist argument against NWICO, on the other hand, held that freedom of information flows across borders was enshrined in the UN declaration and that development journalism was simply a euphemism for the control of the press by governments under the pretext of mobilising economic growth (Kelly 1976: 264). Others of the market school went even further to question the assumption that financial control by foreign enterprise of the media was tantamount to its political control (Vasquez 1983: 265–80). By contrast, left-leaning thinkers have argued that the principle of national sovereignty gave governments a legitimate right to decide their cultural policies and to harness the media in promoting national development. For instance, Hamelink (1983) made an impassioned plea for cultural autonomy and dissociation from the developed world, citing the positive experiences of a number of developing, often socialist countries in resisting cultural synchronisation with the West in the period 1950s to 1970s. He called on developing nations to develop alternative information policies, and offered suggestions of how both local as well as global communications resources could be adapted to support their social and economic development.

In editing a series of articles on the impact of transnational, largely US, television on Europe, Skovmand and Schrøder (1992) rejected the simplistic notion that the effect was unilateral and uniform. They further alleged that public broadcasting in Europe in the past had itself been paternalistic in reflecting only the tastes of the elite, a form of in-country imperialism. While none of the global media conglomerates had achieved dominance in any national market, Albarran and Chan-Olmsted (1998) warned that policy makers have to be watchful over consequences for competition and consumers, even from a rather right-wing media economics perspective. Herman and McChesney (1998) saw the converging media, telecommunications and advertising industries dominated by US conglomerates as new missionaries of global capitalism and a threat to national public spheres. On the other hand, Barker (1997) called for a more plural public sphere in a post-modern globalised world where the nation state has a lesser role. Nonetheless, books on transnational television in Asia such as Bhatt (1994), and Goonasekera and Lee (1998) continue to express concern for the erosion of cultural values and undermining of national sovereignty, if not for civil society and political involvement.

It is quite evident that globalisation of the media, particularly television, has been spurred by greater broadcast deregulation worldwide and the fact that new media technologies such as satellite and cable television render the goal of national media sovereignty quite unrealistic. The consequent rise of global media corporations and the broadcast of media events globally, often "live", have been predicated on the commercialisation of the television medium. Multinational corporations wishing to market their products globally are thus major sponsors of transnational television via satellite, and their advertising agencies the catalysts. Despite being complicit in the growth of global media, advertising and marketing are oft-neglected fields for international communications research, though they have been researched pragmatically by business academics and practitioners. Hence in the next section of this review of relevant academic literature, we examine the growth of international marketing and especially of globalised advertising prior as well as subsequent to the development of transnational television via satellite and cable.

MARKETING AND ADVERTISING

The decline of communism and its alternative world system has been accompanied by even greater liberalisation of economies in the capitalist developed and post-colonial developing worlds. New production technologies in what is now called the post-industrial age make it possible to source, produce and distribute in diverse and multiple locations globally. The media, often transnational in character, as well as tele-communications and universal education, all help create consumer awareness and lifestyle expectations, thus stimulating demand for a wide variety of goods and services even in the more remote and less developed parts of the world. These factors and more have contributed to the globalisation of markets which is accepted uncritically as the environment in which all businesses now need to operate.

International Strategies

Since proof of globalisation was often couched in terms of the production, distribution and consumption of goods and services, Mowlana (1996: 197–98) contended that the multinational corporation was a major catalyst in the process, even though it did not act alone or might have been opposed by nation states. The term "multinational corporation" commonly refers to any firm whose business is conducted substantially across several nation states, though the UN and others prefer to use the terminology of "transnational corporation" (TNC) to describe the same entity. The activities of such corporations could range from trade in goods and services and portfolio investments to foreign direct investments and direct ownership/management. Strictly, a multinational or multi-domestic strategy is one in which a company adopts an independent business strategy for each national market in which it operates. A transnational strategy, on the other hand, is defined as a decentralised one in which all national operations are coordinated to serve several other markets in which the company operates. These two strategies ought to be differentiated from a global strategy, defined as one where the core resources and responsibilities are highly centralised in the corporate headquarters which coordinate a standardised marketing strategy for a unified global market (Hill 2003). But many MNCs also camouflage their so-called global business processes with a local tinge, in a strategy called "glocalisation" which matches their post-Fordist or "dispersed" organisational structures and production processes of today.

Communication technology has been attributed with the converging of consumer demands, enabling marketers to deliver quality at a competitive price through globalised production and distribution, as amply demonstrated by Japanese manufacturers. Thus in a landmark but uncritical business article, Levitt (1983) announced the superseding of multinational marketing by global marketing. Even where there was good reason to segment, he suggested that similar segments could be found across national markets. He dismissed alternative scenarios such as of flexible production of semi-customised products and services as incapable of being price-competitive, offering no systematic research, only anecdotal evidence. Support for Levitt's globalisation thesis may be found, claimed Hill and James (1991), in the fact that products and promotions were generally considered more transferable by the executives of subsidiaries of multinational corporations researched in developing country markets than is realised by their headquarters. But Onkvisit and Shaw (1987) expressed the dissenting view that the world may not be homogenising culturally, citing evidence of a quite opposite trend. Likewise Wind (1986) criticised Levitt for lack of empirical evidence of homogenisation of consumer wants, the irrelevance of production economies given current technology and failing to recognise that synergy of multi-country operations does not depend on standardisation. Based on her research on European countries, De Mooij (2004) argues that despite convergence of macro-level economic development, micro-level consumer behaviour is stable, converging only to a point and then even diverging. This may prove valid also in the context of emergent economies worldwide and further undermine advocates of globally standardised approaches.

Reviewing research on standardisation in international marketing from the 1960s through to the 1980s, Jain (1989) rightly concluded that the issue did not present a dichotomous choice between total standardisation and total customisation, but rests on a number of factors such as similar target market, market share, nature of the product, the environment and organisational factors. Thus there might be numerous permutations of strategies that could be adopted in the process of international marketing to lessen risk of failure. Schultz and Kitchen (2000: 209) advocate the pragmatic approach, convenient to corporations, of standardisation wherever possible and adaptation whenever necessary, not just for advertising but all marketing communications. In a critique of the ongoing process of global standardisation, Ritzer (1996: 143–47) warned it had spread far beyond fast foods to education, healthcare, and the workplace in the US and was a key factor in international business expansion. The reasons for what he termed the "McDonaldisation of society" were the economic benefits to producer and consumer of identifying with positive social experiences, local culture, changes in lifestyles and other consumer products. It was therefore unremarkable that based on their survey of major US agencies, Gould et al. (1999) would conclude that globally integrated marketing communications were strategically important to marketers, regardless of whether these communications were standardised or adapted, contingent on particular environments. Thus the ongoing discourse on the globalisation of marketing tends to revisit periodically a long-standing debate about its strategic aspects, including the standardisation versus customisation of advertising that remains relevant to transnational television in Asia.

International Advertising Agencies

The history of the advertising industry's expansion worldwide in the 1950s to 1970s may be characterised as a series of moves and countermoves by international advertising agencies and national governments. MNCs that entered markets made accessible by new media and deregulated distribution channels were soon followed into those markets by their home-country advertising agencies. In earlier decades, governments in many European and Third World countries had sought to limit US ownership of their domestic broadcasters and advertising agencies or restrict their use of foreign-made promotional materials in the name of nationalism and cultural policy (Tunstall 1977). But with increasing economic integration among countries on a regional basis and new electronic communications media since the 1980s, governments found it difficult to regulate their broadcasting and advertising industries. On the other hand, US advertising agencies discovered strategic advantages in going global early, in terms of size, access to capital, client loyalty, skills and knowledge, and creating barriers to entry, especially since European and Japanese MNCs had earlier not invited their domestic agencies to follow them abroad (West 1996). The rationale for global expansion of US-owned agencies was obvious in hindsight, seeing that their international advertising billings grew six times faster than their domestic billings over the period 1960 to 1989 according to Kim (1995).

While the occasional mergers of earlier decades were primarily of small-to-medium sized advertising agencies, the frequent mega-mergers and takeovers in the late 1980s were of large international advertising agencies among themselves such as BBDO, DDB and Needham to form Omnicom, J Walter Thompson and Ogilvy & Mather under WPP and so on. If agencies were thought to be in crisis in the early 1990s due to loss of the commission system, media cost inflation, rise of retailers' brands and advertising clutter (Brierley 1995), they seem to have overcome it. Much was made of the impending advent of global brands and markets by some advertising agencies in their push to form mega-agencies or to diversify into related industries both to service their existing MNC clients better and to bid for new business worldwide. It took the agency Saatchi & Saatchi to pioneer the expansion into non-communications businesses. What was striking of that era to Mattelart (1991: 8–18) was the willingness of the once-conservative financial services sector to back these highly speculative expansions into marketing super-consultancies. Loosely termed "marketing services" these latter businesses included public relations, graphic design, packaging and so on, which had their proponents claiming to be integrated marketing communications agencies. Initial concerns of global marketers about conflicts of interests in handling competitive advertising accounts were overcome in many cases during the consolidation period of the 1990s by maintaining separate agency identities within the merged ownership structure.

Certainly aggressive mega-agencies raised the profile of advertising as a business, in the West and worldwide. As a result of the mergers and takeovers, Kim (1995) documented that the top ten advertising agencies in the world by gross income in the early 1990s were US, European and Japanese, though in Asia the non-regional agencies numbered two and a half, this fractional figure explained by Young & Rubicam's part-ownership with Dentsu in Dentsu/Young & Rubicam (DYR). The largest marketers/advertisers in most Asian countries were a roughly equal mix of multinational corporations and major domestic ones, though it was not always possible to identify the business and ownership links between them [Asian A&M 1994: 18–19]. With growing deregulation in many markets in Asia there was now a predominance of international advertising agencies or their affiliates over local ones among the top 10 agencies in a number of the countries researched in this book: India, Indonesia and Hong Kong, among others [Tharp 1997]. By 2000, the worldwide market leaders Omnicom and Interpublic had acquired 20 and 30 advertising agencies respectively [Advertising Age 2000] in pursuit of being integrated communications conglomerates. Since First-World-owned agencies or their part-owned affiliates dominate the advertising industry in major markets for transnational television in Asia, the question of whether they adopt a global strategy or one that is culturally contextualised must be addressed.

Global versus Local Creativity

International marketers tend to create a distinctive image around their global brands through advertising, the key creative concept for which may originate anywhere in their markets. De Mooij and Keegan (1991) explained that multinational corporations and their advertising agencies prefer to centralise the concept development but decentralise the creative execution to the various markets which are in a better position to adapt the concept to the local environment. For, on the one hand, there were certain corporate prerequisites of launching a global campaign such as having a standardised brand name and packaging, similarity of the product life-cycle stage and competitive situation transnationally, similar consumer attitudes towards and usage of the product and so on. On the other, there were varying government regulations on advertising to children, of certain products such as cigarettes and liquor, on verifiability of claims, portrayal of human bodies, and so on to be considered in devising or adapting a global creative concept. Shao and Hill (1994) found that while legal regulation of the advertisement of socially-sensitive products were remarkably similar worldwide, traditional social conventions played a more significant role in constraining their advertising in developing countries. Thus there could be numerous impediments to, or at least factors to consider in, devising a thoroughly global advertising campaign.

The standardisation of advertising internationally has been advocated since the early 1960s and somewhat successfully demonstrated at least in the European context at that time. Later, as a result of comparative studies, Green et al. (1978) commended a more moderate approach be adopted by advertisers in which specific sociocultural factors were identified as critical to the standardisation versus localisation decision. This middle path stated simply that global advertising was suitable only for certain product categories, among similar market segments across most countries and under specific conditions. For instance, Domzal and Kernan (1993) observed that personally-relevant products like food and clothing seemed suitable candidates for globalised advertising, especially among the economic elite worldwide and the post-war/postmodern generation in developed countries. But as Bourgery and Guimaraes (1993) highlighted, the critical need was for marketers to distinguish between creative concepts which cross cultures, and the products which do. Research by Kanso (1992) concurred that even though some human needs and wants may be universal, advertising still had to be culturally localised to be effective. Even across Greater China and ethnically largely Chinese Singapore, Tai (1997) found that most multinationals adapted their advertising for each market. In the context of China alone, Yin (1999) found that a combination of globalised and localised advertising was by far the strategy of choice of multinational corporations that cited Chinese cultural values as the primary rationale.

For a tool to diagnose such cultural gaps that may need to be bridged in global marketing communications, Kale (1991) proposed Hofstede's four dimensions of culture, namely individualism–collectivism, uncertainty–avoidance, power–distance and perception of time. Using these as well as economic and media availability/usage indicators, Sriram and Gopalakrishna (1991) outlined an approach for identifying groups of countries for which standardised advertising campaigns may be used. They came up with six clusters in their analysis of 40 countries, but some of the constituent countries of each cluster did not seem to make prima facie sense, as for instance Belgium, Columbia, Italy, Turkey and Taiwan being in the same cluster. While De Mooij (1998: 101–19) was likewise an advocate for the application of Hofstede's typology in advertising, she emphasised also value priorities, acknowledging though that these do not translate easily for cross-cultural comparison. In his ethnography of advertising agencies, Kemper (2001: 51–69) illustrates well the many subtleties of cultural differences that bedevil producing advertising for multicultural societies like Malaysia and Sri Lanka, which render such typologies simplistic. Still, Zandpour et al. (1994) identified four Hofstede dimensions as affecting the style and content of television advertising. But the same research team also found that product types, level of advertising expenditure, presence of US advertising agencies, government regulations, and availability of trained advertising personnel, among other factors, were equally significant influences in the eight countries surveyed. Along those lines, Samiee et al. (2003) would suggest that country-of-origin of MNCs, size of their subsidiaries abroad and organisational structure, among other factors, were influential in standardisation strategies being adopted away from headquarters. While cultural factors may not be sufficient explanation, they certainly remain significant ones for agencies and marketers adopting different creative approaches in advertising for each market. The prospect of a single global advertising campaign needing minimal cultural adaptation in multiple markets holds immense financial appeal for advertisers (Frith and Mueller 2004). A key constraint to such campaigns in Asia seemed to be the availability of transnational media.

Media Buying Transnationally

As a general rule when the international part of an account was held with one agency, the domestic account tended to move to that agency eventually. This resulted in increasing consolidation of media buying by advertising agencies for their multinational clients, usually by the use of a lead agency either in a major market or close to headquarters. However "world brands" were sometimes handled by different multinational agencies in different countries or regions due to account conflicts or strategic diversification, and in fact were even manufactured by different companies through licensing, franchising, joint venture and distribution arrangements (Sinclair 1987: 117–19). In any case the arrival of international advertising agencies in a national market to serve their multinational corporation clients historically was said to have caused a shift in advertising expenditure from print to broadcast media, and from publicly-owned broadcast media to commercial ownership (Tunstall 1977). But there has been a dearth of media research on such impact of advertising, in contrast to programming, a situation which Janus (1981) deplored. This was particularly in the developing world that has seen the expansion of US-owned advertising agencies to serve their marketing clients in new global markets. Researching the impact of satellite television in Europe on advertising agencies, Howard and Ryans (1988–89) found most agency and client executives believing that non-European corporations would be the major beneficiaries and that local agencies would lose some of their business to pan-European or international advertising agencies.

Whether the experience of cable, satellite and pay-TV media in Asia does follow that historically of the US and Europe is something this book will throw light upon. Exactly how marketers allocated spending between domestic and transnational media reaching the same target market depended, according to Mueller (1996: 164–93), on whether budgets were made up of local plans or were a top-down allocation. This would be based on such considerations as use of international versus local advertising agencies, standardisation versus localised campaigns, media alternatives and costs, and media research availability and quality. International advertising agencies have long developed in-house methods for comparing cost of delivering one media programme to different countries, though De Mooij and Keegan (1991) wisely advised that this was a situation complicated by media spill-overs across borders. Besides it was difficult to compare advertising data across countries as Mattelart (1991: 61–62) pointed out, because of discounting in some countries, the use of sample versus census data, the inclusion or non-inclusion of production costs, inclusion or non-inclusion of non-media communications like sales promotion and direct mail, information held back due to commercial sensitivity, different classifications of products and different ways of quantifying products sold. Nonetheless in the light of European research, the advent in Asia of transnational television via satellite might reasonably be expected to result in the consolidation of media spending by multinational corporations into international advertising agencies.

Advertising in the Third World

While there is a relationship between advertising and development, whether it is a cause or an effect is still in doubt. Callahan (1985) set out a number of models on the likely relationships between advertising activity and economic development, and attempted to measure them. He found that advertising was correlated to GNP (Gross National Product) but not to other variables of economic development such as energy, savings and imports, and so concluded, questionably, that advertising changed the composition of consumption but not the level of consumption. In his research on the impact of advertising in developing countries, James (1983: 28–41) found that advertising affected product demand not only by changing tastes but by providing information on brand choices. The economic effects of advertising were therefore difficult to assess because these depended in each case on what was communicated, how it was evaluated by consumers and whether it was acted upon. Although the desirability of instigating changes of taste and creation of wants in developing was worthy of further debate,

James conceded that welfare economics was ambiguous in resolving the issue. Summing up years of research linking marketing and development in the Third World, Joy and Ross (1989) dismissed the more traditional modernisation and institutional approaches, instead favouring the radical world-systems theory approach though they were critical of Wallerstein's assumption of passivity of developing countries. So for the planning of any marketing strategies they recommended intensive ethnographies as the means to obtain "thick descriptions" of the cultural and political contexts of each developing country, in particular the roles of development agencies, governments, local elites and so on. Going further, Maxwell (1997) depicted market research interviews as a secular confessional through which the consumers in developing countries received a hearing of their wants from unidentified representatives of multinational corporations.

Advertising appeared to go through a number of stages in a developing country, according to Kaynak and Ghauri (1986), beginning with the "elite stage" where there was low levels of development and few consumers. Then it went through the "popular stage" when, thanks to literacy, there could be informational appeals to mass audience. Finally advertising arrived at the specialised stage with more persuasive appeals to segmented markets similar to that of developed countries. Kaynak and Ghauri attributed differences in advertising practices, even between two developed countries, to their respective regulatory environments. But the differences between the developed countries and developing ones depended on the relative influence of western concepts in the latter. In any case, advertising content in developing countries tended to mimic that of developed countries because local practitioners have been trained there or by trainers from there. In similar vein, Sinclair (1987) demonstrated that multinational corporations through their advertising agencies were responsible for "taste transfer" or the adoption of mass-produced substitutes in place of traditional products, particularly foods, in developing countries. Since the incidence of advertising has increased with wider developments in manufacturing, marketing and media in capitalist societies, he believed quite rightly that it ought not to be addressed in isolation.

Utilising a dependency model, Anderson (1984) carried out an early critical study of the advertising industry within the Asian region and concluded that the international advertising agencies wielded power over the cultural values of selected nations in a neo-colonial form of domination. It provided specific case studies of three post-colonial nations: Indonesia, Malaysia and Singapore and the then fledgling market of the Peoples' Republic of China. Over a decade later, contributors to Frith (1996) surveyed the state of domestic advertising of 11 nations in East and South Asia, but did not address the impact of transnational television on advertising. However Frith did argue in her own introduction that the advertising scene in Asia has moved beyond dependency to the convergence of professional practice and consumer lifestyles aided by the new media technologies. Jun and Kim (1995) proclaimed the growing number of direct broadcast satellites in Asia as an exciting opportunity for international marketers, but did not provide any evidence of the medium's use or disuse of standardised advertising. While Mazzarella (2003) has documented thoroughly the globalisation of Indian advertising with economic liberalisation of the 1990s, it is without specific reference to satellite television and transborder markets. Arguably, the last comprehensive, critical yet empirical study on transnational advertising across Asia remains that done by Anderson over two decades ago. The late 1970s that he investigated was an era of greater nationalism and well prior to the growth of satellite and cable television, and some of the issues raised in that research are worthy of further investigation in a more globalised Asia of the 1990s.

Marketing and Postmodernity

After the media, the practice of marketing could be said to be another major influence in the development of postmodernity. In terms reminiscent of Williamson's (1978) critique of British advertising, Hebdige (1989: 90–91) expounded on the persuasive power of transnational media not only of products but via them of unwitting participation in new social networks transcending class, gender and even culture. He also decried the emphasis on market research in postmodern economies and how it had popularised so-called social classifications such as yuppies, empty-nesters, dinkies, Generation X and so on. These "aspirational clusters" were based not on traditional social class/sexual polarities of sociological analysis, but on transnational and transcultural "psychographics" for the convenience of global marketers. Furthermore, Firat and Venkatesh (1993) noted that advertising characteristically resignified words and signs, decontextualised products from their physical function, and juxtaposed conflicting images thus contributing to the hyperreality, spectacle and fragmentation in postmodern society. Marketing could then be responsible for commodifying even subcultures, news, education and politics, thus superseding the usual function of the latter as social processes. Hence, Tharp and Scott (1990) underlined the need to research the full cultural meaning of products and ideas introduced into any society and the infinite social consequences thereof, not just their utility and price. Likewise, the contributors to Costa and Bamossy (1995) explored the multiple relationships between marketing and cultural identity, in a globalised world where the resurgence of ethnic groups often across national borders was aided by business practices and vice versa.

As to their role in culture change, Ellis (1990: 39–40) considered television commercials to be the epitome of the medium's propensity to provide a stream of segments independent of each other in meaning. Further, in the view of Cunningham (1992: 71–101), advertising was a long-neglected arena for cultural analysis because of its commercial nature, when in reality advertising was as much a product of a country's cultural identity as a contributor to it. The limited critical studies of advertising have a left-wing bias that assumed audience passivity to marketer strategies, while there was much investment in uncritical market research of short-term advertising effects for corporate interests. Goldman (1992: 37–60) explained the role of advertising in the production of commodity signs as the process by which its viewers provide the labour to interpret the advertisements and thus create surplus value. Similarly, Jhally (1987) illustrated the addictive–compulsive nature of television watching which colonises peoples' free time and theorised that since audiences were sold by television to advertisers, they may be said to work for the medium in return for free entertainment. Jhally was intrigued by how advertising was not just about how products are used but how they were produced in a capitalist society, tapping into our cultural unconscious for their meanings.

With the growth of the Internet in the late 1990s, the obvious issue for academics and practitioners alike was whether it would encroach on consumer use of more traditional media like television, as early research in the US seemed to suggest that it would. But utilising a uses-and-gratification approach, Ferguson and Perse (2000) found that while the Web use was also motivated by time-passing, it differed significantly from television in not being perceived as a form of relaxation. Thus concern with whether particular advertisements were deceptive may be misplaced when advertising's impact on developing countries may be a deeper cultural hegemony within the capitalist world economy aided by newer media vehicles.

This chapter has surveyed both utilitarian and critical thought on the processes of media and advertising globalisation over the latter part of the twentieth century, particularly its last decade in which the phenomenon became highly visible. Dominant themes gleaned from the media literature seem to focus on the growing deregulation and commercialisation of the television, the apparent cultural imperialism of developed countries over the developed, as well as the role of multinational corporations in providing broadcasting hardware and software. The advertising literature touched on issues of how newer transnational media could influence standardisation and adaptation by advertisers, consolidation of media power by international advertising agencies, and the cultivation of consumption behaviour in developing countries. The critical approach to the media and advertising industries needed to address these concerns calls naturally for research methodologies not traditionally utilised, and so these have been elaborated upon in Appendix C for those interested in such issues. Having thus set out the theoretical and empirical orientation of this book, the subsequent chapter comprises a case-history of pioneering transnational broadcaster StarTV, revealing its metamorphosis in the context of Asia.

CLONING STARTV

The entry into Asia of transnational broadcasters on a number of different satellite platforms served as a prelude to the globalisation of the television industries of specific regional and transnational markets. The growth in satellite platforms and transnational television industry in Asia over the 1990s was plainly the most rapid worldwide. This was chronicled in detail in the preceding book by this author, *Imagi-Nations and Borderless Television*. While domestic satellites for telecommunications and television were an integral part of the economic strategies of some developing countries in Asia since the 1950s, only in the last decade of the twentieth century was there explosive growth of commercial satellites utilised for transnational media and advertising. The metamorphosis of the pioneer StarTV from a strictly transnational or pan-Asian broadcaster to one that was more regional, even quasi-domestic, is instructive of realities encountered by all transnational broadcasters in Asia.

HYBRIDISING CHANNELS

Transnational television was introduced to Asia not by some global media conglomerate, but by the family-owned concerns of an Asian businessman. The idea of refurbishing a retrieved telecommunications satellite that had gone errant and utilising it instead to broadcast television came from a son of a Hong Kong billionaire. The satellite purchase and launch in 1991 had the collaboration of the People's Republic of China (PRC), while the broadcast service StarTV stayed in the hands of the Li family and their largely family-controlled conglomerate Hutchison Whampoa. But its much-publicised sale to Rupert Murdoch's News

Corporation over 1993–95 and subsequent programming decisions led to some confrontation with the PRC government. The history of StarTV and its evolution from a pan-Asian broadcaster owned by an Asian conglomerate to a targeted regional, quasi-domestic one owned by a western multinational media corporation holds lessons for all who participate in the transnational media industry, especially those in the developing and emerging markets.

Pan-Asian Phase

Ownership and control: The satellite broadcaster StarTV, with a capitalisation of US$300 million, was initially a wholly-owned subsidiary of Hutchvision, a subsidiary of Hutchison Whampoa. The latter was also a shareholder in the refurbished satellite AsiaSat1 and a private company owned by the family of Hong Kong billionaire Li Ka-Shing. The television service was said to be the brainchild of his son and StarTV deputy chairman Richard Li, and it commenced business in December 1990 immediately after the Hong Kong government granted it a broadcasting license. Between August and December 1991 StarTV launched all its five channels on a pan-Asian basis on two footprints from AsiaSat1. Its broadcasts utilised NTSC colour system on its northern beam which covered Northeast and Central Asia including Japan and China, but utilised Pal-B colour system on its southern beam which covered Southeast, South and West Asia including Indonesia and India [Expression 1992–93].

Channels and programming: StarTV began in 1991 with a package of five channels identical on both northern and southern beams: StarPlus (entertainment), Star Mandarin (entertainment), Prime Sports, BBC World Service (news) and MTV Asia (music). StarPlus, the English-language family-entertainment channel, broadcast 24 hours a day, reaching its target audiences across its footprint through the different prime times (Tables 3.1–3.4). The programming fare included dramas like *Flying Doctors*, comedies like *M*A*S*H*, soap operas such as *Santa Barbara*, talk shows like *Oprah*, documentaries, cartoons like *The Simpsons* and awards shows like *The Oscars*. The counterpart of StarPlus was Star Mandarin, the Chinese-language channel which offered the only non-English programming on transnational satellite television when it was launched in October 1991. It offered a broad range of entertainment and information programming in the Chinese language including drama, sitcoms, variety shows, game shows, talk shows, financial news, documentaries, music and cartoons [StarTV 1992]. Its programming was sourced initially from Taiwan, though audience preferences saw expansion of its sourcing from Hong Kong especially. Although it was pan-Asian in reach, the target audiences of Star Chinese were those of Taiwan, China and to a lesser extent Hong Kong and diasporic Chinese elsewhere in East Asia.

BBC World, an international news channel, had its Asian and in fact worldwide launch in November 1991, and was the only channel in which StarTV itself was not also a programme selector. Its programming drew on the rich resources of the British Broadcasting Corporation, one of the larger news-gathering operations worldwide, comprising 250 correspondents in 50 bureaus and enjoying a long-standing reputation for breadth, credibility and impartiality which CNN has still not achieved. Its leading news programmes were *BBC Newsday* as well as *The World Today* where the reports received in-depth analysis. Presented every half-hour in prime time and every hour otherwise, its news bulletins brought up-to-the-minute news coverage. As Asia's first all-sports channel, Prime Sports broadcast 24 hours per day and initially provided 1,500 hours "live" coverage of major international and regional sporting events including 344 hours of "live" cricket matches in 1993 [StarTV 1994]. In its short-lived stint on StarTV, the 24-hour music channel MTV Asia was established as a joint venture with its parent company Viacom International. The music videos were interspersed seamlessly and at a rapid pace with interviews, news, sports, commercials and "rockumentaries" in a characteristically postmodern collage targeted at the 12–25 age group. Most of the content was US in origin, a situation put down to the lack of music videos of comparable quality and style from the countries MTV Asia was being broadcast to as of the early 1990s. Asian content was said to have grown from 5 per cent when MTV Asia was first broadcast on StarTV to as much as 50 per cent within two years though this was qualified as being only "at certain times of the day" [Balfour 1993].

Penetration and reach: StarTV aimed initially to reach the English-speaking, cosmopolitan, high-earning elite among the potential 2.5 billion viewers in the 38 countries ranging from Israel to Japan under its footprints. This region comprising two-thirds of the world's population was characterised by rapidly developing or "emergent" economies and

Table 3.1
StarTV Entertainment Channels and their Diversification, 1992–2001

Channel	1992	1994	1996	1998	2001
StarPlus	Pan-Asian	Pan-Asian	S.Asian	Indian	Indian
Star World		–	Pan-Asian	Pan-Asian	Pan-Asian
StarPlus Taiwan		–	Taiwanese	Taiwanese	Taiwanese
StarPlus Japan		–	Japanese	Japanese	Japanese
StarPlus Int'l		–	Multi-dom. (Malaysia, Indonesia, etc.)	Multi-dom.	Multi-dom.
Star Mandarin	Pan-Asian	Pan-Asian	(Re-branded)	–	–
Star Chinese		–	Taiwanese	Taiwanese	Taiwanese
Phoenix Chinese		–	Gtr Chinese	Gtr Chinese	Gtr Chinese
Phoenix CNE Europe		–	–	–	Overseas Chn.
Phoenix N.America		–	–	–	Overseas Chn.
Adventure One		–	–	–	Pan-Asian
Vijay TV		–	Indian	Indian & SE Asian	–
Total Entertainment Channels	2	2	8	8	11

Source: Based on StarTV [1993–2001] Media Packs and corporate website.

Notes: Chn.—Chinese; Gtr—Greater; Multi-dom.—Available on either footprint but targeted at two or more domestic markets; Pan-Asian—Identical programming on all satellite footprints across Asia.

thus growing advertising budgets and as yet underdeveloped domestic television media. A survey commissioned by StarTV less than a year after inauguration reported that at least 3.8 million of Asia's households were receiving its programming, 1.2 million of those households being accounted for in India and Taiwan [Expression 1992–93], a situation which will be analysed later in this book. Another survey in February 1993 reported 11.2 million households capable of receiving StarTV, the highest incidence being 4.8 million households in China, followed by 3.3 million in India and 1.9 million in Taiwan [Asian A&M 1993]. It must be borne in mind that these penetration figures represent simply households that had access to satellite and cable television. While these households had the potential to view StarTV the figures in no way give any indication whether these households were actually watching it among all the domestic and transnational channels they had access to. Much less does it show how many viewers there were for each channel, how long they watched and with what degree of attentiveness.

Regional Phase

Ownership and control: In July 1993 News Corporation, better known as Rupert Murdoch's global media conglomerate, bought a controlling 63.6 per cent interest from Hong Kong's Li Ka-Shing and his Hutchison Whampoa group, reportedly for US$525 million in cash and News Corporation shares. Widely deemed overpriced, the purchase complemented News Corporation's other television businesses: the BSkyB satellite television service in Europe, Fox Broadcasting in the US, and a joint venture with Televisa in Mexico, the world's largest Spanish-language broadcaster [Straits Times 1993]. In 1995 News Corporation purchased the remaining 36 per cent share in StarTV with the full expectation that it would lose about US$100 million per year for a few years thereafter. Valuing StarTV was difficult since it had been in operation for only two years, and while officially US$110 million was said to have been invested in it, some estimates had been double that [Ong 1993]. Nonetheless Murdoch recognised the profit potential of the impending boom of the television audience in Asia. Even by rough estimates then, advertising revenues on StarTV were estimated to reach US$1 billion by the middle of 1994 [Nadkarni 1994].

There was some consternation in political circles around Asia about the purchase by News Corporation of StarTV, most notably by Malaysia's then prime minister Mahathir Mohammed. China later responded to a speech by Murdoch about satellite television leading to the downfall of totalitarian governments by banning the personal ownership of satellite dishes. Questions were asked about the financial wisdom both of Murdoch buying StarTV and of Li Ka-Shing selling it, the loss-making status of StarTV adding to speculation that Murdoch had cultural imperialist motives [Yeap 1993]. It was also suggested that Li Ka-Shing sold StarTV because its programming content was antagonising government officials and thus jeopardising his business relations with governments in Asia, particularly China. Murdoch had initially planned to purchase a 22 per cent share of the leading Chinese-language commercial broadcaster TVB, prior to its launch of a satellite channel on ApStar1 as part of a loose consortium with ESPN, CNN, HBO and Australia Television which would have been a threat to StarTV [FEER 1993a]. Ironically the StarTV deal might never have materialised if this earlier bid by Murdoch to buy into the Hong Kong–based TVB had not been foiled by the local government's disapproval.

Channels and programming: The attainment of majority ownership by News Corporation was followed by a major management restructure including the mass resignation of the former chief executive and 30 other executives [Asia-Pacific Broadcasting 1993]. The incoming chief executive gave the first indications of a change of strategy from a pan-Asian one to multi-domestic or even subregional one. For soon StarTV began differentiating its channel offerings on the two footprints, the northern one covering China, Taiwan and the Philippines primarily, and the southern one mainly covering Indonesia, India and the Middle East. The replacement of BBC World on the northern beam with a Mandarin movie subscription channel, while retaining it on the southern beam, marked the start of regionalising StarTV programming. BBC World had run afoul of the Chinese authorities and was believed to have been withdrawn from the northern beam in April 1994 so as not to cause further offence and threaten one of StarTV's major potential markets. It was left on the southern beam where the other major StarTV market of India had a long tradition of listening to the BBC news on radio. By late 1994 the BBC World programme schedule had 25-minute news bulletins every hour on the hour. Effort was directed to make the news relevant to Asia, and particularly to local and expatriate business executives operating in the region. A sampling of other programming in late 1994 included *The Money Programme, World Business Report, Indian Business Report, Panorama* (current affairs documentaries), as well as travel, computer awareness and nature programmes [BBC 1994]. But in 1995 BBC World decided to go it alone in Asia, after the indignity of being removed summarily off the StarTV northern beam over a year earlier.

Star Movies, which replaced BBC World on the northern transponder, initially featured Cantonese movies on a subscription basis to 1.7 million households in Taiwan on 160 cable networks, as well as the Philippines and China to a limited extent. On being available on both transponders, it featured 24-hour movies from around the world, ranging from comedy, action/adventure and romance, to family, western, classics, and kung-fu/sword-play. These movies were in turn adapted and targeted at different regional audiences of StarTV. For instance, English-language movies were subtitled in Hindi for the Indian subcontinent market, Arabic for the Gulf states, in Mandarin for Greater China, and in Thai for Thailand. Star Chinese, superseding the general entertainment channel Star Mandarin, aimed to target Chinese executives and businesspersons more specifically with a financial programme, children and teenagers with cartoons and infotainment, women with Japanese dramas, and families in general. Most of its programming was sourced initially in Hong Kong and Taiwan, though gradually more widely, if still regionally, from China, Japan and Korea [StarTV 1995].

Channel V replaced MTV Asia when StarTV's relationship with Viacom collapsed over a dispute on revenue sharing as well as over the programming direction in early 1994. Since StarTV had a contractual relationship with the key personnel at MTV Asia it was able to launch its own Channel V quickly in May 1994, featuring a regionalisation strategy. This included splitting the channel with the northern beam catering to the China, Taiwan and Philippine pop music markets, and the southern one catering to the Indian and other South Asian ones. Video Jockeys (VJs) based in the regions were able to present music the audience preferred, in a style and language they identified with. By 1994 Channel V broadcast 10 hours of Mandarin programming on the northern beam and another 10 hours of Indian language programmes on the southern beam each day, with some shows like *Gone Taiwan* and *BPL Oye!* shot on location with local VJs. In the remaining 14 hours Channel V continued to provide regional and international programming including *Asian Top 20 Countdown* and *Billboard's US Top 20 Countdown*, using a core team of VJs from throughout Asia who were based in Hong Kong. With its incorporation of both domestic and regional artistes into their otherwise western-oriented programming Channel V became the first and one of the more successful examples of cultural globalisation by a regional broadcaster in Asia.

Prime Sports began to split programming broadcast on the two AsiaSat1 beams, featuring more table tennis, baseball and basketball for the predominantly Chinese and Japanese audiences of the northern footprint and more cricket and badminton for the South Asian and Indonesian audiences of the southern footprint [Asia-Pacific Broadcasting 1993]. In keeping with the regionalisation of its programming StarTV purchased the "live" broadcasting rights of the first division of the Chinese National Football league for 10 years, and three World Grand Prix badminton events from Indonesia, Thailand and China. As a further step it later provided dual soundtracks on its northern programming, namely in English for expatriates and educated elite, and in Mandarin to cater to the viewing majority of China, Taiwan and the rest of East Asia. While programmes on StarPlus, the English-language entertainment channel, were still sourced mostly from the US, they were soon sought from Europe, Australia and Asia as well. Furthermore daytime programming targeted women with fashion, cuisine, parenting, health and exercise programmes as well as talk shows and soap operas, while children were targeted before and after school with adventure series and cartoons [StarTV 1995]. In 1996 StarTV did the previously unthinkable and entered into an alliance with its main competitor ESPN Asia for shared programming on Prime Sports.

Penetration and reach: With the launch of AsiaSat2 in 1995, StarTV had access to even more geographical markets in Southeast Asia and West Asia, even Central Asia and Africa (Table 3.2). Although it continued broadcasting in analog from AsiaSat1, StarTV utilised digital technology on AsiaSat2 that allowed it to increase dramatically the number of channels it could broadcast per transponder. Thus StarTV was in a position in 1996 to adopt specific strategies of each regional market under its footprint, and to tailor its programming accordingly. In Indonesia, for instance, StarTV entered into a strategic alliance with the sole pay-TV licensee Indovision to provide channels that catered to the country's market and a consolidated marketing, distribution and technical operation. For China, StarTV formed a joint venture called Phoenix Chinese Channel with two Hong Kong partner firms

Table 3.2
StarTV News/Sports Channels and their Diversification, 1992–2001

Channel	1992	1994	1996	1998	2001
BBC	Pan-Asian	S/SE Asian	(Ceased)	–	–
Star News				Indian	Indian/UK
Phoenix InfoNews					Gtr Chinese
Sky News					Pan-Asian
Fox News				Pan-Asian	Pan-Asian
National Geographic				Pan-Asian	Pan-Asian
Prime Sports/	Regional	Regional	Alliance with ESPN	(Re-branded)	
Star Sports Asia					
Star Sports Intl.			Multi-dom. (Malaysian, Japanese)	(Re-branded)	(Gtr Chinese)
Star Sports SE Asia				SE Asian	SE Asian
Star Sports Taiwan				Taiwanese	Taiwanese
Star Sports India				S. Asian	S. Asian
ESPN Asia			Multi-dom. (NE/SE Asian, S. Pacific)	Gtr Chinese & SE Asian	–
ESPN Taiwan					Taiwanese
ESPN India			Indian	S. Asian	S. Asian
ESPN Philippines					Filipino
MBC-ESPN					S. Korean
Total News/Sports channels	2	2	4	10	14

Source: Based on StarTV [1993–2001] *Media Packs* and corporate website.
Notes: Multi-dom.—Available on either footprint but targeted at two or more domestic markets. Pan-Asian—Identical programming on all satellite footprints across Asia.

to provide multiple channels with programming attractive to main-land China audiences and acceptable by the PRC government [Bailes and Hollister 1996: 134]. So determined was its change of strategy that StarTV went to the extent of sacrificing its own Star Mandarin channel. Determined to demonstrate its willingness not to impose programming alien to India, StarTV funded a research report into what its public wanted and claimed that future programming would take into consideration the research findings [Khar 1994]. Since selling decoders to unscramble signals meant considerable capital outlay and labour-intensive support operations, StarTV proposed merging its free-to-air and pay-TV services. Thus it developed concurrent plans for a cheaper analogue pay channel in India in recognition of what that market could bear in the interim.

Quasi-domestic Phase

Ownership and control: In furthering its regionalisation strategy following the News Corporation takeover of the network, in late 1994 StarTV increased its collaboration with rival ZeeTV, the regional commercial broadcaster, and UTV, a local programme production house, both of which its parent company News Corporation bought shares in. This resulted in joint production and marketing of two new channels, one free-to-air and another subscription-based. The first, EL-TV, was a Hindi general-entertainment channel which transmitted two hours initially and would expand as it introduced subregional/ethnic programming such as three and a half hours of Tamil programmes in early evening. The second, Zee Cinema, was a pay-TV movie channel that was in competition with Star Movies, which also broadcast English-language movies with Hindi and Arabic subtitles. In January 1995, StarTV sold 50 per cent of its highly successful Channel V to other multinationals in the entertainment industry: EMI Music, Sony Pictures, Warner Music Group and BMG Entertainment. Having thus increased its strategic alliances in the music entertainment industry Channel V was split a couple of months later into Hindi and Mandarin services, the former offering some "live" programmes from Mumbai (formerly known as Bombay) [APT-C 1995: 38–39]. News Corporation also explored investments in leading Indian film and software producers, and began building its own studios to bring about increased domestic programming.

Programming and channels: In October 1996, the StarPlus channel introduced locally produced Hindi-language programmes serials, soap operas and game-shows into its evening prime time, displacing the English-language programming of similar genre for which it was famed. There was speculation that even its English-language programmes would be increasingly produced in India. A case in point was the new Star News slot that was farmed out to a local independent production house, New Delhi Television (NDTV). ZeeTV accused StarTV of breaking an understanding that the latter would not offer more than 10 per cent Hindi-language programming. The new relationship between the two allied broadcasters was characterised as "competitive collaboration" or partners in some channels and competitors in others [Asian A&M 1996b]. This surprise move pitched StarTV not only against ZeeTV but also Doordarshan (DD), SonyET and a host of new Indian commercial channels in the intense battle for advertising revenues. About the same time, StarTV hired as its chief executive in India the former director-general of DD. Soon afterwards, News Corporation gained approval from the Indian government for direct investment in News Television India, paving the way for it to gain domestic broadcaster status [Boulestreau 1996].

Together these developments came to symbolise the completion of StarTV's metamorphosis from a global, pan-Asian up-market broadcaster to a quasi-domestic mass-market one. Having migrated 80 per cent of its channels to digital format, StarTV was able by the late 1990s to offer country-specific channel packages to India, the Middle East, Taiwan and Pakistan via digital compression technology. In 1997, StarTV upset its affiliate ZeeTV further by switching to entirely Hindi-language programming on StarPlus' prime-time, further undermining an unwritten understanding not to encroach on each others' markets. It re-launched the English-language channel that was previously StarPlus as Star World while Prime Sports was subsequently rebranded Star Sports. StarTV's commitment to local content was demonstrated in its financing of local film producers in India to the tune of US$23 million to produce 25 movies a year. Even Channel V was revamped to take on not just the revived MTV Asia but the newer B4U Hindi music channel. In 1999 Channel V was reorganised into four divisions: Greater China, India, International (100 per cent western music) and Networks (a joint venture for programme production).

In mid-1999, StarTV opened a representative office in Beijing, the first foreign broadcaster to do so, underscoring its commitment to

China and its investments, particularly its joint venture with Chinese government and private companies, Phoenix Satellite TV which broadcast Phoenix Chinese Channel and Phoenix Movie Channel. In a trip early that year, Rupert Murdoch expressed his admiration for China's achievements in recent decades and promised to help the world better understand the country [International Cable 1999a]. This followed also his dumping of BBC World from the StarTV stable and cancelling the publication of the former Hong Kong governor's memoirs the previous year. News Corporation was rewarded by China's decision to use its equipment for the national cable system. StarTV bought the exclusive television rights to hundreds of movies to be produced by China Star Entertainment Group and the Media Asia group for its movie channel. By 2000 StarTV offered up to 60 channels of pay-TV services in Hong Kong alone and signed a deal with Cable & Wireless HKT (Hong Kong Telecom) to offer interactive entertainment, digital television and internet services through TVs and PCs throughout Asia. In mid-2001, its Phoenix TV was poised to become the first station with investment from China to broadcast in Taiwan as well [Brown 2000].

Penetration and reach: As of the late 1990s StarTV was running over 30 channels in seven languages in 53 countries and claiming a viewing audience of 300 million [Arenstein 1999]. In 2000 StarTV bought a 26 per cent share in Hathway Cable which operates the second-largest cable network in India reaching some 2.5 million homes in order to run a fully integrated interactive TV and broadband internet service [Leung 2000a]. StarTV provided a 10-channel bouquet of DTH channels called Star Select to 123,000 subscribers in the Middle East via Orbit, many of them Indian expatriates. In the world's second largest television market of Japan, News Corporation was a 11 per cent shareholder in Sky PerfectTV formed by a merger in 1998 of its own JskyB and PerfectTV which had 1.4 DTH households by 2000.

At the time of writing this book it was early yet to analyse the current strategies of StarTV since the early 2000s, and to assess how well they are working and why. Though in a survey of 8,000 business decision makers and another 800 affluent individuals from major cities in East and Southeast Asia in the late 1990s, StarTV and its affiliate channels featured strongly among the top 10 cable and satellite channels watched (Table 3.3). The apparent success of StarTV in expanding the television market in the Asia region, even as a pan-Asian broadcaster, spurred a number of foreign multinational television providers to enter the market, some of them bringing forward long-range plans to expand

Table 3.3
StarTV Music/Movie Channels and their Diversification, 1992–2001

Channel	1992	1994	1996	1998	2001
MTV Asia	Pan-Asian	(Ceased)			–
Channel V		Regional	–	–	–
Channel V Intl.			Multi-dom.	(Re-branded)	Pan-Asian
Channel V Gtr China			(Twn, Phil., India)		Gtr Chinese
Channel V India					S. Asian
Channel V Thailand					Thai
Channel V Korea					Korean
StarMovies	Pan-Asian	(Re-branded)			–
StarMovies India		S. Asian	S. Asian	S. Asian	S. Asian
StarMovies Middle East			W. Asian	W. Asian	–
StarMovies	Pan-Asian	Multi-dom. (S'pore, M'sia)	(Re-branded)		–
StarMovies SE Asia				SE Asian	SE Asian
StarMovies Taiwan			Taiwanese	Taiwanese	Taiwanese
Star Mandarin Movies		Taiwanese	Taiwanese	Taiwanese & Filipino	–
Phoenix Movies				Chinese	Chinese
Star Gold					Indian
Viva Movies			Filipino	Filipino	Filipino
Total Music/Movie Channels:	3	4	7	8	12
Total StarTV Channels:	5	8	18	21	38

Source: Based on StarTV [1993–2001] Media Packs and corporate website.
Notes: Multi-dom.—Available on either footprint but targeted at two or more domestic markets; Pan-Asian—Identical programming on all satellite footprints across Asia; Twn—Taiwanese; Phil—Filipino; S'pore—Singapore; M'sia—Malaysia.

into the region. It also stimulated domestic commercial and public
broadcasters to enter the satellite and cable television business, both
to combat the effect of the foreign multinationals as well as to carve
out their own share of this growing market.

EYEBALLING VIEWERSHIP

By November 1993, just two years after commencing broadcasts,
StarTV was claiming a quantum leap to a potential audience of
42 million homes, as estimated by its commissioned market research.
Of this 30.2 million homes were in China, 7.2 million in India and
2.4 million in Taiwan, which constituted its primary markets. The
next three markets trailed considerably behind: Israel at 621,000, Saudi
Arabia at 369,000 and Hong Kong at 331,000 [StarTV 1994]. Since
the figures were often derived from cable or satellite television access
estimates, the concern of advertisers was not knowing the actual viewership of the channels and particular programmes. Yet even though the
varying methodologies used and conclusions drawn from penetration
figures were questioned both within the industry and beyond, the research indicated clearly that StarTV was reaping some benefits of a
two-year headstart as the pioneer satellite television broadcaster in
Asia (Table 3.4).

Table 3.4
Most Watched Cable/Satellite Channels in 'Last Seven Days', Asiawide 1997

Channel	Business Decision Makers	Channel	Affluent
CNN	21%	Discovery	15%
HBO	20%	HBO	15%
Discovery	19%	CNN	14%
ESPN	10%	MTV	13%
Star Sports	12%	Star Sports	13%
MTV	10%	Star Movies	12%
Star Movies	10%	Channel V	9%
Channel V	10%	Zhong Tian	7%
BBC World	7%	TNT/Cartoon Network	6%
NHK	6%	BBC World	5%

Source: Asian Media Access [1997].

Indian Viewers

By the mid-1990s about a dozen commercial networks, with over 50 channels between them, competed for a share of the Indian television market. It was said that the pioneer StarTV had considerable impact in India because a sizeable proportion of its 900 million population, estimated at over 20 million, comprehended its predominant language of broadcast, English. Soon after it began broadcasting, most of StarTV's four English language channels were available on the unregulated cable networks. Its success was soon emulated by other transnational television networks, among them CNN, ABN, Australia Television and Sony, not to mention domestic commercial ones using the satellite medium such as ZeeTV, JainTV and ATN. This section will examine the performance of StarTV in the competitive environment for satellite television that is India (Table 3.5).

Table 3.5
South Asia and Central Asia Household Penetration of StarTV, 1992–2001

Country	1992 June	1994 January	1996 August	1999 April	2001 October
India	1,282,500	7,278,000	14,000,000	18,000,000	27,000,000
Pakistan	30,195	77,038	150,000	10,000	1,300,000
Bangladesh			205,000	305,000	317,565
Nepal					100,000
Sri Lanka					5,365
Maldives					2,200
Kazakhstan					70,000
Uzbekistan					25,000
Kyrgyzstan					8,000
Georgia					8,000

Sources: Compiled from StarTV [1993–2001] and Couto [1999].
Note: Highlighted countries/regions are dealt with in greater detail in this book and its companion volume (Thomas 2005).

Early to mid-1990s: Almost exclusively urban, StarTV audience was minuscule compared with that of the public broadcaster Doordarshan (DD) with its reach in both urban and predominantly rural India. Still the viewership was achieved despite the fact that audiences had to pay cable operators for the privilege of watching the transnational service. In the early 1990s StarTV catered to the elite—only 10 per cent of Mumbai and 6–7 per cent of Delhi cumulative, or in other words watching StarPlus for a minimum of five minutes per week [Interview Ind03.03]. Especially in the urban slums prior to the growth of local-language channels, audiences would have been watching programming on StarTV. While it was somewhat unrelated to their daily lives, it was no less absorbing television because there were few alternatives then. By the mid-1990s StarTV still had very low viewership, even when audience research panels for satellite and cable television selected primarily the top socio-economic population segment [Interview Ind01.03]. The highest ratings that programmes on StarPlus gained were about three points, compared with ZeeTV programmes at around 35–40 points, and DD programmes around 65–70 points [Interview Ind01.05].

The success of StarTV was primarily because it became part of a cluster of channels on pre-existing neighbourhood cable networks in television-entertainment-starved India then. In the early years of StarTV, cable television in India comprised a significant fraction of urban television households, even if it was a small minority nationally. On an all-India basis, satellite and cable television comprised 20–25 per cent of television homes, though in metropolitan cities it was larger [Interview Ind01.08]. StarTV viewers were a subset of cable subscribers, namely 70 per cent of all cable viewers, though as much as 90–95 per cent of those in cosmopolitan Mumbai [Interview Ind03.04]. The figures in 1994 indicated approximately 45 million households in India with television sets, 8 million households cabled (20 per cent) persons per set. This translated into 300 million viewers for DD1, but only 50 million for satellite and cable television, which nonetheless was about the population of Britain [Interview Ind02.07]. The Indian states with the highest penetration of TV homes were in the north and west of the country—namely Gujarat, 58 per cent; Haryana/Himachal Pradesh, 43 per cent; Madhya Pradesh, 33 per cent and Maharashtra/Goa, 33 per cent [StarTV 1994].

The reasons for the early popularity of StarTV were not uniform across its channels or across Indian audiences, and had to do with specific programming. Each channel had special appeal to particular segments of Indian society, which emphasised pre-existing cultural adaptations such as its colonial experiences. For Prime Sports, the explanation for its popularity had to do with its commitment to broadcasting cricket matches which enjoy a loyal national following, dating from cricket's introduction by the British colonists. In fact Prime Sports was of interest to Indians only when cricket tournaments were shown; otherwise it had a small audience in India. But Prime Sports influenced domestic television, for DD began showing major tennis tournaments from the semi-finals onwards, mimicking Prime Sports which had done so from their start [Interview Ind02.07]. There was little interest in soccer on Prime Sports, however, except in the states of Bengal and Goa [Interview Ind01.11].

BBC World in the early StarTV stable seemed to have benefited from the sizeable and long-standing audiences for the BBC World radio service among the English-educated, especially in India. It had considerable credibility in Indian eyes because of their experience of even-handed reporting by the radio service and also because of the historical experience of the British Raj [Interview Ind01.11]. But the radio service may not have been as unbiased as it claimed since it was funded by the Foreign Office and so not autonomous of the UK government as believed by viewers, unlike the BBC domestic service which is funded by consumer license fees [Interview Ind02.07]. BBC World television service was popular largely for weekly round-ups like *India Business Report*, or when an Indian documentary was shown [Interview Ind01.03]. It was preferred not just for its worldwide news but for its Indian news coverage that provided a counterpoint to the staid DD coverage of the same. Yet, the BBC World television coverage of the Ayodhya mosque destruction in December 1992, a relatively local incident prudently ignored by DD, was widely blamed for provoking or at least fuelling communal riots nation-wide [Straits Times 1992]. This may be one of the more legitimate arguments made against transnational television by governments in the region and may necessitate a code of ethics to sensitise journalists, editors and producers of news services about the consequences of news items put to air.

The only other channel that elicited comment from industry respondents was the StarTV music channel, originally MTV and later Channel V though often mistakenly referred to by the former name. Both music channels certainly had a following among the youth in metropolitan areas [Interview Ind01.02]. There was little doubt that they had revolutionised advertising creativity and consequently had considerable impact on Indian youth, though there were doubts expressed about how long the trend would last. Some believed that parents would not continue paying specifically for it unless it was an integrated part of a pay-TV programming package [Interview Ind02.08]. Channel V did better than MTV only because of top-rating programmes such as *BPL Oye!* that featured Hindi film songs [Interview Ind03.03].

Channel V's popularity with audiences and advertisers was thus attributed to its promotion of a hybrid Indian–global youth culture rather than a purely westernised youth culture.

Late 1990s to early 2000s: As affiliated channels in the mid-1990s StarTV and ZeeTV were an urban phenomenon in India with a quarter of all StarTV households located in the six metropolitan cities of Mumbai, Delhi, Kolkata (formerly known as Calcutta), Chennai (formerly known as Madras) and Hyderabad. Regionally, while western India had the highest penetration at 91 per cent of cable households, the south was a close second at 90 per cent. Since the average StarTV household comprised 5.9 persons, there were an estimated 60 million viewers. These were the more affluent with monthly household incomes of Rs 3,390 (US$110) compared with Rs 2,666 (US$85) of general TV homes, and owned more luxury consumer goods. StarTV household members had a higher comprehension of English at 49 per cent than general households at 42 per cent, and "viewership yesterday" was over 20 per cent of all StarTV households and highest among the upper socio-economic groups. "Viewership yesterday" was also highest in Chennai, Hyderabad and Kochi (formerly known as Cochin) in southern India where Hindi is not dominant and where the number of English-educated is probably higher [StarTV 1998]. Capitalising on the rapid growth of unlicensed cable networks and increasing liberalisation by the government, StarTV penetration in India expanded to an estimated 18 million households by end 1999, while ZeeTV was said to have a reach of 24 million households or some 130 million viewers within the country [Indiantelevision.com 2000]. However, by the early 2000s cable and satellite penetration had reached 40 million households in India, according to the authoritative National Readership Survey. Growing at twice the rate of the television market it had reached a landmark 50 per cent of all television households in the country [Singhal and Ghoshal 2002].

While more recent data on viewer profiles and viewership patterns were not available, expatriate Indian continue to be a significant audience in West Asia for StarTV since there has been no change in their employment trends since the mid-1990s (Table 3.6). In terms of viewership, only 60 per cent of local Arabs and 31 per cent of expatriate Arabs "watched StarTV yesterday" as compared with 83 per cent of expatriate South Asians, possibly due to English-language comprehension [StarTV 1998]. This number increased substantially with the launch of AsiaSat2 and by the late 1990s StarTV had a penetration of 388,000

Table 3.6
West Asia Household Penetration of StarTV, 1992–2001

Country	1992 June	1994 January	1996 August	1999 April	2001 October
Israel	272,000	621,000	800,000		1,324,979
UAE	10,000	116,589	289,000		
Saudi Arabia			388,000		
Kuwait	4,000	31,210	76,000		
Bahrain	3,000				
Lebanon			12,000		
Oman			100,000		
Qatar			25,000		
Total West Asia					115,000
Total Asia	3,029,868	42,126,884	61,443,000	74,168,176	93,822,835

Sources: Compiled from StarTV [1993–2001] and Couto [1999].

homes [StarTV 2000]. Satellite dishes were the prime means of StarTV reception though cable systems were on the increase and some StarTV programming was transmitted terrestrially from Bahrain. In the late 1990s, premier channels such as Star World and Star Movies, as well as Fox Sports, National Geographic, Granada UK, CNBC and Sky News were offered in West Asia as the pay-TV package Star Select [StarTV 2000]. Given the market potential in both South Asia and West Asia, it is rather surprising that the only independent survey of viewership for pan-Asian satellite broadcasting, conducted in the late 1990s, focussed exclusively on East Asia [Asian Media Access 1997]. One reason for this myopia is the tendency generally of thinking of Asian emergent economies as only those countries along the Pacific Rim, and for data to be collected primarily on national markets directly targeted by broadcasters rather than on transnational ethnic markets.

Indonesian Viewers

Given its population size Indonesia has represented another potentially attractive market to advertisers and media-owners, domestic and multinational alike. Its economy had seen steady growth over the last decade, with its GNP growing to Rp. 139,707 billion (US$65 billion) in 1993, although this represented Rp. 711,900 (US$330) per capita, placing Indonesia in the category of developing countries still [PPPI 1996: 37]. Before its economic woes in the late 1990s the World

Bank had expected Indonesia to be reclassified a newly industrialising country by the year 2000 when its per capita income was expected to reach US$1,000 [PPPI 1994: 41]. This economic growth was accompanied by growing affluence of the population as reflected in such indicators as imports of consumption goods, domestic production of vehicles and ownership of television sets. Thus the elite of Indonesia, said to comprise at least 10 per cent of its population or about 19 million, comprised one of the key markets in Asia that StarTV targeted, even under its original pan-Asian strategy. In 1995, StarTV announced that it had reached an agreement with Indovision, the Indonesian pay-TV company, to transmit 15 of its channels. This was in addition to StarTV's composite free-to-air channel available via Indonesia's own Palapa satellite, and its other free-to-air channels on AsiaSat1.

Early to mid-1990s: When StarTV began broadcasting in 1991 there was little immediate consumer response from Indonesia. For one thing the main AsiaSat1 footprint covered only the northern parts of the less-populated, though large Indonesian islands of Sumatra and Borneo. Large and more expensive satellite dishes were needed for reception of StarTV broadcasts in heavily-populated Java island and elsewhere in the country. Furthermore, by regulation in Indonesia all satellite dishes had to be directed towards the domestic Palapa satellite, though this was not easily enforced. Therefore, most of the transnational television watched was that beamed unencrypted via the Palapa satellite including CNN, HBO, ESPN, Discovery and domestic channels from Malaysia, Brunei and Singapore, though most of the commercial channels were later encrypted for pay-TV. Omnibus research utilising a representative national sample carried out by Survey Research Indonesia (SRI, now AC Nielsen Indonesia) confirmed the low incidence of satellite television viewing. Only 4 per cent of respondents reported having the ability to receive transnational television in the household. The higher figures for the provincial city of Semarang (24 per cent) could be explained in part by the more predominant mode of shared cabling of satellite dish reception, as well as the large ethnic Chinese population wealthy enough to purchase private dishes.

Nonetheless commercial research funded by StarTV indicated that the number of households with access to its channels had been growing steadily from 14,335 in January 1992 to 36,211 in February 1993 [StarTV 1993]. This represented a growth rate of 153 per cent within a year of its introduction, though a penetration of only 0.16 per cent of total TV households, estimated at 22.4 million households. Research in the Medan region in Sumatra island directly under the StarTV footprint, showed that StarTV was available in 87 per cent of households which had access to transnational television, though only in 7 per cent of all television households. However, 71 per cent of StarTV households watched a StarTV channel in the day preceding the interviews, a more consistent pattern of viewership than reported by government research. StarTV households in Medan, comprising some 140,000 viewers, were found also to be significantly higher than other television households on such socio-economic indices as ownership of credit cards, cars, VCRs and CD players. In fact, 72 per cent of StarTV households had monthly incomes exceeding Rp. 450,000 (US$225) as compared with only 10 per cent of all TV households [StarTV 1993].

It was difficult to estimate dish ownership and therefore transnational television reception in Indonesia. Based on licenses issued by the government the semi-official estimate was of 500,000 satellite dishes in operation throughout Indonesia in the mid-1990s. But in relation to such statistics in Indonesia, as in many developing countries, any researcher has to settle for some consensus of opinion through different data sources. Working estimates of the government and market research organisations put the number of satellite dishes at between 500,000 to 600,000 [Interview Mly03.05]. But there might have been up to five times the official number operating illegally [Interview Mly03.03]. Based on spare parts exported from the US there could have been as many as 1.2 million satellite dishes [Interview Mly01.03]. Yet only 10,000 were said to be StarTV-capable since larger satellite dishes were needed to receive transmissions from AsiaSat1 in most of the Indonesia archipelago, except in the islands of Borneo and Sumatra [Interview Mly03.06].

The cost of satellite dishes for reception of transnational channels was considerably more than those for domestic channels alone. In the mid-1990s, newspaper advertisements and handbills for the purchase and installation of satellite dishes indicated that manually-tuned receivers suitable for domestic and regional broadcasts, such as from Southeast Asia and the South Pacific, ranged in price from Rp. 950,000 to Rp. 1.6 million (US$500–800). Remotely-controlled, stereo and variable-direction receivers capable of receiving StarTV, American, Russian, Chinese as well as domestic/regional channels cost between Rp. 6.5 and Rp. 12.5 million (US$3,500–6,000) [Suara Pembaruan 1994]. Given the high cost of satellite dishes, they were beyond the means of even some middle-class Indonesians. Consequently there was the practice of "alisan" or mutual-pools for buying satellite dishes, and of cable sharing. Research by Padjajaran University on West Java villages in the early 1990s found many such informal viewer co-operatives and showed therefore that viewership per set was very high [Interview Mly04.01]. Since every satellite dish could be cabled to as many as 20 homes and each home could have a sizeable extended family or neighbourhood drop-in audience, unlike in developed countries, it was difficult to estimate cable/satellite viewership [Interview Mly03.04].

Still, in the early 1990s there was a relatively minuscule audience for transnational broadcasts, estimated at less than 4 per cent of the urban population. These were believed to be largely expatriates, ethnic Chinese or those residing in provinces neighbouring other Southeast Asian countries and watching their stations [SRI 1994]. The impediments to viewing Star TV seemed to be the linguistic barrier, as Indonesia had neither an English-language colonial heritage nor a large ethnic Chinese community, and owning or sharing a satellite dish was an economic barrier for the majority of its population. Thus the most popular form of foreign programming watched was feature films and the most popular foreign channel was TV3 from linguistically-similar Malaysia, largely available via spillover signals in border provinces [Kohei and Idris 1990]. This was in keeping with the majority of satellite dishes owned being of small-to-medium size and suitable for domestic satellite reception on which Malaysian channels were also available. Research conducted by Survey Research Indonesia (SRI) in the mid-1990s indicated that only 2 per cent of respondents watched transnational satellite television the "previous" day and 1 per cent each claimed to have watched it between two to seven days previously or longer [SRI 1994]. None of this negligible number watched it for any significant length of time, though 98 per cent of respondents declared themselves to be irregular viewers of satellite television. The pattern seemed to be that of rather random viewing of channels and StarTV did not feature as a significant choice.

Late 1990s to early 2000s: In 1995 StarTV entered a new phase in Indonesia when it joined the Indovision stable with a 24-hour composite channel of its free-to-air StarPlus, Channel V and Prime Sports channels, via a decoder costing about US$330. In addition StarTV entered into deals with Indonesian production houses to produce local programming for its own channels for the Malay-language region. Among its offerings demonstrating a commitment to regionalisation, even quasi-domestication, were StarPlus Indonesia, Star Sports in Indonesian, and Film Indonesia, a 24-hour movie channel, as well as three channels in partnership with RCTI, namely Citra Junior, Citra Melate and Citra Hiburan [Asian A&M 1997c]. But StarTV and Indovision fell out in the late 1990s over the decision by the latter to migrate from Palapa C2 to the less powerful Cakrawala 1 satellite owned by Indovision's affiliate at the cost of US$1 million per month, as well as a related issue of financial debts to StarTV for programming and management services [Samudera and Hughes 1999]. This entailed installing new dishes for subscribers, free to those that took annual subscriptions but costing Rp. 626,000 (US$74) to those on a monthly plan.

Subsequently StarTV assigned all its channels to one of Indovision's rivals, Metra, which already offered 15 other transnational channels and seven domestic ones [Pardosi 1999]. As of 2000, Metra was said to have a penetration of just 1,000 households, while StarTV's former rebroadcaster Indovision could claim 3.3 million households (Initiative Media Indonesia 1999). Some cancellations of subscriptions resulted, from sports fans, over the loss of Star Sports. StarTV's own 2001 estimate of its Indonesian penetration of about 1 million households (Table 3.7), which would also include direct-to-home reception

Table 3.7
Southeast Asia Household Penetration of StarTV, 1992–2000

Country	1992 June	1994 January	1996 August	1999 April	2001 October
Indonesia	14,335	49,807	50,000		1,070,582
Malaysia			30,000	244,000	619,336
Brunei			30,000	35,400	25,000
Cambodia					25,000
Laos					2,000
Philippines	70,474	187,431	400,000	505,000	944,984
Myanmar			15,000		4,000
Papua New Guinea					10,000
Singapore					282,158
Thailand	9,000	142,805	393,000	340,000	400,000
Vietnam			15,000	3,000	10,000

Sources: Compiled from StarTV [1993–2001] and Couto [1999].
Note: Highlighted countries/regions are dealt with in greater detail in this book and its companion volume (Thomas 2005).

via satellite dishes, appears ambitiously to be slightly midway between these. A survey of Jakarta plus 10 cities by an independent media research firm, placed the viewership of any StarTV channel in Indonesia at 126,000 individuals, with Phoenix/Star Chinese, Channel V and Star Sports topping the list [AC Nielsen 2001]. Quite like Brazil where the terrestrial broadcasters enjoyed political patronage for a long period and resisted change to the free-to-air model (Reis 1999), investment in and adoption of cable television in Indonesia were extremely limited. Thus after over a decade of much business turbulence, StarTV still had a relatively low share of the Indonesian television market in the early 2000s (Figure 3.1), in contrast to its experience in other major markets of Asia.

Figure 3.1
Viewership of StarTV Network Channels in Indonesia, July–August 2001

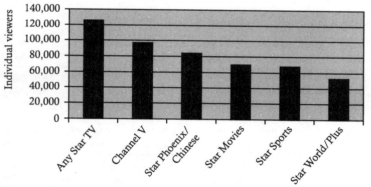

Source: AC Nielsen [2001].

Chinese Viewers

As a transnational broadcaster StarTV has had a chequered history in China, one of its key target markets, ever since it was first beamed into the country from AsiaSat1 in late 1991. It shared its AsiaSat1 satellite platform with some of China's provincial stations and benefited by the growth of satellite dish sales in the early 1990s that gave an estimated 30–70 million Chinese access to transnational satellite television (Table 3.8). This growth was believed to be in large part due to StarTV programming, even though the popularity of the channels varied considerably. Interviewees stressed the critical importance of relevance of music and sports to attracting audiences, a lesson which StarTV seemed to learn early. In fact StarTV split with MTV over the former's decision to go quasi-domestic in the India, China and Philippines markets [Interview Chn03.04]. When the late-coming competitor ESPN generally did better in attracting audiences, StarTV's Prime Sport channel fought back using local sports, for instance cricket for South Asia and swimming for East Asia, using split beams for both sound and visuals [Interview Chn01.09]. StarTV then bought the rights to the popular China football league in 1994 [Interview Chn03.01]. Furthermore a bi-lingual StarTV Movie pay-TV channel was put in place instead of the BBC World Service News for northern beam [Interview Chn01.03].

Table 3.8
Northeast Asia Household Penetration of StarTV, 1992–2001

Country	1992 June	1994 January	1996 August	1999 April	2001 October
China PRC	1,200,000	30,362,966	36,200,000	44,978,776	46,000,000
Taiwan ROC	1,191,419	2,376,433	4,300,000	4,957,000	5,353,000
Hong Kong	150,000	330,827	430,000	750,000	800,000
Macau	5,000		40,000	40,000	
S. Korea	18,945	183,838	1,700,000	3,500,000	6,000,000
Japan	13,400		400,000	500,000	499,000

Sources: Compiled from StarTV [1993–2001] and Couto [1999].
Note: Highlighted countries/regions are dealt with in greater detail in this book and its companion volume (Thomas 2005).

Early to mid-1990s: In China, municipal and provincial governments as well as large state-run firms owned and ran the early cable networks as a service for their workers. Originally municipal governments were unofficially allowed to carry StarTV since they were lower in the political structure and further from central government policy to cause embarrassment. But provincial governments chose to follow suit in offering StarTV on their cable systems due to competitive pressures, resulting from a regulatory policy of "suppressive openness" (Chan 1994). It was believed that some Beijing officials, responsible for regulation of cable television, were influenced towards leniency by junkets to the more liberal and entrepreneurial southern parts of China [Interview Chn04.03]. Thus subtle corruption might have resulted in StarTV being readily available in much of the country in defiance of official edicts. An estimated 10,000 cable operators were said to exist in China, ranging from large ones that controlled up to half a city to small ones which controlled just a street or even one side of a street.

StarTV had researched the incidence of cable access to its channels in China but would not release its data. In 1992 two sets of statistics surfaced about the situation in China, the official statistic claiming 3 million viewers of StarTV, while another from cable operators suggesting a figure of 14 million [Interview Chn01.06]. In 1994 StarTV boldly claimed 30.5 million viewer households in China alone or a penetration rate of 13 per cent of all TV households and that of these StarTV households 37 per cent "watched yesterday". The household monthly income of a StarTV home was found to be Rmb 1,319 (US$160) while that of all TV homes was Rmb 1,044 (US$125), and demonstrated also in higher ownership of luxury goods such as VCRs, compact disc players and personal computers [StarTV 1994]. The impact of StarTV on southern China such as in Quangdong province was low, compared to and because of the spillover from Hong Kong terrestrial television, and where in fact both ATV and TVB had almost equal market shares. The penetration of StarTV in southern China was believed to be as much as 20 to 30 per cent of all households, while the domestic PRC channels' penetration was 95 to 100 per cent, because the former concentrated only on Mandarin and English programming then [Interview Chn02.02].

Late 1990s to early 2000s: The culmination of News Corporation's diplomatic and business efforts in China was the announcement in 1996 later of the establishment of Phoenix Satellite Channel in which StarTV would take 45 per cent, a Hong Kong firm named Today's Asia would take another 45 per cent, and the remaining 10 per cent would be held critically by China Wise International, a sales and advertising agent for national and provincial television stations in mainland China. It was believed that CCTV (China Central Television) was to have been a party to this investment, since new legislation permitted it to launch cable services, but it withdrew either due to objections from Ministry of Radio, Film and Television (MRFT) officials or because it did not wish to yield to pressure from News Corporation. All the same, CCTV contracted to supply programmes through its China Television Program Agency to the Phoenix Chinese Channel which replaced the existing Star Chinese channel [Hughes 1996]. By early 1997 StarTV claimed that its research in 33 major cities indicated the Phoenix channel had a penetration of 36.2 million households in China or 13 per cent of all TV households. This represented a potential viewership of 140 million people, largely under 36 years of age, more affluent and educated than the average Chinese viewer [Asian A&M 1997a].

Survey research conducted in late 1996 by a Chinese market re-search company affiliated to the State Statistics Bureau found that StarTV was available in 19.1 per cent of homes in the coastal regions and 17.2 per cent in the northern regions [Asian A&M 1997a]. But as part of the trend explained earlier it was only in 5.7 per cent of homes in the southern regions, while in the culturally-different and television-deprived northwestern regions the corresponding figure was higher at 9.5 per cent. The audience for the Phoenix channel on which the research focused was relatively young with 54 per cent aged 21 to 40 years, was better educated than that of all TV households and had a 30 per cent higher income. The channel highlighted the fact that 57 per cent of respondents said that they liked Phoenix programming while 28 per cent remained neutral, leaving only 15 per cent with dislikes. By mid-2000, StarTV was claiming an audience of 45 million in China and preparing to launch the world's first 24-hour Mandarin news service [Leung 2000b]. Even discounting the channel's selective reporting, one had to recognise that the revamped and better-targeted

Table 3.9
Peripheral Regions Capable of Receiving StarTV, 1997

Oceania	East Asia	South Asia	W. Asia/ Africa	C. Asia/ Europe
Australia	Laos	Bhutan	Cyprus	Afghanistan
Guam	Mongolia	Maldives	Egypt	Armenia
Micronesia	Korea (N)	Nepal	Eritrea	Azerbaijan
N. Caledonia	Singapore	Sri Lanka	Ethiopia	Georgia
New Zealand	Cambodia		Iran	Kyrgyzstan
PNG			Iraq	Kazakhstan
Solomon Islands			Jordan	Moldova
			Somalia	Russia
			Sudan	Tajikistan
			Syria	Turkey
			Yemen	Ukraine

Source: StarTV [1997].

programming seemed to be making inroads into the Chinese television market, doing better than other transnational satellite television channels that had preceded it.

Despite some popularity of its early western programming among certain elite segments in a number of country-markets in Asia, there were sizeable audiences under the satellite footprint unresponsive to StarTV in its early years. Given its television experience in other continents, notably Europe, News Corporation professed not to believe in global programming and advertising. Disregarding its many peripheral markets (Table 3.9), the satellite broadcaster had to offer something of specific cultural interest to each key market in Asia. In recognition of transborder ethnic segments, StarTV under News Corporation adopted a strategy of broadcasting in subregional and diasporic languages as well. Its partial acquisition of ZeeTV, a transnational channel in Hindi directed at South Asia and West Asia, inauguration of Phoenix Chinese channel, and the substitution of regionally-segmented Channel V for MTV were early steps in that direction. Consistent pursuit of such a strategy has paid off in audiences and consequently advertising revenue in key Asian markets, and thus one that StarTV has continued to pursue into the early 2000s. Its example has been followed by many of its competitors. Nonetheless the varied impact of transnational broadcasters across Asia is best understood first through an analysis of the different politico-economic and sociocultural contexts, as well as the television industries within the regions of South Asia, Southeast Asia and Northeast Asia, which this book will touch on next.

Within the three regions of Asia with which this book is primarily concerned, there are clusters of nation states that share much historically, economically and culturally. India, Pakistan and Bangladesh were once ruled together as the Indian Empire by the British and have had historical connections through previous empires. Hence various cultures and languages cross current political borders. Likewise, Indonesia, Malaysia and Brunei share a similar lingua franca though in their more recent histories they were colonised by the Dutch and the British. China, Taiwan, Hong Kong and Macau are at various stages of adhering to the concept of a Greater China, currently culturally and in part economically, while possibly in future politically. It is these cultural subcontinents with their transborder populations of similar if not identical ethnic groups that are primarily targeted by transnational television broadcasters. Yet in each of their constituent nations there has been a different history of public television, and varied policies on commercial broadcasting which have affected the impact of transnational broadcasters like StarTV.

INDIAN SUBCONTINENT

All countries in the South Asia region, with the exception of Nepal and Bhutan are characterised by once having had the same colonial power; in fact Pakistan, Bangladesh and India were carved of what was administered as the British Indian Empire. Sri Lanka and the Maldives were also colonised by the British, though as separate territories. Although the territories of India, Pakistan and Bangladesh have been independent of Britain for nearly 60 years, a major legacy

has been the dominance of English as the language of the educated
political and economic elite, even the language of government and
business. Furthermore, these three nations share very similar language
and cultural groups, across artificial national boundaries and thus
make interesting case studies of transnational television impact.

India

Geography and history: Dominating the South Asia region geographically, politically, economically and culturally, India is flanked to the
east by Bangladesh, to the northeast by Nepal and Bhutan, to the northwest by Pakistan, and to the south by Sri Lanka. All of these countries
are subsidiary audience markets for television originating from and/
or targeting India. As the world's seventh largest country geographically and second most populous country, India is a market which
can support a large and complex domestic television industry. Its total
population of 1.05 billion or 16 per cent of the world's population
(Daniel 2003: 341) must be the market potential driving the growth
plans of the new commercial television broadcasters, transnational
and regional. India has 16 official languages other than Hindi, many
of them shared by its neighbours—such as Urdu, Sindhi and Punjabi
with Pakistan, Bengali with Bangladesh, Nepali with Nepal, Tamil
with Sri Lanka. Thus it is also a major source of television for the entire Indian subcontinent and diasporic South Asian communities
worldwide.

The Indian subcontinent was the site of some of the oldest civilisations in the world, having extensive trade links with other Asian and
European kingdoms. But it was trade with Portuguese, French and
British, begun in the sixteenth century, which led in the next three centuries to gradual annexation of various regions on the subcontinent.
As a result of wars both in Europe and India by 1805 the British East
India Company came into control of virtually the whole subcontinent,
and this was consolidated as the British Indian Empire by the early
twentieth century. Opposition to British political rule and economic
exploitation in the early part of this century culminated in India gaining independence from the British Empire in 1947, when it simultaneously separated acrimoniously from the newly-formed state of Pakistan
(Speake 1993: 283–90). Upon attaining independence in the late 1940s

the Indian nationalists under Nehru had adopted a socialist economic model of relative self-sufficiency, and thus the country's intelligentsia has reacted negatively since to any form of perceived neo-colonialism such as advertising and marketing by multinational corporations. Only in the early 1990s did India begin to deregulate its economy and open itself to foreign investments, a development that had implications for the television and advertising industries.

Television governance: While domestic terrestrial television remained a state monopoly in the early to mid-1990s despite various proposals for change (Venkateswaran 1993: 15–16), transnational television was one of the few media that was independent of government regulation (Table 4.1). In the government's efforts to restrict it and restore advertisers to Doordarshan, the finance ministry issued a directive to the Reserve Bank of India (RBI), banning the release of foreign exchange specifically for advertisements on transnational TV channels. Thus to advertise on StarTV, a firm had to be a qualified exporter, approved by RBI [Interview Ind01.10]. But this stipulation was dropped after representatives from those channels threatened to take the government to court for acting unconstitutionally [Interview Ind04.01], a legal option not available in most other Asian countries. This episode is illustrative of the difficulty for the government in regulating the industry indirectly in the absence of specific laws, especially given the democratic nature of Indian society. Only through understanding the many players such as the World Bank, transnational corporations, domestic business groups, the state, the middle class, can StarTV's continued reception in India be understood [Conlon 1994]. The advent of transnational television via satellite and cable in Asia and the liberalisation of the Indian economy were concurrent yet independent events that stimulated the development of each other all the same [Interview Ind04.04].

Cable operations were primitive till the early 1990s since there was no government policy statement or any form of regulation apart from the stipulation of the Indian Telegraph Act dating from the 1890s that cables should not cross roads or be buried in the ground. The Act, modified in 1980s, required a licence only for satellite dishes directed at Inset satellites for a nominal one-off fee of Rs 50 (US$1.70) though in practice there was no policing of this requirement. Furthermore since cable operations were private, there was no censorship of its programming [Interview Ind01.02]. The Cable Bill passed in early 1995

Table 4.1
Media Ownership and Regulatory Oversight in India

Medium	Ownership	Oversight
Press	Private	Nominal
Radio	Public	Rigorous
Cinema '	Private	Nominal
Terrestrial TV	Public	Rigorous
Satellite TV	Private	Moderate
	Public	Rigorous
Cable TV	Private	Moderate
Internet	Private	Nominal

Sources: Compiled and adapted from Gunaratne (2000) and Goonasekera et al. (2003), among various others.

required that all cable television operators be registered with their local post office, though after the deadline only those in major towns had done so. A minimum of 51 per cent equity was to be held by Indian residents, which did not faze the multi-service operators (MSOs) run by non-resident Indians. Furthermore every cable operator had to re-transmit at least two DD channels, one of which had to be the sub-regional language channel. All encrypted services were subject to the programming and advertising codes applicable to DD, but whether cable operators would self-censor was uncertain. Dua [1991] argued that with technological development cable networks had the potential to become a form of interactive communication and to influence television programming. The Indian government reserved for itself the right to suspend cable operations on vague grounds of public interest and law-and-order [Lahiri 1995b]. The net result of this Cable Bill was further consolidation of the industry and dominance by big business, both domestic and foreign.

In 1995 the Supreme Court of India ruled, among other things, that there were no geographical barriers to communication, that every citizen should have access to broadcast signals, and that single-source information was at odds with democratic society. More specifically it ruled that the airwaves were not government property but public property that could be used by any Indian citizen and that DD had no right to forbid other broadcasters from uplinking their signals to a satellite [Lahiri 1995a]. Under pressure from the Supreme Court judgements for a new broadcast media law and independent supervisory authority, the government convened two committees to review a previously proposed broadcasting law and propose a new broadcasting policy. One committee recommended that both domestic and transnational channels be allowed to uplink from India, while the other recommended that uplinking be limited only to domestic channels, while foreign equity in them be prohibited. In anticipation of some liberalisation of the law and in order to raise revenue, DD began permitting Indian domestic channels to uplink to satellites or transmit via microwave their respective news bulletins from DD facilities around the country [Wanvari 1996].

The Congress government that returned to power in the mid-1990s was in favour of deregulation of the media industry to permit investment by multinational corporations, though there were reservations among them and especially the opposition. Then prime minister, Narasimha Rao, was inclined to allow foreign equity but was opposed by politicians and the press oligopoly which had the most to lose [Interview Ind02.04]. However there remain considerable inconsistencies across the various media sectors in the Indian economy (Table 4.2). In May 1997 the Broadcasting Bill was introduced in parliament, limiting cross-media ownership to 20 per cent and banning foreign investments in terrestrial broadcasting in India. Just before that happened, the government issued a ban on Ku-band dishes and thus caused IskyB, the News Corporation DTH venture to languish. The government also announced that it would permit satellite channels with at least 80 per cent equity and management control by resident Indians to be uplinked from India, thus saving them the high cost and time lag of uplinking from Singapore, Thailand, Hong Kong and the Philippines [Jifri 1998]. In July 1997, at the behest of News Television India, a subsidiary of Rupert Murdoch's News Corporation that had invested in DTH equipment, the Delhi High Court queried the government's ban on the use of DTH and called for it to be regulated instead.

The Prasar Bharati Act, which had first been proposed seven years earlier, was finally passed by parliament in November 1997, placing Doordarshan and All India Radio under an autonomous board rather than government control. In early 1998 the opposition BJP (Bharatiya Janata Party) came to power and announced that it intended to review all decisions of the Prasar Bharati board and rescind the Act. In May that year, the government announced that it would revive the Act and

Table 4.2
Media Ownership and Regulatory Oversight in Pakistan

Medium	Ownership	Oversight
Press	Private	Rigorous
Radio	Public	Rigorous
	Private	Moderate
Cinema	Private	Nominal
Terrestrial TV	Public	Rigorous
	Private	Rigorous
Satellite TV	Public	Rigorous
	Private	Moderate
Cable TV	Private	Rigorous
Internet	Private	Moderate

Sources: Compiled and adapted from Gunaratne (2000) and Goonasekera et al. (2003), among various others.

honour the autonomy of the board, yet soon after it attempted to remove the CEO. The long-awaited Broadcasting Bill raised a number of concerns. There has not been adequate acknowledgement of convergence of technologies. The requirement of mandatory uplinking, if emulated by other countries, would raise the costs and cause much unnecessary duplication. Given the potential for corruption, auctioning of licenses is fraught with problems and delays. Granting special privileges to Doordarshan to broadcast nationally-significant events could be seen as granting monopolistic rights (Mehta and Iyer 1999). Thus the Indian government moves to domesticate and to some extent control the transnational regional commercial broadcasters which were targeting India primarily, have not been without challenges.

Pakistan

Geography and history: This country of almost 800,000 sq km lies wedged between India and Afghanistan, along the Indus river, and shares a border also with China and Iran. It has a population estimated over 147 million, mainly Punjabi but also minorities of Sindhis, Pushtun, Baluch and Muhajir (Daniel 2003: 563–64), all of which it shares with its neighbouring countries of India, Afghanistan and Iran. Urdu is the official language, which is similar to Hindi in speech but uses a different script—one that is Arabic in origin. Spoken by only 20 per cent of the population it comes second to Punjabi which is spoken by 55 per cent (Goonasekera et al. 2003) and is a language shared with a neighbouring populous state within India. Although constitutionally a secular state despite pressures from religious fundamentalists, Islam is the religion of 96 per cent of the Pakistani population and that was the basis on which the country was formed out of the British Indian empire. Although it is a secular state, periodic agitation for it to adopt Shariah law and the need to appease that constituency has policy implications for television, especially cable and satellite.

Although a relative new country, the history of Pakistan dates back to the Indus civilisation of 2500 BCE. Between the eighth and the eleventh centuries the region was conquered by various Arab generals who spread Muslim cultural influence. From the twelfth to the sixteenth centuries CE, it was part of the Delhi sultanate and from the sixteenth to the nineteenth centuries it came under the Mughal emperors of India. The British East India Company annexed the Sindh and Punjab provinces in the nineteenth century, and after a mutiny and rebellion handed power over to the British government, which then formed its Indian empire together with other territories (Speake 1993: 288–89). In the early twentieth century there was political agitation for the formation of a separate state for the areas of Muslim majority and rejection of a federal nation. Thus on independence from Britain, the empire was divided into Pakistan and India, in what came to be known as the Partition which led to huge displacements of people then and intermittent military confrontations since, notably over Kashmir. In the 1971, East Pakistan, located on the other side of India, fought a war of independence and became Bangladesh. Given the political instability, democratic governments in Pakistan have been relatively short lived as successive coups have brought the military to power, as was the situation again at the turn of the twentieth century.

Television governance: Rather exceptionally for a developing country in Asia, Pakistan Television (PTV) began in 1963 as a joint venture between the government and a foreign corporation, the Japanese NEC (Nippon Electric Corporation), which then expanded slowly over the 1960s and 1970s. In 1989, the democratically-installed Benazir Bhutto government licensed Shalimar Television Network as the second channel initially to 10 major cities. PTV began a second channel for educational programmes utilising the AsiaSat1 satellite in 1992, and a third channel in 1998 for overseas Pakistanis such as in the Middle East and Europe. In 1996, the second Benazir Bhutto government licensed

Shaheen TV as the country's first pay-channel. In keeping with their commercial character, these broadcasters were governed not under specific broadcast legislation but under the company laws (Ali and Gunaratne 2000). Subsequently PTV launched a deliberately transnational service named Pakistan International Television (PITV) also beamed via AsiaSat1 and targeting Urdu-speaking audiences in India, Bangladesh, the Persian Gulf as well as parts of Pakistan not reached by terrestrial television [King 1996].

In 1997, the government of the then prime minister Nawaz Sharif reminded PTV and the private channels of the need to provide healthy dramas and educational programming, rather than competing with foreign channels by adopting western values. Meanwhile, the government licensed the country's first pay-TV channel, Shaheen Pay TV, owned by a local firm associated with retired airforce personnel with 50 per cent foreign equity, and delivered via MMDS technology (Tahir 1996: 113–31). Satellite dishes were commonplace in both urban and rural areas for the watching of foreign news and entertainment channels, including those of India, but no attempts were made by the government of Pakistan to control their sale and use (Ali and Gunaratne 2000). Pakistan's policies towards transnational television via satellite and cable, as with other media (Table 4.2), were consistent with its commitment to controlled access, given its history of authoritarian regimes and the political climate in relation to Afghanistan and India in the late 1990s and early 2000s.

Bangladesh

Geography and history: Located on the coastal plain of the Ganges river which flows into the Bay of Bengal, Bangladesh is surrounded by eastern and northeastern states of India except for a short border with Myanmar (Burma). Its 144,000 sq km territory holds over 133 million people (Daniel 2003: 64), making it the world's tenth biggest population and the most densely populated territory in the world. The population is 98 per cent Bengali which is the same ethnic group dominant in the neighbouring state of West Bengal in India, though Bangladesh is 87 per cent Muslim while West Bengal is predominantly Hindu in religion. It is 17,000 km from Pakistan (formerly West Pakistan), separated by India. As a relatively flat country, Bangladesh is prone to severe flooding and periodic cyclones.

The Muslim-dominated parts of the former British Indian states of Bengal and Assam were partitioned to form East Pakistan on independence in 1947. The first ever elections in the then East Pakistan held in 1970 resulted in the victory of the Awami League of Sheikh Mujibur Rahman that had campaigned for autonomy. When West Pakistan responded with military intervention, East Pakistan declared its independence as Bangladesh and was aided in its war of independence by India with which it has since had an ambivalent relationship. However, like Pakistan, Bangladesh has had a succession of democratically elected governments toppled through assassinations and military coups, which has adversely affected its economic development (Speake 1993: 56–57). Somewhat uniquely, democratic political leadership has been female in recent years, rotating between the daughter of Sheikh Mujibur and the widow of General Zia, both men being assassinated former presidents.

Television governance: Television commenced in 1964 while the country was still part of Pakistan, and it was established as a joint venture between the government and NEC of Japan. After the first station in the capital, Dhaka, further stations were set up in major cities over the 1960s and by the early 1970s it was broadcasting 35 hours per week, mostly in the native Bengali. Even after the revolution that created Bangladesh and the nationalisation of the Bangladesh Television (BTV), NEC remained a shareholder (Bhuiyan and Gunaratne 2000). But draconian media laws were drawn up in 1974 just a few years after the revolution, which successive governments used to curb the autonomy of the broadcast media especially. According to official guidelines issued in 1986, BTV broadcast programmes produced in Dhaka terrestrially through 15 transmitters for 9 hours daily and 14 hours on Friday and Saturdays. About 80 per cent of the programmes were local in origin and 20 per cent imported (Bhuiyan and Gunaratne 2000).

When the Awami League came back into government in 1996 it commissioned a report which recommended an independent authority to oversee broadcast media but there has been reluctance by the government to the relinquish control of BTV. Instead the government has preferred to allow the establishment of private channels to meet demands, though with some restrictions such as the relaying of BTV news bulletins and set proportions of entertainment, news and current affair, and educational and information programming (Page and

Crawley 2001). Under these terms, Bangladesh's first private channel, Ekushey Television (ETV), was granted a 15-year license in 1999 to broadcast both terrestrially as well as extra-terrestrially, thus reaching Bengali-speakers throughout South Asia as well as overseas. By the early 2000s cable operators were licensed by BTV on behalf of the government and provided dozens of satellite channels from India and regionally. However, policies governing all media in Bangladesh, while aiming to be generally stringent (Table 4.3) were subject to some modification upon changes of government, which have been fairly regular.

Table 4.3
Media Ownership and Regulatory Oversight in Bangladesh

Medium	Ownership	Oversight
Press	Private	Rigorous
Radio	Public	Rigorous
Cinema	Private	Moderate
Terrestrial TV	Public	Rigorous
	Private	Rigorous
Cable TV	Private	Moderate
Internet	Private	Nominal

Sources: Compiled and adapted from Gunaratne (2000) and Goonasekera et al. (2003), among various others.

As the second largest market after Greater China, the Indian subcontinent is a fitting site for analysis of the development of transnational television and advertising. Of all the countries in the region, India, with a per capita income comparable to that of China, represents the most attractive consumer market to multinational corporations, even if the figures are still in contrast with those of developed countries. Only in recent years has it sought integration into the capitalist world system, shifting to a market-based domestic economy open to foreign investment and trade. Thus the rapid growth of transnational television in India is symptomatic of the political and economic liberalisation of the country over the last decade or two, despite some reservations about social and cultural impact. While there are cultural affinities across the political borders of South Asia and its diaspora worldwide, it is India that remains the prime target of both transnational broadcasters and international advertising agencies.

MALAY WORLD

Before the Asian economic crisis of the late 1990s, both Indonesia and Malaysia were well on the road to joining the ranks of Newly Industrialising Countries (NICs) or Big Emerging Markets (BEMs), otherwise called the "tiger economies" of Asia, while Brunei has long been an oil-rich mini-state. All three nations have a variant of Malay as their national language, and there are Malay-speaking minorities among their neighbours in Southeast Asia and fellow member nations of the Association for Southeast Asian Nations (ASEAN), namely Singapore, Thailand and Philippines. This made their domestic consumer markets an attractive target for multinational marketers and such were the expectations of the pioneering transnational satellite broadcasters such as StarTV and CNN. This section is an exploration of the estimated 200-million Malay-language/cultural market of Southeast Asia and primarily why it has not been a market conducive for transnational television and advertising.

Indonesia

Geography and history: Located in Southeast Asia, Indonesia comprises about 14,000 islands spread over an area of almost 2 million sq km (over 700,000 sq miles) straddling the equator. Significant islands are Java, Sumatra, Borneo (shared with Malaysia), Sulawesi, New Guinea (shared with Papua New Guinea), Timor (shared with East Timor) and Bali (SBS World Guide 1996). The population of Indonesia as of mid-1999 was 209 million by government estimates. While Bahasa Indonesia, a variant of Malay, is the national language and lingua franca, there are 14 major languages and over 500 dialects spoken by the various ethnic groups that populate the country (Department of Information 2000). A tiny but economically significant Chinese minority has been a part of the territory for centuries, though their language and culture has not been officially recognised post-independence, except when placing or lifting restrictions on their use. Thus it has been a challenge for the media in Indonesia to reach a nation so spread out physically and quite diverse culturally.

The part of the Malay world known today as Indonesia has had a long history of being the site of a number of Hindu, Buddhist and later Muslim kingdoms influenced by similar kingdoms in India from the first to the sixteenth centuries CE. Then it came increasingly under the control first of the Portuguese in the sixteenth century and of the Dutch from the seventeenth century, seeking to dominate the spice trade. It became eventually the latter's colony of the East Indies, though temporarily under British administration during the Napoleonic wars of the eighteenth century. Periodic armed struggles by isolated sultanates in the East Indies were vigorously put down by the Dutch. From early in the twentieth century, there were various socio-political movements in support of independence, which gained some impetus during the Japanese occupation during World War II. Following the end of World War II, left-leaning nationalists under Soekarno proclaimed independence but it was only in 1949 after further armed conflict that the Dutch conceded sovereignty. Hence an era of anti-western sentiment and political non-alignment in the context of the Cold War between communist and capitalist blocs followed, as did economic stagnation subsequently. It was in this context of heightened nationalism that public television was first introduced in Indonesia in the 1960s [Department of Information 2000].

Television governance: In 1987 the Indonesian government decided to revive the domestic television industry by decreeing an encrypted commercial television service for the Jakarta area and later another for the Surabaya area. The government issued another decree in 1990 broadening the provisions to allow for one commercial broadcaster for each provincial or regional capital which was still to broadcast only locally and not network nationally, and allow for a commercially-funded educational channel which could broadcast nationally (Kitley 1994). In January 1993 the Indonesian government issued yet another decree restructuring the television industry to allow up to five commercial broadcasters, all of which would be allowed to use the Palapa satellite for national transmission. Thus the government progressively put in place a domestic commercial industry, which would have significant implications for the impact of transnational television in Indonesia. The government's liberal policy towards transnational satellite broadcasts was related to its interest in attracting foreign investments to the country by demonstrating the openness of the society and its politics [Interview Mly04.03]. Since Indonesia did not allow foreign broadcasts to be made from its territory, this only meant economic gain to Singapore which uplinked television programming to satellites while forbidding the viewing of the same by its own population [Interview Mly04.01].

Desirous that Indonesia not be a dumping ground for western cultural products, the government had advised that broadcasters could face unspecified sanctions if they failed to reduce foreign programming. The recommended ratio was 80 per cent locally-produced programmes and 20 per cent foreign programmes, but only the public broadcaster TVRI met this target while the commercial broadcasters did not. Since the government had set no strict quota, the decisions by stations on that issue were governed largely by the greater popularity of local programming. Broadcasters were also urged to be more selective in their choice of programming; for example music video clips and programmes which had the potential to cause unrest, were to be avoided [Jacob 1994]. The Indonesian government had restricted language of broadcast, regulated news and exercised censorship of programming, though the efficacy of these regulations were in doubt given domestic broadcasters' attempts to circumvent them. For instance, commercial stations were not permitted to have their own "news" programmes, and so they created "current affairs" programmes [Interview Mly03.07]. Censorship of foreign serials on domestic television was undermined when the same programme was available on spillover television from Malaysia [Interview Mly03.03].

In December 1996 a draft broadcasting law was passed by the national legislature to supersede the ministerial decrees under which the media has been regulated. Like the previous decrees the law sought to protect domestic broadcasters from foreign competition and extended to the Internet when utilised as a broadcast medium. Among other matters it allowed for self-regulation by the domestic commercial broadcasters of programme classification, the broadcast of news programmes other than those of TVRI, and allowed TVRI itself to accept advertising against the preferences of the domestic commercial broadcasters [Boulestreau 1997]. More specifically, the law also proposed that the number of television stations be limited, that 80 per cent of programming be locally produced and that all foreign programming be dubbed, not just subtitled, into Bahasa Indonesia [Kwang 1996]. However, the legislation was not immediately signed into law by the then President Soeharto. This prompted speculation that this was because it contained provisions that his family members, who had investments in commercial television, were unhappy with. Instead it was sent back to parliament to review at the request of the president, a situation without precedence in Indonesia [Television Asia 1997]. The long-suppressed agitation for reform in Indonesia finally found its opportunity when the Asian economic crisis of 1997 adversely affected Indonesia. Student demonstrations over corruption, and violence against them by the military compelled the handover by Soeharto in 1998 to his deputy. A number of media corporations had faced delegations from student and other protest movements that demanded changes of management and policies [Interview Mly04.05].

As third president B.J. Habibie formed a multi-party government and set an agenda for reform, including democratic elections for the first time since 1955. This interim government offered eight further commercial television licenses. But critics have alleged that some licenses were granted to business and government cronies, to dilute power rather than remove licenses from existing stations [ASIAcom 1999]. With the 1999 election of former dissident Abdurrahman Wahid as Indonesia's first democratically-elected president came an unexpected outright abolition of the information ministry to allow for freedom of the media which has persisted ever since (Table 4.4). The department was subsumed under the ministry of transportation and communications, which governed technical aspects and had no purview over content (Panjaitan 2000). Indonesia's television broadcasters were not altogether ill at ease with their new-found independence, because editorial staff had made the decision to abandon the Soeharto regime when it became quite evident that it would fall. One outcome was the prevalence of news, current affairs, political forums and talk-back programmes on Indonesian television channels. Concerns about a return to control of the media arose after Wahid was replaced as president by parliament for alleged incompetence in 2001. Under his successor Megawati Soekarnoputri (incidentally, the daughter of Indonesia's very first president Soekarno) the ministry of information was re-established, albeit with less regulatory authority. Despite lobbying by industry and civil society groups, draft legislation on broadcasting made no reference to convergence of technologies, skirted issues of censorship and did not provide for the promotion of subnational cultures by the public broadcaster (Kitley 2003). Still the diversification and popularity of domestic commercial television stifled any significant inroads by transnational television via satellite or cable into the 2000s.

Table 4.4
Media Ownership and Regulatory Oversight in Indonesia

Medium	Ownership	Regulation
Press	Private	Nominal
Radio	Public	Moderate
	Private	Nominal
Cinema	Private	Nominal
Terrestrial TV	Public	Moderate
	Private	Nominal
Satellite TV	Private	Nominal
Cable TV	Private	Moderate
Internet	Private	Nominal

Sources: Compiled and adapted from Gunaratne (2000) and Goonasekera et al. (2003), among various others.

Malaysia

Geography and history: Physically, Malaysia is comprised of the Malay peninsula, south of Thailand, and the northern third of the island of Borneo, shared with Indonesia. Although its 22 million population is predominantly Malay (58 per cent) and Muslim, the country is characterised by ethnic diversity with a 30 per cent Chinese population and 8 per cent Indian, as well as aboriginal peoples (Daniel 2003: 469). Malay is the official language but English is widely used while the Chinese and Indian populations have retained much of their language and culture. In the 1970s there was an effort to standardise the spelling of both Indonesian and Malaysian versions of their common Malay language, though diction remains somewhat at variance—much like UK and US English.

Like the islands of Indonesia, peninsular Malaysia came under the control and cultural influence of various Indian, Chinese, Thai and Javanese empires from the third to the fourteenth centuries. The Malacca sultanate which was established in 1400 was conquered by the Portuguese in 1511 who were in turn superseded by the Dutch in 1641. The Anglo–Dutch Treaty of 1824 clarified spheres of influence and led to the formation of the colony of the Straits Settlements incorporating Singapore, Malacca and Penang. Over the next century British influence and administration extended over the Malay sultanates. Following World War II, the British formed a Federation of Malaya and granted it independence about a decade later. In 1963, the new country of Malaysia was formed by the merger of Malaya with other British colonies of Singapore, Sabah and Sarawak, though the first of these colonies was separated from the new federation within two years [Rayner 1992: 126]. The formation of Malaysia was contested by Indonesia under President Soekarno and a war of confrontation occurred till his overthrow by General Soeharto. The inclusion of Sabah was contested peaceably by the Philippines and is still an unresolved issue. In the 1990s Malaysia, under long-serving prime minister Mahathir Mohammed, adopted a strategy of becoming a developed country by the year 2020, by investing and attracting investments in media, information and communications technologies.

Television governance: Television in Malaysia commenced with a single public channel in December 1963, the year of national independence from Britain, while a second public channel was launched six years later. Radio Television Malaysia (RTM) was organised financially and administratively as a department of the government like any other, with scant regard for its unique characteristics as a media organisation. Although it operated with minimal explicit rules, it assimilated the wishes of the major political parties that through a broad coalition ruled the country following independence. Lowe and Kamin (1982: 6–30) deduced an inventory of unspoken rules which governed producers at RTM such as catering to racial and religious sensibilities, portraying accurately values of particular communities, utilising standard Malay pronunciations rather than dialectic ones, observing political protocols on priority of news items, not implying that government services were inefficient, inculcating national pride, downplaying western lifestyles and so on. These rules were inferred from the decisions of committees, key government officials and national security council as well as the self-censorship exercised by producers.

As in many developing countries, RTM as a whole is funded by a combination of receiver license fees, government subsidies as well as advertising revenues, the last of which has had implications for its programming directions and policies. In order to compete for audiences and more pertinently advertising revenue against commercial competition, RTM began in the 1980s to import more recent, higher quality foreign programmes, catering via programme scheduling to ethnic minorities (notably the Chinese) with greater buying power, lowering restrictions to exempt tobacco brand names being used to advertise other products. Karthigesu (1994: 83–90) believed that there was consequent lowering of standards on sex and violence, such that even local scriptwriters and artistes were permitted to adopt more provocative western formats and styles. Threatened by the popularity of videotape entertainment and Singapore television spillover, the Malaysian government permitted domestic commercial television. Though as Nain and Anuar (2000) assert, the newcomer TV3 was never meant to be politically and editorially independent, owned as it was by a political party in the ruling coalition. Subsequent commercial broadcasters and cable networks licensed were often owned by corporations with links to the political elite in the country.

While Malaysia had banned the use of satellite dishes, their illegal use continued in its more remote Borneo states, as in neighbouring Brunei, to watch largely Indonesian domestic commercial television. In 1996, the Broadcasting Act was amended to license the use of satellite dishes to receive the domestic pay-TV services MegaTV and Astro, also enjoying political patronage, which carried a host of transnational and domestic channels. However all foreign programming was time-shifted by an hour to allow their downlinking for censors to work on them before re-broadcast locally. The same year, the ministry stipulated that 80 per cent of domestic television programming would have to be local by the year 2000 (Hashim 1997). In 1998, a new Multimedia Convergence Bill provided for the creation of a "super-ministry" to regulate the industry and for the corporatisation of the public broadcaster RTM. That would eventually result in greater consistency of policies across media (Table 4.5) in support of then prime minister Mahathir's vision of Malaysia becoming a developed country by the year 2020.

Table 4.5
Media Ownership and Regulatory Oversight in Malaysia

Medium	Ownership	Oversight
Press	Private	Moderate
Radio	Public	Rigorous
	Private	Moderate
Cinema	Private	Moderate
Terrestrial TV	Public	Rigorous
	Private	Rigorous
Cable TV	Private	Rigorous
Internet	Private	Moderate

Sources: Compiled and adapted from Gunaratne (2000) and Goonasekera et al. (2003), among various others.

Though political developments at the national level, such as the conflict between Mahathir and his former deputy that followed the Asian economic crisis of the late 1990s, augured for increasing media control, such concerns have abated with his retirement in 2003.

Brunei

Geography and history: This small country of 5,770 sq km occupies two enclaves rising from the coast with the South China Sea towards interior mountain ranges that separate Malaysian and Indonesian Borneo. It is rich from oil and gas, making its sultan possibly the world's wealthiest person and providing its population of less than 400,000 with the second highest income per capita in Asia outside Japan. The population is 69 per cent Malay and 18 per cent Chinese, the latter not qualifying for citizenship. Malay is official language, though English is in use and the ethnic Chinese minority retains its dialects (Daniel 2003: 45).

The sultanate of Brunei extended over much of Borneo in the sixteenth century before British colonialism in subsequent centuries saw its decline in both territories and political influence. Sarawak was ceded in 1841 to a British adventurer who helped the sultan win some wars and eventually the sultanate itself became a British protectorate in 1888. Brunei did not join other British colonies of Malaya, Singapore, Sabah and Sarawak in forming Malaysia in 1963 upon their independence. Instead under a treaty, Britain controlled Brunei's external relations and maintained troops till the country accepted full independence in 1984. Sultan Hassanal Bolkiah and his family rule by decree with an advisory council, and while there are two political parties, there have not been elections since political instability in the 1960s [Rayner 1992: 127].

Television governance: Television broadcasts began in 1975 as part of Brunei's five-year economic development plans, utilising state-of-the-art technology. In the late 1990s, Radio Television Brunei operated two channels, one terrestrial and the other satellite using Indonesian's Palapa C2. It broadcast in both Malay and English, using both imported and locally-produced programmes. The television media in Brunei was governed by the Emergency (Broadcasting) Order of 1997 which primarily regulated licensing and ownership of local broadcasters. It sought also to control foreign broadcasts allowing the proscribing of channels whose quality and content are deemed unacceptable (Safar and Ladi 2000). In keeping with its conservative culture and politics, as well as its small size, the media in Brunei is limited, government-owned and thus closely regulated (Table 4.6). But while neighbouring Malaysia introduced cable television, which combined both existing global and new local channels, Brunei continued to be somewhat unregulated regarding access to transnational television via satellite dishes. Although the population is relatively affluent, its small size made Brunei a marginal market for transnational broadcasters operating in Asia.

Table 4.6
Media Ownership and Regulatory Oversight in Brunei

Medium	Ownership	Regulation
Press	Private	Moderate
	Public	Rigorous
Radio	Public	Rigorous
Cinema	Private	Moderate
Terrestrial TV	Public	Rigorous
Satellite TV	Private	Moderate
Internet	Public	Moderate

Sources: Compiled and adapted from Gunaratne (2000), among various others.

In its early years StarTV programming for Southeast Asia was precisely the same that it broadcast throughout the continent. Under its new owners, News Corporation, StarTV channels developed regionally-contextualised sports, news and entertainment programming for the South and Northeast Asia audience markets. With little programming targeted at Southeast Asia in the early 1990s there were no ratings published for StarTV or any other transnational channels, and certainly no cult following for any of their programmes. Unlike in India and China, pre-existing domestic channels in Indonesia, Malaysia and Brunei showed programmes of similar genre to that available on StarTV, if not identical programmes, duly dubbed or at least subtitled. Of the other countries around the Malay world, Singapore, southern Thailand and southern Philippines with their small Malay minorities were of limited interest to their domestic broadcasters, but could be collectively to transnational ones. Hence the Malay world constitutes quite a unique, fairly large but relatively untapped audience market within Asia for transnational television.

GREATER CHINA

Though the concept of a "Greater China" dates from the 1930s, it has gained increasing currency with the growth of the transborder economy among the three East Asian territories and expectations of a reunified or federated state eventually (Harding 1993). It comprises the Peoples' Republic of China, Taiwan, Hong Kong and Macau. Hong Kong is the regional headquarters of many transnational television channels and the location of their satellite uplinking facilities for broadcasting to much of Asia. While its territory was a minuscule market for Mandarin-language broadcasters because the local dialect was Cantonese, both its domestic and transnational broadcasters have attracted significant audiences in China and Taiwan. Any discussion of transnational television in Asia cannot ignore one of its major target markets, the approximately 1.5 billion ethnic Chinese resident in East Asia of which the Hong Kong, Macau, Taiwan and PRC populations are inextricable and significant parts. This is discounting the sizeable diasporic markets in Southeast Asia and worldwide estimated at another 30 million.

China

Geography and history: China (PRC) is the largest country in Northeast Asia and third largest in the world at 9.6 million sq km. It is bounded to the north by Mongolia, Russia and North Korea, to the west by the Central Asian nations of Kazakhstan, Kyrgyzstan, Tajikistan and Afghanistan, and to the south by India, Nepal, Bhutan, Burma, Laos and Vietnam. Given its geographical size, the landscape and climate of China is a study of contrasts. It comprises two major intersecting mountain chains through the centre, grasslands in Manchuria in the north, the high plateau around Tibet in the west, desert in the northwest, and large fertile river plains towards the east [Rayner 1992: 113–14]. No discussion of television audiences can ignore the fact that with over 1.2 billion citizens, China is the most populous nation on earth and comprises 21 per cent of the world's population. Despite stringent family planning laws, the population continued to grow and as of the early 1990s 59.1 per cent of the population was less than

30 years of age and 40.8 per cent under 20 years (Goonasekera and Holaday 1993: 167). The Han Chinese constitute 92 per cent of the population, although they share eight major languages and 600 dialects among them. However China uses only one written language in a modernised, simplified script, as well as in a romanised form called "Hanyu Pinyin". The official language, Mandarin or Putunghua, is spoken by over 744 million, while some of the other eight languages such as Wu by 78 million, Cantonese by 53 million, Hunanese by 45 million and Hakka by another 45 million. Only 55 ethnic minorities are officially recognised though the linguistic diversity is in reality closer to 150 [Johnstone and Mandryk 2001: 159].

The ancient history of China was characterised by a series of dynasties, the last of which was the Manchu dynasty comprised actually of non-Han-Chinese nomads from an area northeast of China. During the nineteenth century, the latter part of their rule that was weak and corrupt, the country experienced famines and political unrest. These were capitalised on by imperialist powers such as Britain, Germany and the US who used their success in the Opium Wars to carve out spheres of political influence in China and control all its international trade through their treaty ports along the coast and major rivers. Peasant uprisings, the Boxer rebellion against western imperialism and the defeat in the Sino-Japanese War contributed to disintegration of imperial China, the abdication of the infant emperor, and establishment of the republic under Sun Yat-sen, although that degenerated into warlordism by rival generals and provincial governors. Two political parties surfaced, the nationalists or Kuomintang (KMT), under Sun Yat-sen, and the communists or Chinese Communist Party (CCP) under Mao Zedung. They cooperated initially to unite China and were galvanised by a common enemy in Japan, which invaded the north in the 1930s to set up a puppet state of Manchuria headed by the deposed last emperor of China. But the defeat of Japan at the end of World War II saw civil war break out resulting in the communists conquering the mainland to set up the Peoples' Republic of China and the nationalists, now under Chiang Kai-Shek, retreating to the large island of Taiwan, formerly known as Formosa [Rayner 1992: 114–15].

The communists imposed a Soviet-style constitution, nationalised industry, instituted land reform, and practised economic central planning. When the programme of agricultural and industrial collectivisation in the "Great Leap Forward" spearheaded by Mao in the late 1950s resulted in poverty and famine, a recovery programme was instituted by moderates, which reversed partially the earlier collectivisation.

But Mao fought back in the late 1960s with the Cultural Revolution against perceived creeping capitalism and encouraged the student-led Red Guard movement that removed moderates. The ensuing chaos was rectified in 1970 with the help of prime minister Zhou Enlai, which led to Deng Xiaoping, among others, being rehabilitated. However, the deaths of both Zhou and Mao in 1976 resulted in a succession struggle between leftists or "Gang of Four" and the moderates headed by Deng. When his protégés were finally installed as party chair and prime minister, Deng (as "paramount leader" without any significant official title) was able to push his agenda of modernisation through government streamlining, army downsizing, local autonomy, market incentives and foreign investment, all of which have had implications for the television and advertising industries in China. Student demonstrations in the mid-1980s, which culminated in the 1989 Tiananmen Square massacre, undermined Deng's reforms and resulted in the rise of conservatives in government (Speake 1993: 123–27). Although officially retired in 1987, Deng maintained political influence as a "kingmaker" behind successive national leadership till his demise in 1996. Hailing from business-oriented Shanghai, president Ziang Jemin and premier Zu Rhongji continued Deng's policy of economic liberalisation mixed with political conservatism through to the early 2000s before handing on the leadership to their deputies Hu Jintao and Wen Jiabao respectively in 2002.

Television governance: The Chinese Communist Party typically saw television as a major means of propaganda, communicating the benefits of communism and persuading its population to support their policies. Its role was to disseminate news and government decrees, to provide education and to enrich the population's cultural life (Won 1989: 217). The Propaganda Committee of the Chinese Communist Party's Central Committee held ultimate control of broadcasting through the Ministry of Radio and Television and controlled directly national broadcasters such as China Central Television (CCTV). A second-tier of television channels and local radio existed, governed by the Party's committees at the provincial, autonomous regions and municipal levels. In keeping with its ideology all broadcasting was financed by direct government grants and there were no license fees for viewers and listeners, although advertising had been increasingly used to subsidise operating expenses (Bishop 1989: 113–14). In 1983 the Chinese central government gave governments at provincial level and below the right to build and manage their own broadcasting stations, while CCTV was separated from the direct management of the Ministry of Radio, Film and Television (Won 1989: 218). The commercialisation of China's television bureaucracy was fuelled in part by the competition from spillover television from Hong Kong from the late 1970s and the arrival of transnational television such as StarTV in the 1990s. Domestic public broadcasters thus became semi-autonomous corporations free to pursue financial prosperity, though still subject to the government's political strictures (Hao and Huang 1996).

From the mid-1980s satellite dishes were scarcely used but the launch of AsiaSat1 in the early 1990s created phenomenal growth with sales said to be about 20,000 satellite dishes per month. By end 1993 up to 70 million Chinese were estimated to be watching programmes from transnational satellites such as AsiaSat1, Palapa, Thaicom and others with broadcast footprints that covered China, either directly or via cable systems. In 1994 the State Council Proclamation No. 129 signed by the Chinese premier Li Peng, came into force, banning unlicensed ownership of satellite dishes on the grounds of preserving Chinese culture and socialism. But it might have come too late, for by the mid-1990s there were estimated to be between 600,000 and 1 million satellite dishes already in use. Furthermore the People's Liberation Army (PLA) had been actively manufacturing satellite dishes as a means of supplementing its falling budget grants from the central government of China [Ciotti 1994]. Although domestic television stations were not allowed to re-broadcast satellite television, thousands of illegal cable operators had been relaying transnational programming or pirated videos to neighbourhoods. Thus cable television had become a large-scale industry in China, attracting foreign investment including from Hong Kong and Taiwan, as well as domestic investment including local governments [Stine 1994].

In the mid-1990s CCTV entered into various commercial agreements with Associated Press TV (APTV), US-based Encore Media Corporation and Australia's Channel Nine for supply and exchange of global news, sports, children's programmes, drama and movie programming [AMCB 1996]. Co-productions with foreign television producers included a 90-minute international sports programme which would be broadcast nationwide via satellite on CCTV [Asian A&M 1995]. However by the late 1990s, at the bidding of President Jiang, the Ministry of Radio, Film and Television (MRFT) rescinded the relative autonomy of Chinese television stations via a new censorship system, centralised programme purchasing and evaluation of their performance in relaying CCTV broadcasts [Television Asia 1996c]. Given that the four roles of television are deemed officially to be information dissemination, aesthetic enjoyment social regulation and education/service, programming tends to have a didactic element (Keane 2003). Perhaps the earlier moves towards liberalisation of the programming represented a response to competition from transnational television services, rather than any commitment to the political emancipation of CCTV.

In the early 2000s, mindful of the convergence of communications technologies, China merged its State Administration of Radio, Film and Television (SARFT) with the Ministry of Post and Telecommunications, to form the Ministry of Information Industry (MII). Its new policy allows terrestrial and cable providers to merge and become content providers as well as offer Internet services, video-on-demand, distance-learning and shopping channels over cable networks. While foreign investors are prohibited, Hong Kong-listed companies have been able to enter the China market, even buying shares in local cable networks and establish joint ventures [Leung 2001]. On taking office in 1998, premier Zhu Rongji had called on CCTV and party officials to act as watchdogs in support of China's economic reforms, though later that year president Jiang had warned against subverting state authority (Yan 2000). Of the options Wei (2000) saw before the industry—trading political allegiance for market privileges or using financial clout to assert greater autonomy—which it will take has yet to be seen. Despite mixed messages, the entry of China into the WTO in 2001 holds hope that there might be incremental liberalisation of the media industries (Table 4.7). Certainly foreign suppliers are counting on more opportunities for selling broadcast hardware and software, or both technology

Table 4.7
Media Ownership and Regulatory Oversight in China

Medium	Ownership	Oversight
Press	Public	Rigorous
Radio	Public	Rigorous
Cinema	Private	Moderate
Terrestrial TV	Public	Rigorous
Satellite TV	Private	Moderate
Cable TV	Public	Rigorous
Internet	Private	Rigorous

Sources: Compiled and adapted from Gunaratne (2000) and Goonasekera et al. (2003), among various others.

and expertise. Nonetheless the television broadcasters, domestic and transnational, have had to walk a fine line in China between conflicting political and market pressures.

Taiwan

Geography and history: Taiwan comprises the main island province of the same name, due north of the Philippines and southwest of Japan, as well as a few small and highly fortified islands very close to the central coast of mainland China. In fact it is adjacent to the Chinese province of Fuchien from which much of its population comes. Its warm and moist climate supports agriculture such as sugar cane, tea, bananas and rice crops, largely for local consumption. Although at 36,000 sq km Taiwan is less than half the size of Tasmania, it supports a population 80 times that of the latter [Rayner 1992: 117]. Of the 20.3 million population, local-born Taiwanese represent 84 per cent of the population, mainland Chinese 14 per cent, while about 2 per cent is comprised of Malayo-Polynesian tribal indigenes in the mountain regions. Adult literacy stands at 91 per cent and Mandarin is the national language, though Taiwan uses an older more complex script than that adopted in PRC and does not use a romanised form. Many of the older generation educated during the Japanese colonial era can speak Japanese, while southern Hokkein/Fuchien and Hakka dialects are as widely spoken as they are on neighbouring provinces on mainland China [Johnstone and Mandryk 2001: 186].

After 50 years of Japanese colonisation Taiwan was surrendered to the nationalist government in China at the end of World War II in Asia in August 1945. When the nationalist or Kuomintang (sometimes referred to as Guomindang) government of Chiang Kai-shek was progressively defeated on mainland China by the communists under Mao Zedung, about 2 million nationalist forces, dependents and sympathisers fled to the province of Taiwan between 1947 and 1949. Much to the resentment of the 8 million native Taiwanese, the nationalists established a government in exile for the whole of China and maintained large armed forces in the hope of reconquering the mainland (Speake 1993: 556). Supported politically in their claim of sovereignty over the whole of China by the virulently anti-communist US governments of the time, the Taiwan (ROC) government represented the country in international fora such as the UN. It was ousted from the UN and replaced by the People's Republic of China (PRC) only in 1971, following détente between the US and the latter. Though the US gave full diplomatic recognition in 1979 to China, it still supports Taiwan economically and despite the lapse of their defence pact in 1984, the US has continued to arm Taiwan. Since then Taiwan has enjoyed diplomatic ties with only a few other non-communist nations, though many others have used pseudo-cultural and trade missions to maintain ties unofficially.

Upon the death of Chiang Kai-shek, he was succeeded by his son Chiang Ching-kuo who had the political legitimacy to carry out a programme of progressive democratisation and localisation or "Taiwanisation" of the nation state. This saw opposition political parties condoned so long as they forswore communism, and native Taiwanese allowed into positions of influence in the party, government and military. The process of liberalisation was accelerated on Chiang Ching-kuo's demise in 1984 by the US-educated economist Lee Teng-hui, the first Taiwanese-born president, who soon retired off "old guard" nationalist politicians formerly from the mainland in favour of locals, and in 1987 repealed the 40-year martial law, which has had implications for the development of the domestic television industry as will be explained. In 1991 Lee ended the state of civil war with China and accepted the legitimacy of the communist government in Beijing, abandoning ROC hopes of regaining control of the mainland. However calls for full Taiwanese independence from China promoted by the new opposition Democratic Party were initially rejected by the wider population, which feared a punitive invasion upon such a declaration (Speake 1993: 557). During Taiwanese national elections in 1995, for instance, China was not averse to flexing its military muscle in the Formosa Strait in an attempt to sway voting behaviour against the independence movement. Still, in 1999 the Democratic Party came to power in presidential elections though the new president Chen Sui Bian toned down the independence rhetoric so as not to antagonise China. In a surprise development, Taiwan was welcomed into membership of the World Trade Organization in 2001 at the same time as China was.

Television governance: Under martial law from 1949–87 media content was under the strict censorship of three authorities: the Government Information Office (GIO), the KMT Cultural Work Committee and the Taiwan Garrison Command. The government periodically enacted laws to further control television broadcasting, for instance one to restrict the expression of Taiwanese cultural localisms on television (Lee 1990). Furthermore, through their controlling interests the nationalist government placed ministers, generals, party officials or sympathetic businessmen as directors on the boards of the three broadcasters. Almost half the general managers in the stations were ex-military officers and former aides to the then-president of the country. Even lower-level personnel appointments were influenced such that the vast majority of the television journalists were KMT party members and mostly mainlanders or their descendants, even though these groups comprise less than a fifth in the general population (Lo et al. 1994). Typical of such an identification of media executives with the regime in political power, ideological dissent went unreported, sensitive issues were assiduously avoided, and self-censorship took care of grey areas even before the official censors would have. Hence those in the political opposition had to turn to cable television as a vehicle for their views. The largest cable operators were believed to have 100,000 subscribers, most about 20,000 and some as few as 3,000 subscribers [Interview Chn03.08].

Since many Taiwanese legislators were owners of cable operations and had endured police harassment such as the cutting of cable wires, they were keen to have cable television legalised for their own benefit [Interview Chn02.10]. As the Cable Law of 1993 took effect, there was a shake-out in the cable industry. A minimum of NT200 million (US$7 million) was required for the necessary infrastructure to comply with the law, and consequently between mid-1993 and end 1995 the number of cable operators dropped from over 600 to about 180. As expected, the number of cable networks in Taiwan fell from over 300 in the 1980s to just 140 by 1998 as a result of mergers. Meanwhile subscriptions of cable television had risen from 42 per cent of all television households to nearly 80 per cent over the same period. In 1997 a fourth terrestrial station, Formosa Television (FTV) commenced broadcasting, as a result of the Taiwan government lifting a 22-year restriction on new television channels (Wang and Lo 2000). Under a new Cable Television Broadcasting Law effective early 1999, cable operators were allowed to own and manage telecoms businesses as well. Furthermore, foreign investors were allowed to purchase up to 20 per cent of a Taiwanese cable operator, with approval [International Cable 1999b]. Thus over the decade of the 1990s the Taiwan media market overall became at once better regulated and yet more liberalised (Table 4.8).

Large-scale domestication of transnational channels by dubbing, sub-titling, local hosts, local footage and various other strategies have been critical to their success in the Taiwan market (Chen 2004). Yet despite the proliferation of commercial television channels, Chang (2000) pointed out none featured regular programming catering to the ab-original peoples of Taiwan, being as they are a small and unprofitable market.

Table 4.8
Media Ownership and Regulatory Oversight in Taiwan

Medium	Ownership	Oversight
Press	Private	Nominal
Radio	Public	Moderate
	Private	Nominal
Cinema	Private	Nominal
Terrestrial TV	Public	Moderate
	Private	Nominal
Satellite TV	Private	Nominal
Cable TV	Private	Moderate
Internet	Private	Nominal

Sources: Compiled and adapted from Gunaratne (2000), among various others.

Hong Kong

Geographical background: With a population of over 6 million Hong Kong is one of the most densely populated and urbanised territories in the world, necessitating most of its food, water and raw materials be shipped in from abroad, most notably from mainland China. Hong Kong is located along the tropical south coast of China near the mouth of the Pearl River, adjacent to the Quangdong Province, into which its television signals spill over the border. It is located 130 km southeast of Quangzhou (Canton), capital of the Quangdong province, and 65 km east of the Macau, the former Portuguese colony which reverted to China in 1999. The total land area of 1,071 sq km comprises the Hong Kong island, the Kowloon peninsula, the hinterland bordering China known as the New Territories, and 235 islands, the major ones being Lantau, Lamma and Cheung Chau. Its population is estimated at over 7 million, mostly ethnically Cantonese as in the surrounding southern Chinese province. By contrast, neighbouring Macau has an area of

16 sq km and a population of about 450,000, (Daniel 2003: 157), though also mainly Cantonese.

Being mountainous and lacking in fertile land Hong Kong was relatively unpopulated when the British recognised the value of its sheltered deep-water anchorage to their trade with China and founded a settlement in 1840. Following the First Opium War, the island was ceded by China under duress to Britain as a trading base in January 1841 in lieu of a commercial treaty over British access to Chinese ports. Further hostilities ended with the Peking Convention in 1860 which ceded Kowloon to the British in perpetuity, while another treaty in 1898 leased the New Territories and 235 islands to Britain for 99 years (Speake 1993). The population of Hong Kong grew rapidly from then, fuelled periodically by refugees from unrest on or invasions of the Chinese mainland, and it began its role as a major trading port with China and with Chinese communities in Asia and worldwide. The reopening of China to the world in the late 1970s saw Hong Kong return to its role as a base for international trade with China, especially its southern provinces, and therefore for marketing and advertising to this emerging market. On 1 July 1997 the British colony was returned to China's sovereignty though it remained semi-autonomous as a Special Administrative Region, the practical implementation of which has implications for the transnational and regional channels based there.

Television governance: Television began in 1957 as a commercial service when Redifusion Hong Kong was licensed to provide a wired television service comprising two subscription channels. Then in 1967 Television Broadcasters Ltd (TVB) began operating a wireless television service under an exclusive licence, and has since dominated the market, going to colour transmission in 1972. When the government offered two more wireless licences after a broadcast policy review, Redifusion decided to terminate its wired services and take up wireless broadcasting in 1973. This station subsequently changed owners and was renamed Asia Television (ATV) as it is called to this day. It was a requirement of their licences that both TVB and ATV broadcast a Chinese-language and an English-language channel each and carry specific news, current affairs, children's and educational programming [Hong Kong Government 1994c].

Despite Hong Kong's reputation as a free-market economy, its broadcasting industry was highly regulated in the early 1990s and its authorities have moved with great caution in deregulating the licensing of terrestrial, satellite and cable television. Hong Kong had quite bureaucratic controls on television even prior to its incorporation into China, perhaps in anticipation of that eventuality. The control of radio and television broadcasting in Hong Kong rested with the Broadcasting Authority, a statutory body which used the Television and Entertainment Licensing Authority (TELA) as its executive arm. Domestic terrestrial stations were granted licenses for 12 years, subject to mid-term reviews during which multiple public hearings are held. These stations were subject to programming and advertising codes of practice, and virtually identical codes apply to domestic cable and transnational satellite stations. TELA also commissioned research biennially on viewership, monthly meetings of its television advisory groups in each of the 19 districts of the territory and quarterly meetings of its five audience panels [Interview Chn04.02].

In 1990 the Hong Kong Broadcasting Authority granted a non-exclusive license to StarTV to broadcast five satellite television channels across Asia, taking care to protect its domestic television licensees by restricting StarTV from broadcasting in Cantonese or broadcasting news programmes. The 12-year license was amended in October 1991 to allow StarTV to carry the BBC World Service Television, which must have been seen as logical enough for a British colony. In June 1993 a 12-year cable TV exclusive license was granted to Wharf Cable giving it a monopoly in Hong Kong during its first three years of operation on the condition that it did not accept advertising. From October 1993, StarTV was allowed to operate an Asia-wide regional pay-TV service on condition that the sole distributor of such channels within Hong Kong be the exclusive cable TV licensee, Wharf Cable [Hong Kong Government 1994b].

By the mid-1990s the Hong Kong government shelved plans to introduce a unified bill to cover the satellite, cable, terrestrial and other forms of television. Instead it decided draft regulations specifically for pay-TV and video-on-demand (VoD), in the context of Wharf Cable's pay-TV monopoly expiry and HK Telecom's plans to offer VoD services. Naturally as it was just over a year to the handover of Hong Kong the real reason for the shelving of the bill was alleged to be to please China [Television Asia 1996b]. What would happen in the post-1997 era was uncertain because the Basic Law, or constitution of Hong Kong, was vague on the application of China's mass communication laws [Interview Chn03.02]. Yet even before the handover the government announced that the broadcast laws governing new technologies such as satellite television, VoD and pay-TV would be overhauled over a 12-month period while the existing terrestrial broadcasting laws would not come under review [Asian A&M 1997c]. Ironically, Hong Kong's traditional free-market stance with cautious regulation of convergent media technologies has seen its pre-eminence as a regional production and broadcast centre threatened by Singapore with its government interventionism through both regulation and promoting investment (Lovelock and Goddard 1999). In keeping with worldwide trends in deregulation, Hong Kong allowed telecommunications companies to offer television and vice versa in 1998. Furthermore in order to attract regional broadcasters to use Hong Kong as their media hub, the government relaxed foreign ownership rules that previously restricted them to 49 per cent shares (So et al. 2000). Despite maintenance of media freedoms in Hong Kong into the early 2000s (Table 4.9), a perception persisted about their erosion since the handover to China, under a local legislature largely nominated by the mainland government.

Table 4.9
Media Ownership and Regulatory Oversight in Hong Kong

Medium	Ownership	Oversight
Press	Private	Nominal
Radio	Public	Moderate
	Private	Nominal
Cinema	Private	Nominal
Terrestrial TV	Private	Moderate
Satellite TV	Private	Nominal
Cable TV	Private	Moderate
Internet	Private	Nominal

Sources: Compiled and adapted from Gunaratne (2000) and Goonasekera et al. (2003), among various others.

As with their political and economic contexts, the development of television in the Indian subcontinent, the Malay World and Greater China is a study in contrasts. Still, there has long been some overlap in viewership, programming and advertising within these regions, due to television signal spillover, targeted broadcasting, programme joint productions and sales, as well as direct investments in stations and other parts of each others' cultural industries. This process has been intensified by the growth of satellite and cable television with the consequent need for programming, audiences and advertisers, and with the greater consumer access to television viewing alternatives on a transnational basis. The responses of domestic public and commercial broadcasters in the key markets of China, Indonesia and India to this transnational television onslaught are somewhat varied, given the differing domestic television environments and regulatory policies —developments touched upon in this chapter. The implications for the multinational corporations of targeting these Asian economic regions, via the advertising industry operating out of the pivotal commercial cities of Mumbai, Jakarta and Hong Kong, will be explored over the next couple of chapters.

TARGETING MARKETS

While transnational print media has had a long history in Asia, transnational television is a recent phenomenon to which marketers and their advertising agencies have had to respond. Much of the regional advertising in Asia is handled by the key cities of Mumbai, Jakarta and Hong Kong, though there are other centres such as Chennai, Bangalore, Kuala Lumpur, Singapore, Taipei and Shanghai. Overall Asian television advertising market was worth US$36 billion in 2000 and expected to more than double to US$76 billion by 2010. Asia is also said to have the highest growth rate of television penetration worldwide, rising from 470 million households in 2000 to 660 million households by 2010 [Brown 2001]. Though there is limited secondary data available in the public domain, trends in ratings, media costs and advertising spending may still be analysed in the light of decision-makers' perspectives. From all this it is quite evident that StarTV, in particular, has been utilised as an advertising medium in varied ways in some cultural markets and largely ignored by others.

PERSUADING MARKETERS

The pioneer broadcaster StarTV was initially pan-Asian in its programming and sought to convince multinational marketers and their advertising agencies of this unique advantage in reaching the elite of the continent. However speculation in its early years that there was minimal response from Asian television audiences proved to be true, prompting a belated admission and shift by StarTV to regional programming. Thus the advertising strategy of StarTV in the transition between its two ownership regimes, the advertisers they attracted to the new medium, and the revenue raised, particularly over the turbulent initial half-decade of its transnational satellite television service are worthy of investigation.

Business strategy

The strategy for attracting advertisers under the two ownership eras of StarTV comprised in many ways a study of contrasts between the approaches of a largely domestic conglomerate, Hutchinson Whampoa, new to the business of broadcasting, and of an integrated global media corporation, News Corporation, with considerable experience in transnational television via satellite and cable in Europe and North America. Somewhat paradoxically, the Hong Kong founders adopted a global or pan-Asian approach, whilst the new global owners switched to a regional and quasi-domestic strategy. This shift had much to do with gaining sufficient advertising revenue for the largely free-to-air service to stay financially viable.

Hutchinson Whampoa era: Undergirding StarTV in its initial years were a number of Hong Kong firms that had signed two-year contracts as "foundation advertisers". StarTV had offered them an advertising package that included 4,000 television spots of 30 seconds each for US$2 million and allowed them up to two years to utilise the advertising time so purchased. Alternatively, an advertiser was allowed to purchase a 30-second spot on StarTV for US$1,500, which compared favourably with the CCTV rate set at US$8,000 and TTV rate of US$3,500 approximately, for reaching the Chinese and the Taiwanese markets respectively. Many of these clients had little need to advertise on a pan-Asian medium but were believed to be personal business associates of Li Ka-Shing, head of the family that through Hutchinson owned StarTV then. It is quite a common practice among Chinese businesspersons to draw on their *quanxi* or long-standing business relationships of mutual obligation. However, the founding managing director Richard Li, a son, claimed later that such local advertisers comprised only US$40 million of the estimated US$360 million advertising revenue earned by 1994 and that the rest came from multinational corporate sponsors such as Coca-Cola, McDonalds and Sony which had legitimate business rationales for advertising on StarTV [Straits Times 1994].

With operating costs estimated at US$80 million per year and the business not expected to break even for some years, one cost-cutting business strategy that Richard Li adopted was to pay minimal royalties to channel providers such as BBC and MTV. Instead they were offered a share of the profits and the opportunity of being showcased on the first commercial transnational satellite television station in Asia. He also purchased inexpensive re-runs of *Santa Barbara* and *Hill Street Blues*, popular in the US a decade earlier but not seen before in most of Asia. Another practice developed by Star TV was to offer co-financing to independent programme producers through an associate company that handled such acquisitions [Asia-Pacific Broadcasting 1993]. None of these efforts seem to have made much of an impact on the financial fortunes of StarTV and so its corporate parent Hutchinson Whampoa was soon looking for a new business partner, which it eventually found in News Corporation.

News Corporation era: Once ownership of StarTV passed fully into the hands of the Rupert Murdoch-controlled News Corporation around the mid-1990s, many of its former advertisers abandoned it. Attempts by the new "western" management to enforce contractual obligations on these local businessmen were quite unsuccessful. At the same time, the growth in the number of transnational broadcasters available on the rival satellite platforms undermined StarTV's ability to attract audiences. Its inability to provide local programming content in Hong Kong due to government restrictions, the prohibitions on private ownership of satellite dishes particularly in China and preference given to controlled cable-based access to transnational broadcasts by many governments in Asia inhibited StarTV's marketability to advertisers as a free-to-air broadcast medium. Furthermore, StarTV's change of strategy towards pay-TV was pre-empted by newer rivals such as HBO Asia and ESPN Asia, which adopted that mode almost from their very start. So as we have seen in an earlier chapter, under News Corporation, StarTV had by the late 1990s become increasingly differentiated into specialised regional channels and attracted new advertisers by targeting regional, even quasi-domestic audiences.

Products Promoted

By the second full year of its operation, the largest number of advertisers on StarTV by product category, were "travel, hotel, leisure and airlines" (Table 5.1). Their choice of the transnational satellite television medium was understandable since by the very nature of their service the target markets were primarily transnational and pan-regional. "Corporate image" advertising, largely by multinational banking and financial institutions, followed closely behind with fashion and boutiques, automobiles and accessories, and alcoholic beverages. Somewhat surprisingly, StarTV did not attract significant number of advertisers in the categories of audio and visual equipment, or watches and clocks, often global in production and marketing. Over the years, the category of "food and confectionary" came to attract the largest number of advertisers on the medium, followed by "corporate image" and "fashion and boutiques". While corporate advertising was a natural use of the transnational television medium, the other two categories reflect both the growing affluence of Asian consumer markets, despite occasional setbacks, and the aggressive involvement of marketers, both regional and global. But it is noteworthy that the numbers in some categories such as "construction and real estate" and travel, hotels, etc. have stagnated generally, even declined on occasion.

Table 5.1
Top Product Categories Advertised on StarTV, early to mid-1990s

Product Category	1993	1994	1995	1996
Albums and cassettes (music)	13	15	36	61
Alcoholic drinks	34	47	52	55
Automobiles and accessories	34	42	68	65
Beverages	20	27	34	45
Construction and real estate	15	22	15	25
Corporate image	40	50	68	89
Electrical appliances	41	52	48	54
Fashions and boutiques	33	43	60	73
Food, confectionery	26	32	61	101
Medicines and eye care	15	15	11	20
Telecommunications	11	14	26	21
Toiletries, personal care and cosmetics	21	37	36	75
Travel, hotel, leisure and airlines	49	64	42	49
Total	385	493	577	762

Source: StarTV [1993–97].

It is worth reiterating that these rankings by the number of advertisers may have little correlation with actual expenditure by product category or brand/corporate name, the latter being considered proprietary information by StarTV under both ownerships and not available for analysis. Nor did the limited data provided by StarTV give indication of which advertisers may have withdrawn from further advertising or increased their advertising spending, of what their countries-of-origin were, or even of what their target markets (domestic or transnational) were. There was some evidence of changes in how the products were categorised such as by the creation of new product categories such as health foods in addition to food and confectionary, and airlines in addition to travel, hotel and leisure, thus making comparison across the years difficult. It was also not clear how, for instance, the category "corporate image" was differentiated from clients in the banking and telecommunications industry who tend to use such advertising liberally, especially as some corporate names seem to fall under different categories in different years. Certainly in the data provided there were no clues as to what specific brands, products or services of each corporate client were advertised, and of what specific type of persuasive appeal was used. Still the growing number of advertisers in most categories does provide some indication of the relative success of this particular strategy of StarTV in attracting certain products and services as advertisers.

In the late 1990s StarTV began to categorise the information on advertisers and products first by the type of channels in which they advertised rather than consolidating them across their stable of now almost 20 channels. Furthermore, it changed some of the product categories making comparison across years problematic. Analysing StarTV advertiser lists then, its sports channels attracted 238 advertisers, the music channels 335 advertisers, its Chinese channels 417 advertisers, its general entertainment channels 491 advertisers, its news channel (then only *BBC World*) 76 advertisers and its movie channels 240 advertisers [StarTV 1997]. Considerable overlap of advertisers was apparent, as were multiple listings of advertisers within each channel to represent different product lines and brands or national offices as suggested by differing client account numbers. Indicatively, the general entertainment channels had the largest number of advertisers, though whether their total spending was the highest source for StarTV was unclear. Certainly on most channels, a significant majority of the advertisers and brands were now domestic or regional, that is from within Asia rather than being of global source. In keeping with the change of strategic direction, it was now competing in different national markets with domesticated specialist channels in news, entertainment, sports and movies. Consequently consolidated data became irrelevant, and by the early 2000s StarTV had ceased making such advertising data publicly available, making further analysis of trends simply impossible.

Advertising Revenue

As estimated by an academic researcher, StarTV advertising revenue was around US$10 million in 1992. This was believed to have doubled the following year, boosted by liquor and cigarette advertising banned on many terrestrial broadcasters (Wang 1993). But a few years later StarTV reported to the television industry media that its advertising revenues had risen to US$37 million in 1993 [APT-C 1995]. Another industry source placed StarTV's 1994 revenues at US$112 million, but its 1995 revenues at US$88 million—a significant 21.5 per cent decline [Bailes and Hollister 1996: 133]. However in early 1997 StarTV claimed to have earned US$17 million of advertising from China alone in November–December 1996 for a single channel, namely its Phoenix Chinese Channel [StarTV 1997]. Given StarTV's reluctance to declare its full financial situation, there were considerable gaps in information and discrepancies between industry estimates and self-claims.

While Frith (1996) acknowledged that StarTV and other regional broadcasters caused multinational marketers to consider pan-Asian advertising strategies, data on how much of an effort has been made in this direction was not available. She cited this as just one of a number of trends in Asian advertising which include tapping undeveloped markets, increasing use of local managers, more localisation of campaigns and less censorship. StarTV had aimed initially to tap into the burgeoning advertising expenditures in Asia by targeting the cosmopolitan, English-speaking urban elite across the continent. But it failed to make a dent in the fortunes of domestic and regional commercial broadcasters that provided tailor-made programming to various national audiences. So StarTV was forced to switch from a pan-Asian to a regional or quasi-domestic strategy including alliances with domestic cable networks and the use of pay-TV. Up until the pay-TV channel Star Movies was introduced in 1994, the broadcaster had only one income stream, namely advertising [APT-C 1995]. Insufficient revenue, whether from advertising and subscription, was believed to have precipitated the financial woes of smaller transnational satellite broadcasters in the region such as Hong Kong's CETV and CTN, and Thailand's UTV and IBC (International Broadcasting Corporation—somewhat presumptuous for a mid-size Thai cable operator!).

Such challenges remain true for StarTV since the formerly pan-Asian medium has diversified into channels that are more subregional and quasi-domestic in focus. Its ownership by the media conglomerate News Corporation allayed any concerns from advertisers about its long-term financial viability in the mid-1990s. Then by the early 2000s, having achieved programme ratings superiority in India over its main rivals ZeeTV and SonyET, its StarPlus channel alone was said to be reaping 70 per cent of all advertising revenue during prime time. Furthermore StarTV was estimated to be earning US$18 million in subscriber revenue from cable networks in India alone. Though there were losses of about US$40 million the previous year, in the second quarter of 2000, StarTV's consolidated revenue was said to have grown by 54 per cent to US$221 million, boosted by advertising sales in India, China and Taiwan [Couto 2000].

Having evaluated the strategy of StarTV for attracting advertising in this section, the process of managing advertising on this transnational medium will now be looked at from the perspective of three key markets. Although Ha (1997) pointed out the strengths that pan-Asian media had—less clutter, more prestige and targeting the elite—she also cautioned of the limitations of small audiences, high cost and unsuitability for localised campaigns. The next section will report the viewpoints of decision makers in Indonesia, India and China on how transnational satellite television was utilised for advertising over the 1990s. It examines why the medium was considered variously unsuitable, of limited value or ideal by advertising agencies, domestic broadcasters, market researchers and broadcast regulators.

MANAGING ADVERTISING

Historically, academic literature on advertising globalisation has suggested that the advent of transnational television would undermine government regulation of domestic broadcasting and advertising. Domination of domestic advertising industries by international advertising agencies serving multinational marketer clients would continue to escalate, with the transnational medium prompting the realignment of advertising accounts to take advantage of the economies of scale of global or regional campaigns. In other words, the experience of Europe and the Americas was thought to be likely to replicate itself in Asia. But the perspective from Mumbai, Jakarta and Hong Kong of the advent of StarTV, its impact on strategic advertising decisions made by advertising agencies and their marketer clients, and the responses of media owners and governments appeared quite different.

Mumbai-based Advertisers

Government regulation: As to regulation of domestic television advertising, agencies needed to adhere to the Doordarshan (DD), policy regarding no liquor or tobacco advertising, while in the press media there were some laws governing the advertisement of certain products, for example health warnings on tobacco [Interview Ind04.03]. The DD commercial code incorporated social objectives such as not offending moral, racial or religious susceptibilities, not infringing on the rights of the consumer, not projecting a derogatory image of women, and not promoting tobacco, liquor and such goods [DD-ARU 1999].

The guidelines used to insist on the non-promotion of foreign goods and financial services [DD-ARU 1994] but this was no longer mentioned by the late 1990s. Perhaps this was simply economic pragmatism because Doordarshan now competed for such advertisers who used to support the transnational broadcasters as the only television media available to them to reach Indian markets. In any case, such past regulations were a reflection of India's earlier, if only partial, socialist commitment to a mixed economic model in which government approval was needed for manufacture and each product category had only 6–8 producers [Interview Ind03.07]. This had bred a bureaucratic public system inimical to capitalist production and marketing, including advertising and distribution of products [Interview Ind01.01].

With the advent of transnational television, notably StarTV, the Indian government attempted to thwart its growth in India by enforcing its existing foreign exchange rules. These required a marketer to earn over Rs 1 million in export earnings before it would be permitted by the Reserve Bank of India (RBI) to utilise part of that to purchase advertising time on a foreign medium via licensed agents, ostensibly to further promote export sales [Interview Ind01.10]. The three or four advertising agents in the country approved by RBI were paid in rupees, deducted their commission and then claimed for foreign exchange [Interview Ind04.01]. But the finance ministry's directive to RBI, banning release of foreign exchange specifically for advertisements on transnational television channels targeting India, particularly StarTV, was withdrawn after representatives from foreign channels held meetings with ministry officials and threatened to take the government to court for flouting a basic constitutional clause [Nag 1993]. Thus the Indian government's attempts at control of commercial satellite television, whether transnational or domestic, within the framework of existing laws did not succeed. Almost all advertising practices prohibited on Indian domestic television were commonplace on StarTV and ZeeTV, since their broadcast signals were uplinked in Hong Kong and so did not come under the jurisdiction of the Indian government.

Agency–marketer alignment: In the mid-1990s there was some realignment of the Indian advertising accounts of multinational marketers because their worldwide advertising agencies had returned to India, often as joint ventures with local agencies [Interview Ind01.01]. This was generally attributed to the liberalisation of India's regulatory environment that fortuitously coincided with the arrival of transnational television, and not as a direct impact of the latter [Interview Ind01.04]. Thus the response of interviewees to the question of whether StarTV in particular or transnational television in general had prompted realignment of advertising accounts was equivocal. Even the transnational television executives admitted then that there was little pan-Asian advertising. This was because MNCs still used different agencies around the region and their marketing programmes had differing objectives in each national market.

Given budgets and financial control issues, each national subsidiary of the MNC or its advertising agency bought advertising time from the local representative of the transnational broadcaster, resulting in little coordination of advertising regionally [Interview Ind03.07]. There were also few transnational campaigns, not only because prime times were not in common across the time-zones under the footprint, but because products were not available throughout the region yet [Interview Ind01.08]. Most of Indian television advertising campaigns were domestic because there were fairly few global products in India at the start of the 1990s. Though products advertised on StarTV and ZeeTV tended to be from the MNCs, especially the Japanese such as

Sony and Panasonic, there were others like Colgate-Palmolive's Lux, and P&G's Pampers that preferred domestic campaigns and media. Thus even global brands available in the country had different positioning, packaging, and brand equity from other markets—problems that needed to be solved at the marketing end before advertising [Interview Ind02.01]. Thus markets were considered quite diverse even within a region like South Asia, more so than Europe.

Domestic markets: From observation, the products from India that were advertised on transnational television in the mid-1990s tended to be high-value consumer durables. These were extremely expensive for the average consumer in India, for example cars such as Maruti 1000, or lifestyle products such as credit cards [Interview Ind01.03]. The major advantage of transnational television has been that it allowed Indian advertising agencies for the first time to target brands at specific market segments, which had generally not been possible with the mass-market oriented Doordarshan. Advertising of luxury goods on transnational satellite television was believed to bring about a positive predisposition to these global brands, especially when encountered overseas by Indians. Corporate advertising was another use of transnational television, though even then it was identical to commercials used on Indian domestic television. In the early to mid-1990s only the StarTV channels StarPlus and BBC had significant audiences among the upmarket segments in India [Interview Ind01.07]. Still, by the late 1990s Gupta (1998: 131–33) had reported that for about 40 per cent of all households with cable, watching foreign programming was not the motivation for their subscription. Even though it would never strictly become a medium catering to the masses it was thought by some advertising executives that Star TV ought also not to relinquish its original strategy of targeting the pan-Asian elite [Interview Ind02.04].

The arrival of the satellite television medium did not result in a rush of multinational product advertising directed at India, because as the interviewees pointed out such products were either unavailable then in India or not well distributed in that market. MNC products were not readily available in India till the late 1990s, but were available elsewhere and sought after by Indians abroad as tourists and expatriates. Instead transnational television was used to advertise domestic brands to the Indian market thus stimulating consumer demand and as a consequence its pull, expanding their distribution. Gupta (2000) suggests that this strategy is particularly effective in India, as it helps heighten the traditional social-class structure by providing the elites with symbols of snobbery. However some South Asian products were expected to grow markets worldwide, especially with the "greening" of consumer markets [Interview Ind01.07]. For example, pickles from Pakistan were advertised out of Dubai to its major market in Middle East [Interview Ind02.02]. Unintentionally, primarily domestic advertising on a transnational medium had resulted in some export orders from other national markets, notably in South Asia or West Asia that saw the same advertisements via spillover television signals. Furthermore, cable operators and networks garnered advertising for domestic or regional products, services and events for insertion particularly in movie channels, earning about Rs 5 billion thus (Kohli 2003: 83).

Transnational markets: The use of split beams and programming differentiation by StarTV meant that it was possible for Indian advertisers to target specific markets abroad as well. This was increasingly done as successive channels were thus split, beginning soon after the takeover by News Corporation [Interview Ind02.02]. As a result, advertisers were able to target specific geographical and cultural segments of the Asian market, such as expatriate Indians in the Middle East, Pakistanis and Arabs. Commercials on satellite television channels seen after 11 P.M. in India were targeted for Pakistan and Dubai prime time because there is a two and a half hour difference of time-zones [Interview Ind01.01]. Thus a pan-Asian Indian audience segment may exist to a certain extent, and corporate advertising was directed at these expatriate non-resident Indians (NRIs) in the Gulf states, Saudi Arabia and the Far East. StarTV carried corporate advertising to the 2 million NRIs there to attract investments in Indian firms in the increasingly deregulated domestic financial market.

Though StarTV's penetration in West Asia was then equivalent to ZeeTV, the latter was far more influential as a Hindi-language channel in catering to all expatriate South Asians there, especially from Pakistan, believed to number 5 million by an estimate in the mid-1990s [Interview Ind02.07]. ZeeTV, then an affiliate of StarTV, could be said to have become a transnational broadcaster over the 1990s as it gained a sizeable audience in the Persian Gulf region of both Arabs and South Asians, who were seen as consumers of Indian food exports. ZeeTV programmes were mainly film-based and so were popular as far away as Egypt, while similarly the Pakistani films played on its channels became popular in India [Interview Ind01.02]. Pakistan television audiences were attracted to ZeeTV because their Urdu language is similar to Hindi, unlike Bangladesh where the populace lacks facility with Hindi [Interview Ind01.04]. Pakistani advertisers also actively used ZeeTV and StarTV because they faced no foreign exchange restrictions on funds transfer to pay for the advertising, unlike Indian advertisers. ZeeTV was used to reach non-diasporic markets in the Gulf: for instance some commodity advertisements were directed at Arabs, though these were generally ad hoc [Interview Ind01.05]. Till the mid-1990s this was done in only a limited fashion since the primary target of Indian advertisers was rather short-sightedly the domestic market in India itself.

There were believed to be approximately 16–18 million ethnic Indians resident around the world who were emerging as major investors in India. Repatriation of savings and venture capital by NRIs placed the group as the fourth largest investors in the country behind the US, Switzerland and Japan, and invaluable in augmenting India's foreign exchange reserves. Reasons given by NRIs for their investment in India were said to be, in order of importance, emotional ties, prospects of higher return, and familiarity with Indian conditions [Haeems 1994]. NRIs were also a valuable target market since they were allowed to buy Indian export-quality products abroad to bring back to India, exempt from local excise and luxury taxes. Kohli (2003: 81) estimates their income as roughly half of India's GDP and a lucrative market for pay-TV given the minimal programming costs. Thus the then StarTV affiliate ZeeTV positioned itself as a truly South Asian channel reaching Indian expatriates worldwide. In a form of reverse globalisation through ethnic identity, it began in the mid-1990s to identify Indians resident in West Asia, Africa, Southeast Asia, Fiji, Mauritius, the US and the UK as valuable markets. So together StarTV and its then affiliate ZeeTV stumbled into the business of being transnational broadcasters for expatriate and diasporic Indians who were of interest to some domestic advertisers, especially exporters.

Jakarta-based Advertisers

Government regulations: By law all advertising in Indonesia had to be placed via a local advertising agency with a domestic medium, which therefore precluded multinational marketers from buying transnational media time through their Indonesian operations. As a public broadcaster TVRI did not accept advertising except of a community and public interest nature [Grafik McCann-Erickson 1994]. But 12 per cent of the advertising revenue of the domestic commercial channels was remitted to TVRI as their licensor [Interview Mly04.01] and as a means of financing the latter's operations as nationwide public broadcaster. According to the government's Decree 111 of May 1989 all commercials on Indonesian television had to be produced locally, though full exemption was granted for airlines [Interview Mly02.01]. Advertising agencies in Indonesia were also self-regulated by a code of ethics which specified adherence to national laws and ideology, sensitivity to local culture and religion, restrictions on promotion of certain products and so on [PPPI 1996: 167]. On the surface it appeared difficult for Indonesian advertising agencies to participate in the creation, production and utilisation of regional advertising, via transnational television or otherwise. Yet, foreign commercials were adapted for use on domestic Indonesian television even before the toppling of the Soeharto regime in the late 1990s and certainly the practice has been more common since [Interview Mly01.11].

Agency–marketer alignment: There had been a shift of marketer–client accounts in Indonesia to international advertising agencies with the reintroduction of television advertising in the late 1980s, motivated in part by a search for skills in producing commercials. Creative "hot-shops" specialising in television commercial production as well as local advertising agencies able to undercut prices competed then with transnational ones for MNC accounts. These smaller agencies even began to network on a regional basis [Interview Mly02.07]. But there had not been any corresponding multinational client–agency realignment in the country prompted by transnational satellite television [Interview Mly03.05]. Industry opinion held it unlikely that there would be a sizeable shift to advertising on transnational television as marketing strategies and positioning of products and brands were quite different, even among culturally similar countries such as Malaysia and Indonesia.

Transnational markets: Data on spending on StarTV by Indonesian advertisers was virtually non-existent, certainly unavailable throughout the 1990s, largely because the amounts were thought to be negligible. This was attributed to the fact that regional headquarters of MNCs, typically located in Hong Kong or Singapore, handled such media buying [Interview Mly 03.05]. On the one hand, if there had been any moves by such regional headquarters to require contributions by domestic marketing subsidiaries in Indonesia, they would have been resisted strongly on account of the fact that most MNCs were operating as joint ventures by law. So there were no apparent cutbacks in domestic media spending to fund regional advertising [Interview Mly02.06]. In any case, all advertising expenditure figures were somewhat inaccurate in Indonesia because of the widespread practice of discounting [Interview Mly03.05], as was the case elsewhere in Asia.

Domestic markets: Pan-Asian advertising was believed by respondents not to work in Indonesia because of language and cultural barriers. This was reflected in the fact that local programming in Indonesia, however badly produced, enjoyed higher ratings than any imported programming. In any case foreign programming, similar to that available on the transnational satellite channels, was available on the domestic commercial channels either dubbed or subtitled, and therefore more popular. Even if they were English speaking, Indonesian audiences preferred programmes that were dubbed because it made them easier to understand and otherwise the wider family would not be able to appreciate them [Interview Mly02.08]. Furthermore it was relatively expensive to purchase a satellite dish and so the approximately 600,000 viewers of transnational satellite television in Indonesia were believed to be mainly the wealthier ethnic Chinese, expatriate executives or English-educated Indonesians. Transnational television would only have greater impact in Indonesia if costs of satellite dishes or cable access were lowered [Interview Mly02.07].

As the government anticipated the arrival of transnational television by deregulating its domestic television industry, there has been considerable loyalty to domestic commercial channels that were available nationwide and free-to-air. On the other hand there was a language barrier to watching transnational television and a cost hurdle to owning private satellite dishes. Even when cable television was later introduced, subscription was relatively expensive and so did little to make transnational television more attractive to domestic audience markets. So long as domestic broadcasters offered advertising to mass and segmented markets for less cost, upmarket segments accessible primarily by transnational television held little interest to Indonesian advertising and marketing executives. Therefore, despite the size of its market, Indonesia was neither a target of transnational advertising via satellite or cable television, nor was the medium used much by multinational marketers operating in the country for advertising targeted at its elite domestically or around the Malay World.

Hong Kong-based Advertisers

Government regulation: Regulation of advertising on transnational satellite television channels uplinked from Hong Kong was virtually identical to those governing that on its domestic terrestrial channels. These included broad guidelines on good taste, exaggerated claims, disparaging remarks on competitors, advertising to children, among others. While tobacco products, gambling, nightclubs and the like faced a total ban, liquor was permitted though subject to restrictions on promotion to children or young people. As with many countries in the region and around the world there was qualified approval of advertising by financial institutions, property developers, pharmaceutical manufacturers, educational institutions and so on [Broadcasting Authority 1993]. Hong Kong's Television and Entertainment Licensing Authority (TELA) stipulated a maximum of 10 minutes of advertising per broadcast hour. But StarTV was then said to utilise only a small fraction of that allowance [Interview Chn02.01], mostly due to advertiser disinterest. The prohibition of advertising on the Wharf Cable and ban on the use of Cantonese on StarTV ensured that there was no domestic target market for transnational television via satellite or cable [Interview Chn02.05]. Though transnational television broadcasters to the region were not subject to the broadcasting and advertising regulations of the countries in which their signals were received, they were subject to Hong Kong regulations, which while less stringent than many other countries within the region were not totally liberal either.

Agency–marketer alignment: There was no realignment of advertising accounts as a result of the availability of transnational television, though for other reasons. Some shifts of advertising accounts had occurred in the 1990s to align agencies and marketers regionally, though these might have been part of a worldwide trend, rather than because of transnational television [Interview Chn01.07]. Of the criteria for selection of an advertising agency, internationally or in Hong Kong, the ability to handle transnational satellite television was thought to rate quite low. The more important criterion was whether each agency had a regional network of agencies for coordinating a comprehensive marketing strategy [Interview Chn01.08]. So, executives in Hong Kong saw such moves as a result of multinational marketers' decisions at corporate headquarters level, as part of a worldwide realignment [Interview Chn01.09].

As explained earlier, the first advertisers from Hong Kong on StarTV were charter advertisers who had a form of "equity" participation in its launch by Hutchinson Whampoa but most did not sign up as long-term advertisers after its sale to News Corporation. This helps explain why some of the advertising of this transnational medium was primarily targeted at the domestic Hong Kong market. Some early clients were incredibly local, for example, HK construction firms [Interview Chn03.01]. Domestic advertising was still important for product sales in Asian countries in the mid-1990s, even though regional advertising was growing in importance [Interview Chn01.07]. In other cases advertisers had utilised it as a relatively inexpensive new medium to reach upmarket target segments in their own domestic markets. For though its actual audiences in each country were actually small, being the first households to be cabled they were certainly of high income [Interview Chn01.03].

Transnational markets: The consensus opinion among international advertising agencies in Hong Kong was that regional advertising was not being driven by transnational television media but was being achieved via or in conjunction with domestic television in multiple countries. In the interim pan-Asian advertising largely duplicated what was already being done on domestic advertising [Interview Chn01.01]. StarTV was recommended by agencies in its early years on the basis of what satellite television would deliver in the future through the establishment of an early and strong relationship of the brand with the medium. It claimed to deliver large numbers of viewers at low cost, especially if the advertiser did not mind the wastage since it was a blunt instrument for targeting market segments. Transnational satellite television has to be used in conjunction with, and never to the exclusion of, national terrestrial television [Interview Chn01.09]. Transnational broadcasters were confident that regional advertising was growing rapidly especially for travel and tourism, and for corporate advertising [Interview Chn02.03]. The applicability of transnational television to all advertising markets within Asia was questionable since, in general, packaging and distribution were not standardised across the region, but the situation could change with the increasing subregionalisation of channels.

Realising that marketers and products were seldom pan-Asian or transnational, StarTV changed into a sub-regional or quasi-national medium, by itself as well as in conjunction with domestic cable networks. By the mid-1990s the multinational marketer Philips segmented its domestic appliances into five markets because it was more cost-effective and because some products were geared more to India/Middle East, only the southern beam of StarTV was used [Interview Chn01.08]. Through localising via language the transnational broadcaster ended up focusing on the domestic mass markets of Taiwan, China and India, which was at odds with some multinational clients' emphases on the more affluent Singapore, Malaysia and Hong Kong markets instead. As in the case of India, StarTV was utilised as an advertising medium for products in Taiwan such as liquor that faced restrictions on domestic television [Interview Chn01.08]. Still, a number of multinational clients such as United Airlines, Cathay Pacific Airlines, Kelloggs and Procter & Gamble remained on StarTV as part of global media deals [Interview Chn01.09].

Domestic markets: Advertising on StarTV from Greater China declined after its switch to broadcasting on separate beams and providing subregional programming, following the News Corporation takeover. Perhaps the new subregional/ethnic audiences had failed to make up for the pan-Asian expatriate/cosmopolitan audience it had lost in the process of change. One of the objections raised had to do with the fact that the mass audiences targeted in the mid-1990s were not prime prospects for the sort of products and services handled by the international advertising agencies based in Hong Kong. StarTV may have claimed to be in 30 million households in China, out of its 40 million households Asiawide. But multinational marketers were not enthused by that statistic since few of them were operating in all of China at that time, and especially when 15 million of those households were in the remote Sichuan province. They were keener on more urbanised Taiwan which had a high incidence of cable TV [Interview Chn01.09], though Liu (2001) confirmed that Taiwanese cable operators were prone to insert local advertisements over the broadcasters' ones despite the practice being illegal. Product distribution and market share varied considerably across countries under the satellite footprint and so posed a problem for marketers wishing to use the medium on a pan-Asian or even subregional basis [Interview Chn01.08].

However the true successor to StarTV in China itself, Phoenix Satellite Channel, its joint venture with local interests, seemed to progress well from its start. This was helped by the fact that it was soon available in 36 million households nationwide or a penetration of 13.2 per cent of all TV households. The penetration was higher in the cities and stood at 19.1 per cent of households in coastal provinces and 17.2 per cent of households in northern provinces, which constituted the most affluent in the country. By the time Phoenix was officially permitted to broadcast in the Guangdong region in 2001, an audience of 42 million was said to have already had unofficial access to it for some years [AMCB 2001]. It had also diversified into news, movies and general entertainment channels, and was available also to diasporic Chinese audiences, including in Europe, North America and Australasia. Hence StarTV's ability to attract significant advertising revenue from China via Phoenix in the early 2000s was unquestioned.

With the advent of the transnational medium of satellite television in Asia the long-debated issue of globalising advertising has been revisited in the region, along with concerns about the consolidation of strategy, media-buying and creativity, and market domination by international advertising agencies. The views of advertising agencies, domestic broadcasters, market researchers and media regulators towards transnational television in the three regional cities of Jakarta, Mumbai and Hong Kong in the early 1990s to early 2000s, were quite varied. Since these cities serve as hubs for advertising and broadcasting in Indonesia, India and Greater China, the views of the decision makers may well point to broad trends for their respective regions. The next chapter examines the different ways in which StarTV in particular was utilised as an advertising medium by some marketers and why it was largely ignored in other cases in Asia. Furthermore the creative practices of advertising agencies and their clients with the broadcasters StarTV and others in the regions of South, Southeast and Northeast Asia are instructive of the challenges faced by all transnational television.

With increasing media choice, such as offered by StarTV and the other transnational broadcasters, there appeared naturally to be greater scope for advertising creativity and sophistication in media buying in Asia, to overcome clutter on limited domestic media and achieve cost-efficiencies. But the availability of a new advertising medium like transnational television was no guarantee of its use, at least not in the manner originally envisaged, namely as a pan-Asian medium. In any case the use of a global advertising strategy via transnational television may be limited because of factors such as the availability and popularity of domestic television channels, culture and language, literacy and print media preference, affluence and consumer sophistication, non-standardisation of products to be advertised and relatively high costs of satellite access for consumers. All of these may have made media planning and cross-cultural creativity issues for advertising very complex in the early years of transnational satellite television when it was a global, pan-Asian or regional medium.

MEDIA SELECTION

Research in Europe in earlier decades suggested that there might be increasing consolidation of media buying to achieve greater cost-efficiencies with the coming of transnational television. Yet in Asia transnational television was first used largely as a niche medium for reaching upmarket segments of domestic markets and often by advertisers of products restricted on domestic media. Since then the transnational broadcasters have regionalised and domesticated their programming increasingly and thus compete with newer domestic or regional broadcasters delivering their commercial channels via satellite and cable. The historical choices confronting media planning staff of leading advertising agencies in Mumbai, Jakarta and Hong Kong in the early to late 1990s are described. In particular, the rationale for their media-buying decisions for or against StarTV as a pan-Asian advertising medium, and the consequences for the development of transnational and domestic broadcasters will be analysed.

Mumbai-based Agencies

Shifts in adspend: With the commercialisation of Doordarshan (DD) in 1986 television took 16 per cent of the total advertising expenditure in India, then Rs 6 billion (US$200 million), compared with radio's 3 per cent and cinema's 2 per cent (Kumar 1989). Television's share of advertising expenditure rose steadily to 22 per cent in 1991 when transnational television first appeared, whilst print declined from 72 per cent to 66 per cent [Indian MIB 1993]. The Indian advertising industry was estimated to be growing at 25 per cent rate per annum over the 1990s [Interview Ind01.04]. Television industry leaders were optimistic about a three-fold increase over the decade, aided by diversification of the manufacturing sector, expansion of the services sector, increase in advertising media alternatives, liberalisation of the economy and re-orientation to export markets [Saggar 1993: 32–35]. In the mid-1990s television was growing at the rate of 22–25 per cent per year [Interview Ind01.10]. By the year 2000, total advertising expenditure in India was estimated to be around Rs 10 billion (US$330 million) with the television medium's share at about 30–32 per cent of that [Interview Ind03.07]. Thus Indian advertising expenditure or adspend, for short, was growing rapidly in the 1990s, while the television advertising growth rate was even faster than overall adspend.

Transnational television adspend: The initial euphoria over transnational satellite television led to advertisements being placed on StarTV regardless of rationale [Interview Ind01.04]. About 1 per cent of all Indian marketers were said to be on transnational television but even then targeted at the domestic market [Interview Ind01.05]. With the arrival of ZeeTV at end 1992, there was a significant switch of advertisers to it and so the growth of ZeeTV income in 1993 was estimated by one multinational advertising agency to be Rs 750–800 million (US$25–27 million) [Interview Ind01.04]. Reviewing the television advertising spending for 1993, another multinational advertising agency estimated that Indian brands spent Rs 300 million (US$10 million) on StarTV and a further Rs 500 million (US$17 million) on ZeeTV. This was a pittance compared with the Rs 4,500 million (US$150 million) spent the same year on Doordarshan which represented a 10 per cent increase over 1992 but still its lowest increase since in the past the growth rate had ranged from 19 to 67 per cent annually [HTA 1994]. DD Metro channels in the major state capitals had collectively gained advertising market share at the expense of DD1 (The main DD channel) rather than mitigating the effect of the transnational channels.

The advertising growth rate of DD declined from its peak of 88 per cent between 1984 to 1990, to 29 per cent between 1990 to 1992 with a sizeable amount lost to StarTV and ZeeTV, and for this DD's inertia was to blame [Menon 1994]. On the basis of the advertising association's 1993 adspend figures published in Mumbai, DD estimated that their advertising revenue loss to StarTV was Rs 200–250 million (US$65–80 million) [Interview Ind01.03]. As an indication of the media-buying pattern on DD versus ZeeTV, a major multinational joint venture spent 20 per cent of its total advertising budget on DD, and only 10 per cent on Zee [Interview Ind01.11]. DD1 experienced a shrinking of its commercial revenues over 1993, as advertisers displayed a decided preference for the Metro channel (DD2) where the proceeds went to the private programme producer and not to the national broadcaster. In the first half of 1993, the Metro channel got 24 hours of advertising, of which 10 hours was a shift from Doordarshan's main channel, whose share of the advertising pie shrank from 21 per cent to 17 per cent while that of its subregional channels dropped from 79 per cent to 73 per cent [Kang 1993].

There were no definitive figures on advertising spending in India in the early to mid-1990s, but most advertising agencies and market research organisations published working estimates, all of which pointed to the fact that compared to DD, advertising expenditure on StarTV and ZeeTV was minuscule then. However, data from the late 1990s demonstrated a dramatic reversal in the advertising expenditure situation for India (Figure 6.1), with satellite channels exceeding those of DD. The growth in the number of satellite television channels of domestic origin and the greater domestication of transnational broadcasters in order to target India specifically have resulted in their ability

Figure 6.1
Advertising Expenditure on Doordarshan versus Satellite Television Channels

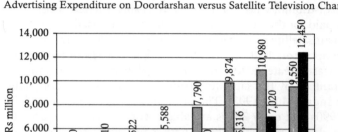

Source: Hindustan Thomson Advertising, cited in DD-ARU [1999].

to attract much greater advertising spending. This was achieved at the expense of DD despite its best efforts at proliferation of channels and diversification of programming. The share of the television medium has grown from a mere 15 per cent of total advertising in the early 1990s to over 40 per cent in the early 2000s. For the satellite broadcasters to India such as StarTV, ZeeTV and SunTV, unlike in developed countries where subscription predominates, advertising represents 70 per cent of all revenue [Equitymaster.com 2004]. So as of the mid-2000s this trend towards advertising growth continues unabated, regardless of rapid changes in financial fortunes of individual commercial satellite broadcasters in the highly competitive Indian television environment.

Cable advertising: In the early 1990s local cable operators or associations of cable operators sold television commercial spots because they sometimes substituted their own advertising in the commercial breaks of the then pan-Asian satellite channels. End-of-video movie advertisements tended to be very local in character, such as for a neighbourhood grocery or restaurant. First-run movies broadcast on cable television had advertisements running throughout on the bottom and top portions of the television screen, occupying up to a third of the screen.

Called "crawlies" in the advertising industry, these were superimposed by the film distributor who retained the advertising revenue. Most cable operators paid for the movies on video that they utilised, but not for the free-to-air satellite-broadcast programmes that they re-transmitted. The cable operators had on occasion blacked out Hindi movies on ZeeTV, or least threatened to, unless their legal rights as re-transmitters were guaranteed by the satellite broadcaster against their copyright owners in India [Mitra 1993]. The situation changed considerably in the late 1990s and early 2000s as cable networks were increasingly consolidated and variously affiliated with major media conglomerates such as News Corporation and Zee Telefilms that also broadcast television via satellite to India.

Media trends: The increasing complexity of advertising media in India over the 1990s came to be acknowledged by every media planner. Media planning became a complicated task due to the growth of publications and television channels, in an increasing number of subregional languages. By the mid-1990s there were already 19,000 publications, 400 of them with circulations over 100,000, while 20 of them were over 300,000. It was a situation compounded by the growth of television from two national channels initially to over 100 at the end of the 1990s with implications for advertising media trends. While the more professional marketers operating in India (often the affiliates of multinational corporations) sought to utilise gross ratings points in their media planning, the less professional resorted to conventional practices, invariably rules of thumb. Media choices by advertisers were said to be simplified by going for the familiar [Interview Ind02.01] with budgets being allocated first on the basis of quantitative audience profiles, only then on some qualitative considerations [Interview Ind01.12]. Yet one agency estimated that the decision was about 90 per cent quantitative and only 10 per cent qualitative. As with a number of other agencies, it cited the increased availability of hard data from market research companies, which use both people-meters and diaries that covered all metropolitan cities and major towns [Interview Ind01.14].

There was some scepticism in the early 1990s about advertising on StarTV's pan-Asian channels in the face of its minuscule audience within India (Table 6.1). This was in contrast with the early commercial Indian channels that were targeting largely domestic market segments which advertising agencies were primarily interested in. Then there was also the restrictiveness of having to generate export earnings in order to be permitted to advertise on the medium. Exporters were allowed to retain 25 per cent for promotional purposes and then for export markets only [Interview Ind04.01]. Nonetheless StarTV was acknowledged as the catalyst for transnational advertising by Indian firms because there had been no advertising expenditure going abroad previously [Interview Ind04.01]. Using reach figures alone, perhaps certain advertisers ought not to have bought advertising time on StarTV, but they did so for qualitative reasons such as audience lifestyle [Interview Ind01.10]. In India, Unilever was the first to advertise on StarTV but when the numbers did not support the decision, it was also among the first to opt out [Interview Ind01.11]. Yet Unilever's support was subsequently instrumental in SonyET's entry into the market in the late 1990s, at a time when ZeeTV was still dominant [Interview Ind01.16].

Table 6.1
Ratings and Cost Comparisons of Indian Channels, mid-1990s

Channel	Type	Audience	Programme	Rating	Cost US$
StarTV	Transnational satellite	50 million	Soap opera (*The Bold and the Beautiful*)	3	1,600
ZeeTV	Domestic satellite	50 million	Serial (*Tara*)	30	3,482
DD 1	Domestic terrestrial	310 million	Hindi film	50	8,571
DD 2	Domestic terrestrial	50 million	Serial (*Dekh Bhai Dekh*)	45	5,143
SunTV	Domestic satellite	4 million	Tamil film	50	685
Asianet	Domestic satellite	1 million	Malayalam film	50	514

Source: Chaitra Leo Burnett [1994].

As the transnational channels became more regional, there was a tendency to clearly target one constituent national or subregional market over another. In the South Asia region, this was invariably India rather than Pakistan or Sri Lanka, for instance. One advertising executive explained this in terms of the much larger size of the Indian market as well as its relative cosmopolitanness of culture. Nonetheless, MNC marketers were wary of advertising on programmes and channels that were clearly politically or nationally partisan [Interview 01.14], as was a concern during the India–Pakistan conflict in Kashmir that was re-ignited in the late 1990s. Even in the late 1990s, diasporic and expatriate Indian markets were still not considered by advertising agencies in India in their media-buying decisions on transnational television. It was only said to be a factor if the marketer/advertiser was also operating in that market [Interview Ind01.12]. So until satellite television ceased being a pan-Asian medium it was dominated by multinational corporations like Coca-Cola and Sony able to afford using it in targeting multiple markets simultaneously.

Media budget sources: Despite government regulations that discouraged such expenditure in the early 1990s, the new medium of transnational satellite television attracted additional funding for advertising, from the discretionary budget sources of marketers in India. The general view among advertising agency executives then was that advertising budgets for transnational television were being siphoned from that normally designated for other media. Though there was some divergence of opinion on whether those funds were originally meant for domestic television (four interviewees), press (seven interviewees), or both (three interviewees). Consumer non-durables such as toilet soaps, detergent powders and toothpastes reduced their adspend on press and increased it on television dramatically. Prior to the arrival of domestic television advertising in 1986, the press medium had 75 per cent of total adspend in India but by 1993 this had dropped to 65 per cent though space taken in the press by advertisers had actually grown a measly 16.8 per cent in the five years between 1988 and 1993 [A&M India 1994]. The general view though was that the press would not be affected by further proliferation of domestic satellite channels, as they had already been forced to respond to the onslaught of public television and then transnational television [A&M India 1994]. With Indians increasingly preferring to get their news and entertainment from television it was thought by some that the domestic Indian press was in danger and that this trend would escalate as consumers began judging even domestic television by the sophistication of transnational alternatives.

Although press advertising had indeed been losing its market share over the mid- to late 1990s (Table 6.2), it was said to be gaining in value because of the inflation in media rates and also because a number of newspapers could carry colour advertisements. Using the literacy yardstick, television had greater potential, but if one considered the growth market to be among the middle class/educated, then print might have more potential [Interview Ind02.01]. Thus the

Table 6.2
Media Trends in Indian Advertising Expenditure, mid- to late 1990s

Year	Press	Television	Outdoor	Radio	Total Adspend
1994	66%	25%	6%	3%	Rs 30.46 billion
1995	63%	29%	6%	3%	Rs 39.06 billion
1996	59%	33%	6%	2%	Rs 47.26 billion
1997	58%	34%	6%	2%	Rs 57.86 billion
1998	56%	34%	8%	2%	Rs 63.06 billion

Source: Ammirati Puris Lintas research, cited in DD-ARU [1999].

growth trend for television should not detract from the importance of print in the future, for a number of reasons including increasing literacy and the resurgence of subnational ethnic identity with regional language newspapers [Interview Ind03.10]. Likewise, growth in television advertising was expected to be in subregional channels that would erode national television budgets but not print budgets [Interviews Ind03.07 and Ind01.14]. Media buying in India was expected to become increasingly psychographics-driven via narrowcasting of audiences made possible by the growth of transnational and domestic television, and the role of cable operators. By the early 2000s, with over 100 satellite and cable channels available in India ranging from regionalised global channels through national public and commercial channels to subnational ethnic ones, broadcasters like StarTV represented just one media alternative of the many facing the advertiser.

The growth of television channels, both transnational and domestic, in India rendered increasingly controversial and obsolete the diary methods of measuring audience viewership used previously by market research companies. This led to the two leading research companies IMRB and MARG launching two different people-meters in conjunction with overseas affiliates, and both claiming to have the more sophisticated technology, extensive coverage and accurate data [Lahiri 1995c]. Subsequently in 1997 another market research firm ORG with its affiliate Taylor Nelson AGB launched a different form of people-meter because the previous one was prone to error due to cable operators frequently switching channel frequencies [Asian A&M 1997d]. Towards the conclusion of the fieldwork for this book there still did not seem to be a definitive measurement of Indian television audiences, at least available to an outside researcher. Though there were industry estimates such as published by chambers of commerce (Figure 6.2) which projected the steady growth of advertising expenditure into the mid-2000s.

Figure 6.2
Projected Indian Advertising Expenditure, 1999–2005

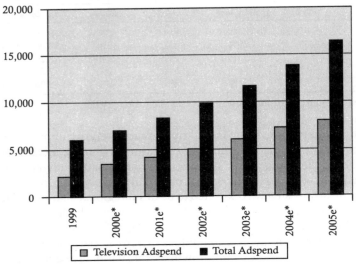

Source: FICCI [2000].
Note: *e—estimate.

With the number of multinational marketers/advertisers and their television media alternatives in the nation, subregion and region increasing, television advertising expenditure in India was expected to outstrip other media. More patently such advertising trends attest to the rescinding of India's earlier socialist ideals and its increasing incorporation into the capitalist world economy.

Jakarta-based Agencies

Shifts in adspend: The consensus of opinion among the interviewees in Indonesia in the mid-1990s was that there had been no known shift of advertising media spending from domestic television to transnational television, nor was any anticipated. The latter was deemed an inappropriate if not also an expensive medium for the vast majority of goods and services advertised to the national market, with the possible exception of luxury goods for an upmarket segment. Advertising agencies in the early to mid-1990s considered domestic television still to have a lower cost per rating point than StarTV [Interview Mly02.06]. Indonesian advertisers were not unfamiliar with transnational advertising as they had been forced to utilise Malaysian television in the early to mid-1980s to reach border provinces when commercials were banned on domestic public television. Prior to 1987 because of the ban, Indonesian advertisers spent US$2.5 million on Malaysia's TV3 in order to reach Indonesian consumers via spillover broadcasts in border areas such as Medan, Pekan Baru and Riau [Interview Mly04.10]. But it was only a temporary measure by a limited number of advertisers, and such advertising expenditure returned to Indonesia as soon as commercial television was introduced because of the tremendous popularity they soon achieved.

Advertising expenditure had an abnormal increase with the reintroduction of commercial television, but it soon stabilised at approximately 43 per cent of all media [Interview Mly04.02]. For entertainment, domestic television channels were still preferred by audiences and thus 65 per cent of advertising expenditure in Indonesia remained in that medium [Interview Mly02.01]. Even though the growth rate was not sustained with some products returning to the print media, domestic commercial television has been the dominant advertising medium in Indonesia ever since the early 1990s, a trend that continued unabated into the 2000s (Table 6.3) despite a major economic downturn. While spending on the print media over the same period remained more or less constant, this growth of television advertising seems to have been funded from the sales promotion budgets of marketers. Although data on advertising expenditure in Indonesia was readily

Table 6.3
Indonesian Advertising Expenditure by Media, 1992–98

Medium	1992		1994		1996		1998		2000 est.	
	Rp. b*	%	Rp. b*	%	Rp. b*	%	Rp. b*	%	Rp. b*	%
Television	390	38.0	1,062	46.5	1,638	49.1	2,213	58.9	4,201	60.6
Newspaper	377	36.7	743	32.5	1,538	32.8	956	25.4	1,803	26.0
Magazine	95	9.3	155	6.8	211	6.3	191	5.1	266	3.8
Radio	100	9.7	139	6.1	170	5.1	136	3.6	215	3.1
Outdoor	55	5.4	176	7.7	230	6.9	261	6.9	309	4.5
Cinema	10	1.0	11	0.5	12	0.3	n/a		n/a	
Total	1,027	100.0	2,286	100.0	3,335	100.0	3,757	100.0	6,927	100.0

Sources: PPPI [1996] and PPPI [2000].
Note: *Rupiah billion.

available, this researcher was cautioned by interviewees that it was not reliable, since they did not reflect the discounts repaid to advertisers by media owners.

Transnational television adspend: Till the late 1990s StarTV was believed to deliberately not solicit for advertising in Indonesia, for it invariably would have meant taking market share from the domestic broadcasters. This would have jeopardised its good relations with the government of then president Soeharto whose family controlled most of the domestic channels. This astute policy paid off with its eventual strategic alliance with the country's sole pay-TV franchise, Indovision, owned largely by the same business conglomerates that owned the dominant domestic channels. Not only were StarTV channels and most of the other transnational broadcasters' channels on the service, Indovision was also required by the terms of its license to carry the domestic commercial channels unencrypted. Unfortunately this arrangement collapsed in the mid-1990s and StarTV entered into a new alliance with another pay-TV operator. Nonetheless, in Indonesia, StarTV succeeded not by competition but cooperation with domestic media interests, and in the early 2000s gained most of its revenue from cable subscriptions rather than advertising.

Hong Kong–based Agencies

Shifts in adspend: There was no major shift in advertising expenditure to transnational television in Hong Kong in the early 1990s, for only a few marketers were thought innovative and proactive enough to trial the new medium upon its arrival [Interview Chn01.04]. Even though the advertisers on StarTV tended to be marketer clients that already had regional business, there were questions raised about signal wastage when the satellite footprint did not coincide with the countries those firms marketed to. Objections to siphoning advertising budgets from any domestic market around the region were raised especially when the specific market was itself not reached by transnational television [Interview Chn01.05]. Furthermore, there were the issues of whether there was consistency between the varied positioning of the product in the various markets and in the advertising being done on a regional basis. Generally, if the positioning and brand personality were not already consistent across the region, then the advertiser would not choose to advertise on StarTV [Interview Chn01.04]. For this reason, even regional television channels were thought not to work as well as national channels for advertisers. With new transnational television providers entering the market in the late 1990s, multinational marketer clients were able to buy a "patchwork quilt" of domestic and transnational media, that is to buy whichever media were stronger in specific geographical areas targeted [Interview Chn01.08]. Clearly advertisers preferred different regions to be put together or tailor-made for their media needs.

Transnational television adspend: Since there were plentiful alternatives, such as print or domestic commercial television, the case for transnational television was harder for Hong Kong–based advertising agencies to make. Furthermore in the early years there was little hard data on transnational television audiences for agencies and their marketer clients to make valid comparisons. Hence some industry executives believed that the best way to reach the pan-Asian elite remained via print, primarily magazines. The prior lack of television stations in some countries, for example in Taiwan and India, had resulted in a supply-led media market and therefore advertisement agencies were keen on transnational television [Interview Chn03.01]. The domestic terrestrial stations in Hong Kong had experienced a growth of advertising revenue in the early to mid-1990s and StarTV had seemingly no adverse effect on this [Interview Chn02.02]. As found elsewhere in the region, there was some resistance by local distributors of global products to siphoning of the advertising budgets towards regional campaigns such as on transnational television. It was difficult to draw on budgets for domestic markets because of the differential impact of transnational television across Asia [Interview Chn01.08]. Nonetheless, in their capacity often of being regional coordinators of advertising, Hong Kong agencies succeeded by the late 1990s in persuading some of their multinational clients by negotiating attractive deals with transnational broadcasters [Interview Chn01.09].

Media budget sources: The limited advertising from Hong Kong on transnational television in the immediate years after the advent of the medium seemed to come from regional print media that then suffered a drop in revenue (Table 6.4). Some funds for advertising on transnational television also came from overall regional media budgets of multinational clients, while other funds came from their various domestic television budgets, depending on footprint coverage of each country. Previously the funds came strictly from regional print budget

Table 6.4
Hong Kong Advertising Expenditure by Media, 1995

Medium	HK$ million	US$ million	Growth
Television	7,432.76	960.61	+19%
Newspapers	4,375.83	565.53	−12%
Magazines	1,795.56	232.06	+9%
Radio	977.66	126.35	+20%
Outdoor	392.72	50.76	+14%
Cinema	47.46	6.13	−24%
Other	91.22	11.79	+10%

Source: Asian A&M [1996b], citing SRG Adex reports.

but because that pool was huge there was only minimal impact [Interview Chn01.03]. The budget for transnational television could also have come from domestic television because the former was more cost-effective on a cost-per-thousand basis for just one country [Interview Chn01.04]. While it was said that the budget for these excursions might have come from both domestic print and television budgets, the most likely scenario was that it involved fresh funding to trial the new transnational medium. In the case of one advertising agency's clients, some used new funds, others re-allocated funds though they left print budgets static [Interview Chn01.09]. Hence the pattern in Asia appeared to be similar to that following broadcast de-regulation in Europe where budgets for television advertising increased without a corresponding decline in print budgets.

Although regional advertising budgets had been growing in Asia, regional print media was not giving up revenue to transnational television without a fight. In response regional print advertising was marketing itself on the basis of flexibility in targeting regions through sub-regional editions, since such targeting was not possible on StarTV in the early 1990s. While there was cost inflation through sub-regionalisation, or in other words cost per thousand is higher thus, there was less wastage though [Interview Chn01.08]. One consequence has been complex negotiations on pricing for regional versus subregional media [Interview Chn01.07]. Thus regional advertising budgets were growing but very slowly, perhaps even plateauing if inflation were considered. On the other hand, some advertising agencies and marketers in Asia were not into buying low-rating programmes such as on StarTV because they were considered not cost-effective to administer [Interview Chn03.01]. Ultimately, advertisers were being persuaded with cost-effectiveness, namely by the argument put up by both print and television media that the higher costs involved in sub-regionalisation were more than made up for by less wastage.

Transnational television adspend: It was impossible to arrive at definitive advertising revenue figures because StarTV and other transnational broadcasters declined to release them, stating that they were commercially-sensitive and proprietary information. Advertising expenditure figures in the mid-1990s (Table 6.4) did not differentiate between transnational and domestic television media, though they seemed to indicate growth of television revenue at the expense of newspapers and cinema which are primarily domestic in reach. This may have been as much due to the growth of transnational as of domestic commercial channels. Although most advertising on transnational television was placed by regional offices of advertising agencies based in Hong Kong or Singapore, this did not preclude domestic offices in Asia making bookings as well, in coordination with the former or otherwise [Interview Chn01.07]. Information on country-of-advertiser-origin was not disclosed by the transnational broadcasters because there might sometimes have been conflict between national offices of MNC marketers over the media-buying decision [Interview Chn02.01]. Sponsorships were another form of revenue that distorted assessment of the income of transnational channels, not to mention the latter's increasing dependence on subscriptions and carriage fees. A prime example was Channel V's use of promotion or non-discrete advertising, resulting in it having three streams of income: sponsorships, subscriptions, and carriage fees [Interview Chn03.01].

The increasing complexity of media planning in Asia following the growth of transnational television has meant that advertising became less marketer-directed and more advertising agency-led. Over the 1990s in Asia, media planning staff rather than account management staff served the marketer as the prime source of marketing communication strategy. In Indonesia where there are ample domestic media alternatives, including commercial television, and little regional marketing ambition, transnational satellite television has been largely ignored. For India, StarTV and the other commercial satellite broadcasters have been utilised primarily as domestic advertising media with regional markets being considered largely incidental, almost accidental. So it does seems that with the possible exception of Hong Kong where advertising agencies have at least a de facto regional role, marketers have steered clear of buying satellite television as a new transnational medium and have been abetted in this by their advertising agencies in each domestic market within Asia.

CREATIVE EXECUTION

The most visible expression of the globalisation of advertising, at least to the general public and consumers, is the production of transnational commercials. But the decision on whether to standardise or localise advertising creativity rests on a number of factors including consistency across the region of product positioning, consumption purchase and usage patterns, attitudes towards the product and brand, and sociocultural taboos. This section examines the products and brands advertised on transnational television in Asia such as StarTV in the early to mid-1990s, the creative approaches adopted by those which did, as well as the insurmountable difficulties perceived by advertising agencies which did not. The extent to which each advertising centre responded to the pressures to globalise or at least regionalise their creativity was symptomatic of their incorporation with the global consumption marketplace.

Mumbai-based Agencies

Products and brands advertised: The few Indian products advertised on StarTV in its early years were largely those meant for export markets such as liquor, financial products and white goods produced in India and targeted at regional markets [Interview Ind01.01]. There was little pan-Asian advertising originating in India because most products were not exported and the average Indian businessman was not thinking of marketing his products abroad. India had no internationally-known consumer products of its own to promote, except some to NRIs [Interview Ind 02.04]. If StarTV did enjoy some support from Indian marketers, a number of interview respondents alleged that it was primarily financial services and liquor advertising which had no outlet on the domestic television channels due to restrictive Indian laws. StarTV and ZeeTV allowed freer expression due to more liberal advertising regulations in Hong Kong from which they uplinked [Interview Ind01.07]. Thus StarTV was alleged to have survived on liquor advertising in its early days while hoping for more advertising income by starting its own Hindi channel [Interview Ind01.11].

Other advertisers from India on StarTV in the mid-1990s, apart from liquor and financial services, included a broad range from cosmetics to car tyres. One view was that there was no clear differentiation between types of products advertised on transnational television and on domestic television, with the former being simply utilised to boost frequency among the upper-income, English-speaking target audience [Chaitra Leo Burnett 1994]. An alternative view was that lifestyle products and upmarket brands with small budgets used ZeeTV and StarTV almost exclusively because of the lower rates per television spot offered. As one executive pointed out, the products advertised on StarTV and ZeeTV tended to be high-value items of appeal to upmarket, often male segments, such as cars and credit cards [Interview Ind01.03]. One agency named its clients on transnational television as Ponds cosmetics and Titan watches on StarPlus, TI cycles on Prime Sports, the *Hindu Business Line* newspaper on BBC [Interview Ind01.08]. Another advertising agency had commercials on StarPlus for products such as Denim cologne and Ceat tyres [Interview Ind01.05]. Most advertising from India placed on the transnational medium was directed at the domestic market and the common explanation proffered by industry executives for this was the dearth of global products distributed in the domestic Indian market in the mid-1990s.

One advantage that StarTV enjoyed over domestic Indian media was the patronage of multinational or, rather, global corporations, which had the same marketing strategy in more than one country and could benefit from the cost savings of transnational advertising. Still even though an MNC may market globally, across Asia or even a region like South Asia or West Asia, it often had to develop separate advertising campaigns for each national market. For instance, Unilever deliberately made specific advertising for each country, its Lux soap using movie stars from India, Pakistan and Dubai for those respective markets [Interview Ind01.11]. In part this was because Unilever soaps were also not standardised across the footprint, so much so that Pakistani viewers once thought their products were fakes because the packs in their country were different to those shown on the commercials on the transnational channel [Interview Ind02.02]. Thus advertising out of Mumbai on StarTV in its early years was complicated by the fact that products or brands were not standardised in the South Asian region or that they were at different stages of their life cycle in each market, and so needed to be positioned differently. For instance, Kemper (2001: 135–42) would illustrate how Sri Lankan advertising had to be more conservative culturally and appropriate local idiom in order to gain mass appeal. But by the late 1990s, StarTV as well as regionalised global channels like CNN and BBC came to be used for both corporate and product advertising. Though whether a regional and local strategy was adopted, was contingent on the brand, product and its target market [Interview Ind 01.12].

Cultural adaptation: Respondents were virtually unanimous that with the possible exception of liquor products no television commercials (TVCs) were created specially for the transnational medium in the early to mid-1990s [Interviews Ind01.02 and Ind01.07]. Whenever TVCs were created for transnational television, often only English language versions were done for the "image", even though the audience that could understand the language was relatively small compared to the total audience in India. This was the case of advertising for a luxury car, targeted at an upmarket segment which was not necessarily cosmopolitan but local businessmen without an English-language education and more comfortable with Hindi-language television [Interview Ind01.08]. Sponsorships of programmes by Indian, Hong Kong and Japanese firms were also gaining ground. From the marketer's point of view it did not matter where the programmes sponsored originated from, unlike advertising [Interview Ind01.07].

In the mid-1990s Indian advertising agencies held on to the hope that the situation with regard to the non-production of TVCs specifically for transnational television would change in time. They seemed confident that Indian consumers were getting more sophisticated in their advertising tastes and that India's expertise in film production would see it take the lead in creating TVCs for the region [Interviews Ind01.04 and Ind01.10]. But there were some reservations expressed about regional cultural differences within South Asia, not to mention subregional ones within India, pre-empting collaboration on creative strategy [Interview Ind01.11]. For the Indian market itself, TVCs were usually created with actors and attire that did not betray any ethnic group, and then dubbed over in different languages [Interview Ind01.12]. They were designed to tap into emotions and were quite nationalistic, even chauvinistic in character. Often sports celebrities and movie actors were used who were acceptable to all ethnic groups and their voices lip-synched to the different languages [Interview Ind01.14]. These were possible with products whose usage is quite universal such as soaps, shampoos, food and confectionaries [Interview Ind01.13]. By the late 1990s, transnational channels such as StarTV and CNN had become so domesticated, that the commercials on them were identical to those used on quasi-domestic satellite channels such as ZeeTV and SonyET. The commercials of multinational corporations targeted an urban youthful market especially were characterised by a synthesis of global/ western and local/regional elements of culture (Butcher 2003: 209–20). While thus accessible to similar market segments in the South Asian region, such advertising was clearly rooted in Indian cultural identity, however artificially constructed.

Jakarta-based Agencies

Products and brands advertised: The only Indonesian products known to have advertised on satellite television in the early 1990s were airlines and hotels, because the medium was considered ideal for such products given its access to their target markets in many of the countries under the footprint [Interview Mly02.04]. But Indonesian advertising agencies preferred to place corporate and image advertising for up-market consumers in domestic print media rather than regional television, for example in the then popular *Tempo* magazine [Interview Mly02.06]. The only example of a successful transnational campaign cited was that for the Dimension 2-in-1 shampoo where Unilever produced a single commercial for three markets, namely Malaysia, Thailand and Indonesia [Interview Mly02.07]. But no comment was volunteered about its effectiveness in creating brand awareness or delivering sales in Indonesia, only that it was a rare and successful collaboration of advertising agencies within the region.

Indonesian advertising agency personnel seemed to have reservations about the practicality of devising a pan-Asian, let alone global, advertising campaign that could be used on transnational satellite television. One advertising agency expressed the view that it was not a question of whether the advertising of global products had to be integrated with the local culture of Indonesia, but how it was to be done. Still it was deemed cheaper for advertising to reflect local culture than to attempt to change it. For while certain consumption habits could be changed, influencing the culture as a whole was not possible [Interview Mly02.02]. Hence Indonesian advertising agencies were acutely conscious of the cultural diversity within Asia, even within their Southeast Asia region, and the difficulty of transcending this or of attempting to change some aspects of it in relation to consumption behaviour. Globalisation of markets and advertising, whether via transnational television or otherwise, was treated as rhetoric rather than reality by advertising agencies and media owners alike in Indonesia right through the 1990s.

Cultural adaptation: Executives in advertising, market research and domestic broadcasting seemed to consider the cultural barriers virtually insurmountable and pointed repeatedly to examples of multinational marketers who had opted to create multi-domestic advertising campaigns within Asia. For instance, in the Marlboro commercials the US version had only a lone cowboy, but in the Malaysian version there were four herdsmen to represent collectivism, while for materialistic Hong Kong the version featured the urban owner of the ranch arriving via helicopter [Interview Mly02.02]. Advertising agencies in Jakarta implied that cultures were distinctly different within the region of Southeast Asia, not to mention the whole continent of Asia. Thus regional advertising would be inappropriate for Lippobank, which positioned itself as "the bank for Chinese investment" in Hong Kong, but this was a politically unacceptable message in its other markets of Indonesia and Malaysia. Even in the neighbouring and culturally-similar Malaysian and Indonesian markets there had to be separate national advertising campaigns for global brands like Toyota, Salem and Dunhill [Interview Mly03.05].

Whether or not the cultural differences were insurmountable objectively speaking, the fact that they were so perceived explained the non-involvement of Indonesian advertising industry in pan-Asian campaigns. But there might be other explanations, including the fact that the cultural issue was used as a publicly espoused rationale for non-consideration of this medium, when the true reason might well have been the loss of local revenue and power which would have accompanied the decision to collaborate in a regional strategy. Regardless of their motivations, the reality was that transnational satellite television exemplified by StarTV acting as a pan-Asian medium in the early to mid-1990s had no impact on the practice of advertising in Indonesia. Thus advertisers in Indonesia could not envisage a major shift to using pan-Asian television commercials given the significant social and cultural differences they perceived across the region, even within their region. There did not seem to be even a recognition of a regional Malay-culture market, despite some evidence of programming exchange and transborder audiences. Given the fact that there was a doubling of the number of domestic channels in the late 1990s despite political crises, and that few transnational broadcasters had specifically targeted Indonesia with their programming and channels, this situation remained relatively unchanged into the early 2000s.

Hong Kong-based Agencies

Products and brands advertised: As far as advertising agencies in Hong Kong were concerned, transnational media such as StarTV in the 1990s were suitable primarily for corporate advertising, and not for consumer goods that needed national and sub-national advertising [Interview Chn01.01 and Chn02.08]. The only clients of one international advertising agency to advertise StarTV were corporate ones that had sales strengths in the countries where the channel was accessible [Interview Chn02.07 and Chn01.07]. StarTV claimed to deliver large numbers at small cost but that was true only if marketers did not mind the wastage. It was still considered a blunt media instrument in its early days [Interview Chn02.08]. Most marketing clients were not prepared for the introduction of StarTV, though some clients were already using TVCs regionally, which had been created and previously used domestically with local soundtracks [Interview Chn01.09]. Unlike the earlier owners of StarTV who were promoting it as a pan-Asian medium, international advertising agencies and their MNC marketer clients were quite sceptical about the applicability of Levitt's (1983) globalisation thesis in the Asian market for the majority of their products [Interview Chn03.04].

Believing in the concept of transnational advertising, nonetheless, some advertising agencies helped put together a package for media buying on StarTV which was then subleased to their marketer clients. However it comprised primarily clients whose marketing operations were already transnational which were amenable to the idea of utilising StarTV, and it was not the arrival of the new medium that triggered their commitment to transnational advertising. One advertising agency spent an unspecified substantial sum advertising on StarTV because its clients—Coke, Tourist Authority of Thailand, Cathay Pacific and

UPS—were all products with a global strategy [Interview Chn01.03]. But target markets for each advertiser did not always align with the satellite footprint. For instance, while Thailand might have been a market leader for one client, India was a poor performer, or while Hong Kong and Singapore were more services-driven, China might have been more into packaged goods [Interview Chn01.04]. Hong Kong itself was not much of a market for StarTV since the latter was prohibited in its early years from broadcasting in Cantonese, the dominant language of the colony, so as to protect the domestic commercial channels. Therefore, even in the late 1990s StarTV was used by those multinational advertisers in Hong Kong which had already been marketing regionally in Asia, but not to the exclusion of domestic advertising media in constituent countries. Transnational satellite television was found to work only for a select group of products and services, and even then the reach of the medium did not quite fit the market priorities of the multinational marketers in the region.

Cultural adaptation: Agency and media personnel were of the opinion that transnational and domestic advertising were not distinctly different but quite complementary. The commercials that were used on the transnational medium were often a subset of those used on the domestic television in the country, if not elsewhere in the region, but considered to have wider applicability [Interview Chn02.01]. For regional advertising, advertising agencies often looked first at what was available domestically which might be useable regionally. But the result could be mixed: Adidas ran a global commercial in Asia successfully, while a Milo commercial did not work within Greater China because the boy featured did not have a "Hong Kong face" [Interview Chn01.07]. Transnational television was used in conjunction with domestic television, and never to the exclusion of the latter [Interview Chn02.09]. In other words, no commercials were created specifically for the new medium and pan-Asian advertising simply duplicated and extended domestic advertising. Though the language is similar for China and Taiwan, the creative strategy for China needed to be different, due to its different social, cultural and economic environment. Besides, the written language used in Taiwan was not the simplified form used in China [Interview Chn01.08]. As with their counterparts in Indonesia, Hong Kong industry executives had reservations about whether a regional campaign was feasible or at least not problematic.

Coordination of advertising was important so as not to be different at different levels such as in much of the 1990s when dealer/local advertising was often unprofessional, national advertising featured different benefits in each country, and regional advertising attempted to maintain the brand image. The coordination was mainly via the marketer clients' structure along national lines, which was not always effective [Interview Chn01.03]. Generally packaging was not standardised, and would not be for a while yet [Interview Chn02.09]. Thus there were issues of sub-cultural differences even within Greater China, consistency of image and lack of coordination of regional advertising with domestic advertising. Despite its reservations, Hong Kong's advertising industry has been reasonably active in supporting StarTV as an innovative alternative for marketers based there, more so than most other countries in the region. This may be largely due to the fact that Hong Kong is the regional headquarters for a number of multinational marketers operating in Asia. The medium was also utilised not only as an pan-Asian medium but as a more limited regional one for the Greater China market, increasingly so as transnational satellite broadcasters themselves position themselves as regional or quasi-domestic. Furthermore StarTV was considered as having to have a role in conjunction with, rather than in opposition to, domestic television.

While the Indonesian attitude towards this transnational television might be characterised as disinterested avoidance, the Indian attitude was one of enthusiastic embrace, and the Hong Kong one was of thoughtful consideration. Indonesia's advertisers saw little response to the new transnational medium by audiences satiated with multiple commercial channels domestically and so largely ignored it. Indian advertisers chose to use StarTV and domesticated satellite channels which followed as a means of circumventing some local restrictions on advertising, as well as reaching expatriate and diasporic Indians elsewhere. Hong Kong domestic advertisers likewise had little use for the medium locally but did see potential for targeting other constituents of Greater China as it became regionalised, while its multinational advertisers were keen to dabble in this new transnational medium. All of them saw, though, little scope for globalised or pan-Asian advertising across the whole of the StarTV footprint, except perhaps in the limited cases of corporate advertising and upmarket services. As this became patently obvious in the mid-to-late 1990s, transnational broadcasters in Asia adapted their programming to regional and quasi-domestic markets for which they were rewarded with advertising, a trend that has persisted into the 2000s.

A conceptual framework was introduced in the companion volume *Imagi-Nations and Borderless Television* to focus and compare the findings from all three regions selected as sites of in-depth investigation, namely, the Indian subcontinent, Malay world and Greater China (Figure 7.1). This analytical grid will be expanded upon further in this book, highlighting the factors influential in the highly complex interaction of transnational television and advertising. Inductively derived from the interviews, secondary data and content analysis conducted, these explanatory factors will demonstrate the highly complex impact of transnational satellite television in each of the representative countries. Across the selected regions, countries and supranational sub-regions investigated, it is quite evident that the globalisation of media in Asia has developed in distinct ways. As such this analytical framework serves as a basis for a critical understanding of the management of transnational television and advertising, as this chapter will attempt to demonstrate.

EXPANDING THE GRID

As it is simply not feasible with case studies to segregate strictly events from causes, problems from solutions and description from analysis, the preceding chapters of this book have alluded to the contributory factors in the impact of transnational television and not just the historical facts in various countries in Asia. Still an overarching framework is invaluable for systematically analysing the interacting factors of globalisation in the study of transnational media. Each factor may be

Figure 7.1
Grid for Analysing Impact of Transnational Television

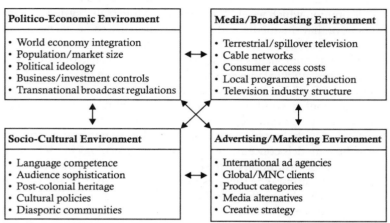

Politico-Economic Environment	Media/Broadcasting Environment
• World economy integration • Population/market size • Political ideology • Business/investment controls • Transnational broadcast regulations	• Terrestrial/spillover television • Cable networks • Consumer access costs • Local programme production • Television industry structure
Socio-Cultural Environment	**Advertising/Marketing Environment**
• Language competence • Audience sophistication • Post-colonial heritage • Cultural policies • Diasporic communities	• International ad agencies • Global/MNC clients • Product categories • Media alternatives • Creative strategy

represented by a continuum that is relevant selectively to the phenomenon of transnational television, especially in the context of developing countries. For comprehensive analysis of borderless media markets, every factor could and should be applied to each of the countries in the region, but here different yet comparable countries from each region are used under each category of factors simply for the purpose of illustration.

Discerning Levels

A review of the level of analysis possible and the one adopted in this research is pertinent at this juncture. Theories of global communication may be classified as being either micro, mid-range or macro theories. Micro-level theories deal with the human mind, its motivations, needs, thoughts, fears and desires. Learning concepts garnered from psychology such as selective perception, frustration–aggression, cognitive dissonance, stereotyping and gaming have their usefulness in explaining the ways in which audiences utilise the widely available media and all the global information it provides access to. Macro-level theories emphasise the vital importance of the constant flow of information to the maintenance of relations between countries, without which diplomatic, economic or military confrontation might result. Idealist systems theories believe that the media could be a forum for public opinion which would lead to peace, while realist systems theories believe that the media and public opinion are to be harnessed to serve the ideology of the state.

Mid-range approaches to analysis deal with social groups, classes, communities, political movements and institutions in relation to global communications. Frustration–aggression is often cited by governments in the developing world as their underlying concern for seeking to control western programming and advertising which would lead to dissatisfaction with their economic state and thus to political instability. Since these models concentrate on the television ecology in each country, comprising institutions in the broadcast industry and their decision makers, such mid-range theories match the objectives of the present research. In analysing the growth of transnational television and advertising in this book, a "media-strategy" approach would seem to avoid the polemics of the earlier mentioned schools, especially of political economy and cultural studies, by taking into consideration the full complexity of its national contexts. Yet, bridging the political economy and cultural studies pillars, such an approach analyses government policies and regulation, the positioning of channels by media-owners, the programming appeal to audiences, the role of marketers and advertising agencies, in representative countries and regions.

Bigger Picture

Politico-economic environment: While recognising that earlier modernisation paradigms had been inadequate, many economists claim that promoting the growth of the information sector via investments in telecommunications would transform developing economies. Although structural-functionalism has its roots in the developed world, its modernisation theory variant is still held to have some relevance to developing countries facing a dilemma over the conflicting values needed for modernisation versus nationalism. Despite their earlier socialist, nonaligned, and somewhat isolationist policies, all three countries have sought greater integration into the capitalist world system in the last decade or so. Whether China will be able to maintain its communist political system while pursuing a market economy, India its socialistic bureaucracy while liberalising, or Indonesia its military-authoritarian government while privatising has yet to be seen. Quite obviously, it would appear that countries which adopt a free-market approach in their economies are the most integrated into the capitalist-dominant world economy, and by implication would be the most likely to experience globalisation of its television. Thus regardless of their particular politico-economic shade, India, Indonesia, China and most other nations in Asia, have experienced globalisation of their television industries, if not directly via transnational television, at least indirectly as their domestic channels faced up to the challenge of global or regional competition. All countries in Asia exercised some form of regulation of access to transnational satellite television on a range from "active suppression" to "liberal access" though these do shift over time.

All three countries used as comparative case studies on politico-economic environment are populous and that explains in part their interest to broadcasters and advertisers, though the differing levels of interest can be explained by other contributory factors. But the role of population size in the potential impact of transnational television in the case of Indonesia needs to be qualified by the relative level of cultural sophistication and economic affluence of the population of each country or geo-linguistic market. The foreign investment in the media industry in particular attracts attention on the grounds that it is a national cultural resource and involves issues of national security. Still, in one form or another, the three key countries studied maintained strict controls over investment in the media, especially the television industry, though in reality this is being progressively eroded. As a general rule, a policy of allowing access or at least of not overtly restricting is favourable to the growth of transnational television in a particular country, though this needs to be qualified by yet other factors. Regulations alone have not been sufficient to deter access, for they often serve to drive the industry "underground" and consequently difficult to regulate.

Sociocultural environment: In essence it was the commercial and political capital cities which had driven the demand for transnational television, and so the markets in Asia were largely defined by the greater metropolitan areas of Mumbai, Karachi, Taipei, Hong Kong, Shanghai, Jakarta and Kuala Lumpur rather than their respective countries. In general terms, these urban consumers are cosmopolitan in their outlook and consumption habits, given their exposure to western culture. While there might have been affluent audiences in other urban or rural regions of the various countries under the satellite footprint they were better described as being local in outlook by contrast. They often represented a secondary market for transnational television, one better catered to by subregional or subnational language programming. Critical as audiences are to the performance of transnational broadcasters, advertisers are less interested in their size per se as with their buying power and cultural sophistication.

Like many developing countries worldwide, Pakistan, Malaysia and Taiwan have utilised public television as means of promoting national integration, social development and economic modernisation. But their concern about past colonialism or neo-colonialism has been responsible for restrictions on access to transnational television by their citizens who by virtue of culture and education may appreciate such broadcasts. The more stringent the cultural policies of a nation in its commitment to national integration, the more likely it is to control domestic television broadcasting. Ironically, the more restricted the domestic programming fare, the more motivated are consumers to gain access to transnational television regardless of governmental controls on access. While accusing transnational satellite broadcasters of cultural imperialism, government leaders often remained blinkered to the same phenomenon within the nation state by one dominant ethnic group over its minorities. Ironically, as national public television broadcasters worldwide compromise their public service ideal of nationwide appeal in order to survive in a commercialised broadcasting market, ethnic minorities often have even less hope of gaining a cultural voice within their nation state.

Where satellite television may not be economically viable a domestic market basis, there might be a market for it on a subregional-ethnic or global-diasporic basis as some transnational channels have demonstrated. There are South Asian expatriates such as in the Middle East, or immigrants historically in Southeast Asia, Fiji, East Africa, the Caribbean and more recently in North America and Europe. A parallel situation exists in Greater China and among overseas Chinese, predominantly in East Asia such as in the urban areas of Thailand, Philippines, Malaysia and Indonesia, and also practically worldwide. But there are few ethnic Malay migrants outside the Southeast Asia region, largely confined to the Netherlands and its former colonies of Surinam and South Africa, where the regional-origin languages are in disuse. Thus while pan-Asian English-language television did not work well, regional South Asian–language and Chinese-language channels have proven very successful. There is therefore considerable correlation between the existence of migrant and expatriate markets, and the growth of transnational television using one of the major languages of Asia.

ANALYSIS BY INDUSTRY

In a hypothetical causal model, the advent of transnational broadcasters might constitute the independent variable, the changes in the media and advertising industries being dependent variables, with politico-economic and sociocultural factors constituting intervening variables. Given the complexity and multi-directional nature of the relationships between the factors elicited inductively through this research, such a model seems overly simplistic. In this section the impact of transnational television on the media and advertising industries, and vice versa, in Asia will be explicated via the analytical framework and its inventory of key factors. While it can be applied to all constituent countries, and could be for comprehensive analysis, the applicability of the framework will be demonstrated using comparable minor country-markets as well as major advertising centres from each subregion.

Media/Broadcasting Environment

Terrestrial/spillover television: Small markets such as Macau, Bangladesh and Brunei that are accustomed to spillover television would normally be primed for reception of transnational television via satellite. Bangladesh had only a moderate number of domestic public or pseudo-commercial television channels, which precipitated the establishment of quasi-legal cable networks utilising videotape programming, which in turn were catalysts for the penetration of satellite television from within the region. Acknowledging its citizens' interest in the wide variety of Greater China channels, Macau granted access via cable to satellite channels. Even if audiences have access to limited domestic channels as in the case of Brunei, if there is ample choice via both spillover and domestic sources, they are unlikely to be keen on transnational satellite television. This is especially so if it is in a foreign language or dialect and it is more costly. Thus the more diversified and liberal the domestic television industry and/or greater the access to spillover terrestrial television in a country or subregion, the less of a market for transnational television it is (Table 7.1).

Cable networks: The success of transnational television in Asia has been highly dependent on the development, even pre-existence of cable networks, whether legal, illegal or quasi-legal. In Bangladesh, StarTV took off largely because neighbourhood cable networks had preceded the arrival of the new television medium, created by the demand for alternatives to the government-controlled media. Brunei did not have a cable industry and thus difficulty of access explains in part why it had among the lowest penetration for transnational television. Macau came belatedly to have cable networks because the demand was limited due to ease of spillover television from Hong Kong and southern China. The cable networks in much of Asia existed in a legal vacuum caused by the regulatory lag over technology change in communications, and the belated attempts to legalise the medium were dictated largely by the status quo of an established cable industry. Often governments seized on the opportunity provided by the introduction of new broadcasting legislation to attempt to control citizens' access to transnational television via domestic cable networks. Multi-service operators (MSOs), a consequent development, are relatively recent entrants into the transnational satellite television equation, and so it is somewhat premature to ascertain their impact on transnational broadcasters and advertisers.

Consumer access costs: A critical factor with the penetration of transnational satellite television in Asia has been the cost of access to the average consumer. In Brunei, where cable networks have not existed,

Table 7.1
Media/Broadcasting Environment of Transnational Television

Selected Factors	Macau	Bangladesh	Brunei
Terrestrial/spillover television	Wide choice/high-entertainment	Moderate/mixed programming	Limited/ high-info
Cable networks	Oligopolistic/ MSOs	Extensive/ neighbourhood	Monopolistic/ non-existent
Consumer access costs	Moderate cost/ pay TV	Low-cost/ cable	High-cost/dish or DTH
Local programme production	Limited production	Limited production	Limited production
Television industry structure	Local/private	Joint ventures/ strategic alliances	Government/ family-owned

the cost of access via satellite dishes was high, and so transnational channels were confined to the upper socio-economic classes. Even in the late 1990s, cable access in Macau was through pay-TV monopolies which were relatively expensive for the average consumer, whereas the neighbourhood cable operators in Bangladesh had brought the cost of access down to a level where even the lower middle class could afford it. The development of these networks into oligopolistic multiservice operators under government regulation has not significantly lowered cost of access. Direct-to-home television by the transnational broadcasters could be a threat to the cable industry, but only if and when they are able to lower their hardware and subscription costs to the level that consumers in many Asian markets have become accustomed.

Local programme production: The more extensive and productive a domestic film and video production industry in a country, the more likely it is to be able to provide sufficient programming to sustain its own television channels and/or contribute to transnational satellite channels. In the case of India and Hong Kong, the prodigious domestic film and video industry has been a source of programming on domestic channels and have also contributed to the establishment by their countries of regional commercial channels often via satellite or cable. By contrast, Bangladesh, Brunei and Macau have much less productive if not virtually non-existent film and video industry, which have therefore had difficulty sustaining anything more than its domestic television channels. In any case while programming for the StarTV channels was sourced worldwide, increasingly they were from the very countries and subregions to which these now quasi-domestic channels were broadcast. It might be argued that the more accustomed domestic audiences were to imported programming, the more likely they were to accept transnational television via satellite. However, how one defines imported programming and locally-produced clones is critical. For though Greater China, the Malay Archipelago and Indian subcontinent were not very dependent on imports from the West and had locally-produced programme clones, these were not readily transferable between the constituent territories due to minor language and culture variations.

Television industry structure: The ownership of transnational channels by global media corporations has been assumed by governments to imply their domination of any regional market they expand into. In reality, however, the impact of ownership is far more diffused, as the history of StarTV illustrates. This pioneer of transnational satellite television in Asia was originally not part of a global media corporation owned by western interests, but owned by business family from within Asia. Furthermore, transnational satellite channels are often carried by locally-owned cable operations in the various countries of Asia, ranging from neighbourhood entrepreneurs to large domestic firms with political affiliations. A recent development has been the formation of formal strategic alliances and joint ventures between transnational and domestic broadcasters such as ZeeTV and AOL Time Warner, as well as with domestic programme producers such as UTV with StarTV, cable networks and the like. In terms of corporate citizenship then, whether one might classify a broadcaster as being primarily foreign, regional, local or some hybrid is now an open question. The experience of StarTV and its followers into the Asian market demonstrates the principle that the greater the number of strategic alliances or joint ventures formed, the more significant the impact of transnational television on the domestic broadcasters, advertisers and audiences in that market, and vice versa.

Advertising/Marketing Environment

International advertising agencies: The most positive responses to the use of transnational television as an advertising medium were from Hong Kong where the international advertising agencies have had a direct presence and dominate the advertising industry. Invariably these agencies act either as formal or de facto regional or subregional coordinators of advertising for a number of multinational marketer clients. To them, a transnational medium such as StarTV was an attractive option over dependence on multiple branch or affiliate agencies to deliver consistency of advertising via domestic broadcasters across a regional market. In Jakarta, where the international advertising agencies and their MNC clients were compelled by law to operate as joint ventures with local firms, there was considerable pressure to advertise domestically, and thus resistance towards regional advertising initiatives. In Mumbai there were restrictions on the purchasing of advertising time or space on regional television media, primarily via foreign exchange constraints. Still, India-based agencies were marginally more responsive to the new medium than Indonesian ones, because they felt some responsibilities for other subregional markets, even if only to expatriate/diasporic Indians there. Thus the stronger the presence of international advertising agencies in a country the more likely that a transnational medium such as StarTV would be utilised for advertising in that national market as well as for the region, subregion or diaspora of which that market was a part (Table 7.2).

Global/MNC clients: It appears that the greater the number of multinational clients operating directly in key markets of a region, the more significant the commitment to advertising regionally via transnational satellite television. This is closely related to the situation above with international advertising agencies which tend to service the MNC marketers. Both these advertising agencies and their MNC clients were likely to have had experience with regional advertising via satellite television in Europe or North America, or even global advertising, and were therefore more interested in replicating that practice in Asia once the option was available. In some cases advertising of a global product via domestic media could be coordinated through national offices, joint ventures or sole agents in various countries of the region. But apart from this being a cumbersome process, it was fraught with difficulties given the varying regulations on content, not to mention restrictions on the use of foreign-produced television commercials imposed by many governments in the region including India and Indonesia. In analysing the clients of StarTV, this research uncovered different national offices of MNC marketers purchasing advertising time on the same transnational medium primarily to target a domestic market, whether in collaboration with or independent of their regional office. As a general rule, wherever the regional headquarters of MNCs

Table 7.2
Advertising/Marketing Environment of Transnational Television

Selected Factors	Jakarta	Mumbai	Hong Kong
International advertising agencies	Via affiliates/ national	Via affiliates/ national–regional	Direct presence/ regional–continental
Global/MNC clients	Via agents	Joint ventures	Regional offices
Product categories	Corporate/ services	Domestic/luxury	Global/services
Media alternatives	Moderate	Wide	Moderate
Creative strategy	National/ customised	Regional/adapted	Global/standardised

were predominant as in Hong Kong, there was greater openness to experiment with the new transnational television medium as a viable alternative or at least as a complement to domestic advertising.

Product categories: Generally, advertising on the transnational medium tended also to be of upmarket products and services targeted at the socio-economic elite of regional markets, since these were the innovators and early adopters of this new medium. Advertising which originated from Hong Kong was primarily of a corporate nature or promoted financial services, the line between them being not always distinguishable. Therefore where the clients handled by advertising agencies in a country required a considerable emphasis on corporate advertising or services advertising, the more likely was transnational satellite television to be utilised as a medium. Financial advertising and liquor were placed on StarTV through Mumbai because Indian advertisers were not permitted on domestic television and the primary target market was the relatively wealthy expatriate Indians in the Middle East. Together with upmarket cars, electronic appliances and fashion-wear these were placed on what was considered a strategic medium for also targeting domestic Indian consumers of the middle class and above. The only advertisers initially allowed to utilise the transnational medium through Jakarta were those of upmarket services targeted at foreigners such as Indonesian airlines and luxury hotels. So where there were restrictions on using transnational media for domestic markets, a medium such as StarTV was used to advertise domestic products for transnational markets. Thus analysis of the products advertised on StarTV was revealing of the strategies adopted deliberately or unwittingly in the use of a transnational television medium.

Media alternatives: Developing countries which have a wide range of advertising media, especially television, are less likely to utilise the transnational medium, as illustrated by Indonesia which has five quasi-national television networks. On the other hand advertisers in a country like India which had limited access to domestic television embraced a transnational medium such as StarTV in its early days even though they utilised it as a quasi-domestic medium. If a product was distributed solely to urban areas of a country, it was likely that transnational television would be considered, though this was only true when there was no commercial television or a second public channel which had a more urban reach than the national broadcaster. Thus in India, StarTV,

ZeeTV and SonyET found themselves competing with DD2 for the urban markets of South Asia, while in Indonesia RCTI and Indosiar were the unquestioned choice for the same purpose though only within the country. Quite accurately Reeves (1993: 152–67) surmised that advertisers are quite indifferent towards the privatisation of the media if they can achieve the same ends through a monopolistic government broadcaster that they could through multiple commercial ones, especially when there is a limited consumer market as is the case in many developing countries. Hong Kong represented a special case since the territory was largely urbanised, and both TVB and ATV had territory-wide as well as southern China coverage. But since the domestic television media were mass market–oriented and the cable/pay-TV service was prohibited from carrying advertising, some upmarket products utilised StarTV to reach the expatriate market in Hong Kong. Thus despite their availability, the domestic media was not strictly viable alternatives and a transnational medium enjoyed considerable demand from advertisers in particular product niches.

Creative strategy: Where the perception among advertising executives was that cultural differences between their country and those of other countries were almost insurmountable, then there would be a decided preference for local creativity. Advertising executives in Jakarta were the most forceful in arguing for the imperative of domestic creativity, albeit of a cosmopolitan nature, as necessary for effective marketing communication, though it might also be a rationalisation for retaining advertising budgets domestically and not challenging government restrictions. Those in Mumbai seemed equivocal about the need for domestic creative styles and an informal review of their commercials shows that they opted for a more regional–cosmopolitan style than a domestic–traditional one for the upmarket products and services advertised on transnational and domestic channels alike. Invariably the same commercials for upmarket products were placed on StarTV as well as the more sophisticated DD2. Executives in Hong Kong were almost indifferent but most prone to choosing a more global-creative style in domestically-produced commercials, if not using global commercials of western origin or adapting the concept slightly in domestic remakes. The preference of an advertising agency for a more global or at least a hybrid global–regional creative style for multinational clients generally commends the use of transnational media over any strictly national one.

EXPLICATING INTERACTION

It is no small challenge to discern the cultural and economic impact of transnational television and advertising, and vice versa, as they have not happened in isolation. For the advent of transnational television in Asia coincided with the end of the Cold War, the transformation of GATT into the World Trade Organization, the rise of democracy movements, and so on. Critical commentary on the growth of transnational television via satellite has been overshadowed by hasty attempts to grasp the implications of the extraordinary development of the Internet. The related preoccupation with e-commerce ignores the digital divide which runs right through the continent. While the middle classes and upwardly mobile in most countries of Asia are plugged into that revolution, the vast majority of the population has little access to computers, let alone the skills to utilise them. Still, among these information have-nots, only a small minority is not connected to the television revolution thanks to relatively inexpensive access. Even if they do not have access to satellite and cable television, they invariably have access to domestic terrestrial television that has become quite globalised due to the competition of the former.

The advent and growth of transnational television however has a clearly discernible impact on the media and advertising industries in the various countries and vice versa in the scramble for ratings and revenue. Much programming on the largely commercialised television in post-media liberalisation Asia is entertainment—soaps, variety shows, game-shows and the like—seemingly distracting the people via "bread-and-circuses" instead of addressing the causes of their poverty and other socio-economic injustices endured. However the portrayal of affluent consumerist lifestyles on both local and foreign programmes must contribute to the urban drift and even economic migration by the poor who have few options where they reside. The wide choice of television channels now in much of Asia's urban areas does mean that television has shifted from being a window into the rest of the nation state or geopolitical region, into being wallpaper representation of the world marketplace, alternatively alienating or alluring. What is insidious is that the accessible medium of television is shifting its viewers from being citizens of a nation state, however flawed in its design, to being consumers vital to capitalist production and marketing systems, if not global, at least regional or subregional. With the decline of public broadcasting the government was left as a referee among the players, one that was sometimes ignored, seeking to balance national cultural agenda with global economic imperatives. It is this drama played out over a decade from the early 1990s to early 2000s that this book has focused on.

The end of the first decade of transnational television in Asia is now sufficiently past for the kind of critical reflection, long-term perspective and broad-based comparison across the region that this book seeks to provide. For those seeking up-to-date information on transnational television in Asia, there is always the World Wide Web, though finding comparable data across half a dozen or so countries in the region is not always easy. For those interested primarily in more current data, some relevant websites are listed in Appendix E to this book. However, other data is proprietary and strategically precious in the highly competitive media and advertising arena. The inductively-derived analytical grid sketched in this chapter was devised to elucidate the major factors in the development of transnational television in Asia, largely as perceived by key decision makers in the region's cultural industries. At this stage of the diffusion of transnational television in Asia, the descriptions of the selected factors are perhaps more accurate concerning the urban-metropolitan areas of each country than as generalisations about each country as a whole. The penultimate chapter which follows will revisit the research issues first stated in Chapter 1 in the course of summing up the findings of this study. Through answers to these questions the macro issues surrounding the environments of transnational television and micro issues concerning the strategies adopted by key players in the industry will be expanded upon, and generalised with caveats to other developing countries in Asia and beyond.

The impact of transnational television on the Asian continent defies any preconceived notion that it should be unilateral and uniform. Transnational broadcasters and their audiences in any country have a relationship within the context of a society often comprising multiple co-existent cultures, and any globalisation of the media has to paradoxically involve some localisation. The new medium has also to contend with quite varied politico-economic environments in each country, which may curtail or even enhance its impact. Therefore the contingent corporate strategy for transnational broadcasters and advertisers may not be global but rather a multi-domestic or hybrid global–local one. Since globalisation in Asia has not been uni-directional, with westernised global cultural products obliterating traditional local cultures, this chapter will examine how and why transnational television programming and advertising have often been characterised by both globalisation and localisation strategies concurrently. It will analyse how transnational broadcasting has became an advertising option utilised in divergent ways by each market, precipitating a re-thinking of the notions of global, regional and local strategies.

Globalisation/Localisation

Early transnational broadcasters such as CNN and StarTV adopted a global or pan-Asian strategy when they first entered the continental market, clearly differentiating themselves from the nationally-oriented domestic broadcasters. But Asia proved more diverse culturally and economically than these transnational broadcasters had assumed from their experience in North America and, to a lesser extent, Europe with its bilingual and multilingual citizenry. Hence transnational broadcasters learnt that it was not simply a matter of targeting programming or advertising at some pan-Asian elite market. Realising that it was not able to attract much advertising and sponsorships, StarTV diversified into Greater China/Mandarin, Indian/South Asian, Indonesian/Malay and even further market segments. Making appropriate changes in programming and even language of broadcast, they took on the domestic broadcasters compelling the latter to respond with changes to their strategy in turn. Latter transnational broadcasters took their cue from this change of StarTV's strategy.

Genre Specialisation

While domestic television broadcasters have been generalists in their programming in their attempt to cater to a wide range of audiences, pan-Asian television broadcasters are usually quite specialised. For instance, CNN specialises in news, ESPN in sports, while the StarTV stable had specific channels for music, news, sports and entertainment, although the last of these comprised a fair assortment of programme genre. This strategy of the transnationals was their strength as they were able to provide far more programming attractive to market segments of sports fans, music lovers or news-sensitive politicians and businesspersons, than any of the domestic broadcasters. Nonetheless, the early transnational broadcasters soon realised that this was not sufficient to attract a critical mass of audiences across Asia. The exceptions seemed to be the ethnic/language channels of Phoenix Chinese and ZeeTV that enjoyed broad-based audiences in specific countries or regions within Asia. Without abandoning its strategy of specialised programming, StarTV began expanding each channel's offerings by language, culture or region. Thus Star Sports/Prime Sports was soon offered in multiple language versions that coincided with different satellite footprints, providing more of the sports that obsessed each market, for example badminton for Indonesia, cricket for India, and basketball for China. Similarly, it offered Channel V in multiple versions catering to Greater China music fans who appreciate "Canto-pop" (see glossary), Filipino music fans who prefer a higher content of western rock, and to fans in both South and West Asia with a higher content of "Bollywood" (see glossary) film music to cater to subregional tastes.

Programming is not altogether distinct from advertising so far as the former too bears a marketing agenda. Despite adopting a critical position towards the dominant culture, Kaplan (1987: 143–53) believed that a television channel such as MTV lets itself be co-opted by the commercial establishment. She argued that it is a continuous advertising medium promoting consumption on a variety of levels from the sponsors' products and the programme itself to an entire youth subculture. Baudrillard (1988) would suggest that this illustrates how the media are paradoxically both instruments of power for mystifying the masses as well as the means used by the masses for the denial of reality. However Habermas (1989) would counter this post-structuralist relativism with the view that reciprocal meanings arise from the dialogue between speaker and hearer, medium and viewer/listener, and out of that may come new consensus and social norms. The impact of the domestic public broadcaster DD on village life in India amply documented by Johnson (2000) is a harbinger of greater change as satellite and cable television makes inroads in the first decade of this century. As such, both programming as well as advertising on domesticated transnational television whether they be MTV, CNN, StarTV, ZeeTV or SunTV involve collation of cultural fragments from around the world. Such programming decisions are made primarily to communicate with quite heterogeneous consumer markets across Asia and appeal to advertisers by providing a conducive context for promoting their goods and services.

Geo-linguistic Segments

It appears feasible to segment the Asian media market by regional mega-cultures, which have a major geographical focus but are also scattered across the whole continent and beyond. One may speak of a Chinese-Confucian segment centred on Hong Kong, yet extending to Taiwan and PRC and to overseas Chinese throughout Southeast Asia, even worldwide. Other Northeast Asian countries such as Japan and Korea might be considered "cultural cousins" due to historical links, even if there has been understated animosity since. There might also be said to be a Hindi–Hindu segment centred on India but extending to other South Asian countries by language if not religion, and to their expatriates and migrants in West and Southeast Asia, East Africa, Europe and North America. The role of transnational television in extending the hegemony of "Hinglish", a mix of Hindi and English, over South Asia as well its globalisation via the diaspora has been aptly demonstrated by Thussu (2000). A Malay-Islamic culture could be seen as located in Indonesia, Brunei and Malaysia but diffusing also to southern Thailand, Singapore and the southern Philippines, as well as having religious, though not ethnic, affinities in Pakistan, Bangladesh and the Middle East. Finally there is a Anglophone–cosmopolitan segment, having a limited yet affluent membership among the urban elite and expatriates of Asia especially in the world-class business capitals within each region such as Hong Kong, Singapore, Mumbai, Kuala Lumpur, Manila and the like.

In spite of the superficial non-homogeneity of nation states which comprise our world there is a socio-economic elite of both developing and developed countries who have more in common with each other than with the lower classes of their own countries. While not ignoring the existence of the nation state, Sklair (1991) conceptualised the global system as comprising three interlinked levels: economic, political and cultural–ideological, associated respectively with transnational corporations (TNCs), a transnational capitalist class and global consumerism. The nation state then may be dismissed as a myth used by world capitalism to deflect criticism from its hegemony of the global system. Though Sklair attributed the global capitalist system with having improved significantly the standard of living of billions through a form of materialist socialism, he questionably stated this was without imposing a political and cultural ideology. In actual fact a capitalist class has arisen worldwide, often including the economic elite of developing countries, who identify with the global capitalist system particularly through its culture–ideology of materialism and consumerism, even if not language and secularity. Multinational marketers and media owners have certainly been in the forefront of targeting these lucrative market segments through their advertising and programming, as may be observed with transnational television in Asia.

Multi-lingual Broadcast

There has been considerable scope for pan-Asian channels in Chinese and Hindi, since both are more widespread as languages and cultures throughout Asia than Malay/Indonesian, Japanese, Korean and the like.

But regional programming for Northeast Asia, South and West Asia, or Southeast Asia respectively may not work very well, for though the languages may be similar across national borders cultures are quite distinct as indicated by the fact that the highest rating programmes in many of the constituent countries are very much productions with a local idiom. Pan-Asian programming received a new lease of life when it became technically possible to have different sound and video tracks accessible simultaneously to viewers using decoders. It was also another way for satellite broadcasters to utilise the increased channels available to them through digital compression, inexpensively yet highly effectively. Thus most transnational broadcasters have been able to go a step further to customise channels for subregions, if not for specific countries, a practice that could be characterised as fragmentation and hybridity. Such domestication of transnational television in Asia makes it difficult for social critics to allege media or cultural imperialism, unless one takes the extreme position that it is the programme genre that counts rather than country-of-production.

It would be well-nigh impossible to deny that certain genres such as drama and comedy have had a long popular tradition in most local cultures, well prior to television. It might be argued instead that television, whether transnational or domestic, has been instrumental in their preservation in rapidly-modernising countries. Certainly it may be said that in Asia, local cultures are being co-opted in the process of the globalisation of their cultural industries and postmodernisation of cultures. But no medium can be subversive if the dangers are understood and anticipated. Postman (1985) recommended that we educate ourselves on how the television medium works, teach children how to interpret symbols of our culture and learn to talk back to it, at least figuratively. Despite the pervasiveness of television in the developed world, he deemed that some attempt to reach some form of accommodation with it was possible without losing one's integrity. There must be growing recognition that media ecology and cultural hybridity work in concert for transnational television to gain acceptance in any country. Perhaps what needs to be realised by transnational broadcasters in developing countries is that their markets may neither be regional, national nor subregional, but comprise intersecting and overlapping segments based on multiple dimensions of culture and affluence within their satellite footprints.

Global–Local Co-habitation

Over the past decade, transnational television in Asia has been increasingly characterised by strategic alliances with domestic broadcasters and programme producers. This has been partly due to domestic firms lacking finance to expand their own operations, as well as government restrictions on foreign ownership that prevented global firms from entering on their own. Furthermore the convergence of technologies in television, telecommunications and information prompted firms to seek out expertise in related areas in the course of business expansion. One characteristic development has been the strategic alliances between film and television producers and cable/satellite broadcasters and other distributors, many of them via ethnic (sometimes family) businesses which span continents such as the overseas Chinese and non-resident Indian networks. The result has been that transnational broadcasters are tapping the very same sources of programming as domestic broadcasters, bringing both types of broadcaster into direct competition in national, though often largely urban, markets.

This does imply that domestic production houses do not truly represent a post-Fordist mode of cultural production because they are so closely allied to global media conglomerates, if not actually part-owned by them. As Schiller (1989) warned earlier, the critical issue in international communications seems to be the increasingly commercial ownership of the broadcast, information and cultural sectors of all countries and their consequent dependence on multinational advertisers. By the 1990s global media had come to be dominated by a few multinational corporations, when similar developments took place in other cultural industries such as Sony's acquisition of CBS Records and Columbia Pictures, and the merger of Time Warner with Turner Broadcasting. In the context of the US, McAllister (1996: 47–51) underscored the media agenda-setting propensity of advertisers in their push for programming which delivers large audiences, with desirable demographics and made pliant to the commercial message. The prediction of Waterman and Rogers (1994) that the more economically well-off countries of Asia would continue to produce more domestic programming seems to be borne out by the evidence in Asia of the late 1990s, even if it has been in concert with global media corporations.

COMPETITION/COLLABORATION

Domestic terrestrial stations in Asia, particularly those which were previously public bureaucracies, had in the past focused on programming of educational and informational value to its audiences. But they have now come under pressure to provide quality and variety in programming comparable to that available on transnational television. Given the dearth of entertainment on domestic television, national audiences have turned to transnational broadcasts for it, wherever it is accessible economically and culturally. Thus most of the domestic broadcasters have since been compelled to respond by increasing channels, adapting western television genre, and providing more subregional ethnic programming which though popular involves higher costs in local production. Domestic terrestrial channels in Indonesia, India and China have been quite resilient in the face of new competition from transnational television, even entering into some collaboration with them instead of outright competition.

Cloned Diversity

As we have seen in earlier chapters, one strategic alternative for terrestrial broadcasters has been to segment their domestic market along linguistic and subcultural lines, and position themselves as providing a superior service in those areas. Thus over the decade of the 1990s, Doordarshan launched over a dozen new or revamped channels with the express intent of weaning Indian audiences off StarTV, even ZeeTV and other domestic commercial satellite broadcasters. They included offerings of movies, sports, business news, current affairs, music and "enrichment" or educational, religious and nationalistic programmes, all of them in very localised languages. Similarly Indonesia and Malaysia liberalised their domestic television industry, encouraging the entry of commercial channels broadcasting nationally but with some differences in programme positioning. Even the more cautious China permitted strategic alliances in programme production and imports for its domestic channels, as well as re-packaging of transnational broadcasts by its public broadcaster CCTV for pay-TV cable channels. The consequence for consumers in almost all Asian countries and various Asian diaspora worldwide has been immense expansion of channel choice and improvement of programme quality.

Although there may be economic pressures from changes in government policy that favour consumer sovereignty over public regulation and funding, Tracey (1988) was persuaded that the public service broadcasting in most countries would remain well funded. Citing the popularity of locally-produced drama over American soap operas, he felt that domestic public broadcasters should not be underestimated by those fearing media imperialism. But back then Tracey also observed that ethnic minorities especially used VCRs as an alternative to free-to-air broadcasting controlled by governments which was often geared to development programming. In a UNESCO study on television programme flows in the developing world, Sepstrup and Goonasekera (1994) had found transnationalisation of consumption by audiences to be much smaller than supply of imported programming by domestic broadcasters. Though they noted in passing that some locally-produced programming consumed bore the strong influence of US or British production styles, a phenomenon documented and christened "copycat television" by Moran (1996) and demonstrated in Asia (Moran and Keane 2003). In the context of India, various contributors to Brosius and Butcher (1999) highlight numerous permutations of the global–local fusion particularly on the regionalised transnational channels. Localised programming on many of the television channels in Asia, whether of transnational or domestic origin, typically mimic western genre such as sitcoms, talk shows, soap operas, game shows and the like, and are often outright clones, licensed or otherwise.

Downlinking and Upgrading

There has been increasing incidence of domestic commercial and even public broadcasters downlinking transnational programming from satellite for re-broadcast terrestrially, either incorporated in their channels or via cable/pay-TV under license. On the one hand the growth of programming hours has meant that domestic or regional film and television producers (often terrestrial broadcasters themselves) have been able to market programmes produced previously for domestic consumption, to satellite and cable channels for re-broadcast transnationally. On the other hand since domestic channels have proliferated, they are in need of programming to fill the time, and find it pragmatic to re-broadcast transnational television programming not available otherwise to most of their terrestrial audiences, duly subtitled or dubbed. Furthermore due to a glut of transponders, domestic television channels are able to utilise satellites inexpensively to broadcast within the region, thus catering to audiences of similar culture and language located across national boundaries, though sometimes this is done for political standard-bearing rather than out of commercial astuteness.

Comparative media law affords some models for democratic countries worldwide in the drafting of broadcast laws that seek to protect a plurality of voices within, against the pressures of media globalisation as in the case of India (Price 1998). The Asian situation might find some parallels with the experience in Western Europe where, despite exploiting weak national government regulation undermined further by European Union directives and being backed by major media conglomerates, satellite television channels have not been very successful. Collins (1992) argued that the new medium ultimately depends rather on their ability to attract subscribers which in turn is dependent on cost–benefit analysis by consumers of satellite channel offerings versus terrestrial television and video. Still, Browne (1999) contended that satellite broadcasters have often radically influenced the programming schedules and content of terrestrial television, including the public broadcasters that have learnt to be more creative and cost-efficient given the increased competition. Yet, long-time critic of the commercial monopoly of broadcast media in the US, Bagdikian (2000) was no more optimistic about the character of new media like the Internet as a viable alternative since they are likewise relatively unregulated by government and increasingly under the ambit of media conglomerates. Thus transnational television, domestic terrestrial or cable television and even the Internet ought not to be thought of as mutually exclusive alternatives for citizens but simply as media alternatives to options for marketers wishing to advertise to consumers.

Opportunities and Opportunism

Most formulations of cultural imperialism have been largely based on economic perspectives but on the issue of the media, capitalist domination may be no more or no less acceptable to Third World countries than socialist control. To avoid ideological polemics, Lee (1980) had sought to re-define the more specific media imperialism as the composite of programme flows, ownership, transfers of broadcast systems and promotion of capitalist worldviews/lifestyles. The term "cultural imperialism" was then preferred by those with a Marxist bent to imply wholesale domination of culture in which the media was a mere symptom. Believing that developing countries could not shut out technological change without widening the gap with developed countries, Lee suggested a compromise solution of regional cooperation, creative use of the media, and the synthesis of modern and traditional media as possible antidotes to media imperialism. Similarly Ayish (1992) contended that developing nations might have to rethink their authoritarian orientation if they wished to be integrated into the information-based global economy. He proposed that they think of international communication primarily as information vital to politico-economic planning, rather than as cultural imperialism via the mass media. Accepting media imperialism as a correlate of development, both had thinkers suggested ways of contextualising, even capitalising on it as an economic sector for developing countries. Their ideas have found expression in the Asian media scene even if their contribution is unacknowledged or unknown by industry and governments.

In the wake of an expanding television industry in the region, one strategy of domestic commercial broadcasters has been the export of their television management expertise and programming to newer terrestrial broadcasters in the region. For instance in the late 1990s, TV3 of Malaysia helped Vietnam develop its domestic television station and been a provider to it of sports and other programming, Shinawatra of Thailand was a partner with the Cambodian government in the setting up and provisioning of programming for Cambodia's first UHF television station, and TVB of Hong Kong assisted in the setting up of Indosiar in Indonesia. The practice of countries importing programming from within a region or other culturally similar source calls for a revaluation of the past accusation of First World dominance of television programming worldwide. In the maturity stage of their existing business life cycle, domestic terrestrial television broadcasters in Asia are finding new market niches elsewhere in the region, even globally. In seeking thus to revive their business fortunes, Asian broadcasters may constitute a case of what world-systems theorists like Wallerstein (1979) would cite as semi-periphery countries exploiting the periphery.

Global Parallels

It is a naïve argument indeed that global media would supersede domestic media, especially when that has not happened in other industries, whether they be food products or airline services. Schiller (1989: 115–17) had argued that the on-going trend towards deregulation in broadcasting resulted from lobbying by First World MNCs faced with the increased competitiveness of a global marketplace made possible by the new communications technologies. Once these privatised cultural industries established by government policy are dependent on corporate sponsorship, analysis of any single programme's effects on audiences was futile since cultural, economic even political imperialism by the capitalist West was self-evident. The deregulation of media industries in Asia is acknowledgement of these developments there, but it is also a worldwide trend in most industries and represents a symptom of a new relationship between weakened states and ascendant corporations, in a relatively unchallenged capitalist economic world system. The reason for the growth of transnational television in Asia may have been supply-driven in that the global media corporations have been motivated to maximise returns on their existing investments by expanding internationally. But their growth in Asia is also consumer demand-driven, having been given impetus by economic affluence and technological change, areas which deserve more extensive and intensive research.

Arguing that US programming was rapidly constituting a smaller percentage of a growing international television market, Cunningham and Jacka (1996) charted the export success of Australian television programmes not just to the English-speaking markets of the UK, Ireland, the US and Canada, but also to elsewhere in Europe and East Asia, if for different reasons in each. Likewise the contributors to Sinclair et al. (1996) document the growth not only of alternative English programming exporters in Canada and Australia, but also of new television production centres for the Hispanic, Arab, Chinese and Indian markets which are regional, diasporic and geo-linguistic. Together these writers have argued that changes like the growth of transnational television, convergence of electronic technologies, regulatory changes that accompanied shifts in political ideologies towards media privatisation, lowered costs and decentralisation of production, the rise of global media conglomerates and the integration of national economies into the capitalist world system have all contributed to the establishment of a far more complex global television industry and market than was in place when the earlier studies of US programming dominance were made.

TRANSNATIONAL/MULTINATIONAL

The debate over the globalisation of markets has raged for some decades now. Quite a few MNC marketers still believe in global advertising, or, in other words, that the same advertising campaign can be minimally adapted for use effectively worldwide and cite the fact that this is cost-effective and helps build a consistent corporate image internationally. Others point to the near-impossibility of a single campaign communicating well in all nations because it would have to conform to local cultural distinctives, government regulations and local product usage patterns. The advent of transnational television was expected to remove the need to comply with multiple national regulations and so facilitate the use of global advertising campaigns. This was the original positioning strategy of StarTV which argued for the cultural similarity of the pan-Asian elite segment. Yet global or regional advertising did not take off with transnational television in Asia and the reasons for why this was so will be reviewed in this subsection.

Agencies Quasi-aligned

Advertising agency executives in the US did tend to believe that transnational satellite television would become the leading advertising medium while their marketing clients had their doubts (Howard and Ryans 1988–89). But both groups concurred that it would affect agency–client relationships as local agencies lost clients to global agencies, as regional campaigns increased despite the cultural heterogeneity, and as marketing activities grew increasingly globalised and centralised. The respondents also believed that there would be greater emphasis on visual communication and on pan-European themes. Although they perceived a number of barriers to international advertising such as language, culture and regulations, both advertising and marketing executives expected satellite television to lead eventually to the control of strategy, media planning, budgeting and creativity by their corporate headquarters. Contrary to expectations, in none of the countries researched for this book was there any significant realignment of advertising accounts with international advertising agencies admitted to be a result of the advent of transnational television.

With growing deregulation around the world there now is a preponderance of global marketers over local ones among the top advertisers, and of global agencies among the top advertising agencies that often had similar rankings worldwide as well as locally. That has been true of Asia where, with the exception of Japan, most of the largest agencies are foreign multinationals, and that certainly was the case in the advertising centres scrutinised in this book, namely Jakarta, Mumbai and Hong Kong. But often these are local affiliates or subsidiaries of global agencies servicing global and local/regional marketers and so the terms "global" and "local" are somewhat imprecise, given their complex ownership structures and diverse spheres of operation. Mattelart (1991: 37) had anticipated that as US advertising agencies grew dominant worldwide, they would no longer be considered hegemonic because their ideology and practices would become institutionalised in the profession and contextualised in the countries in which they operate. Furthermore it may be argued that the local agencies and marketing communications industry as a whole which global marketers have helped spawn around the world have in time come to assert their independence of practice, developed their own hybrid cultural idiom and actually come to compete with US-owned agencies for advertising accounts of MNCs.

Creative Tension

Liberalisation of the advertising content regulations, and the availability of transnational media which is not subject to much regulation, was expected to see some advertisers switching agencies or to media brokers as a consequence of no longer needing creative services or preferring to use commercials produced by their global agencies. International advertising agencies have long tended to side with their global clients in lobbying regulatory bodies against the local film/video production industry concerning foreign content in commercials or rather for the freedom to decide when a global campaign is appropriate and when a multi-domestic campaign, requiring local production, is. Despite the apparent cost-effectiveness of transnational television, Asia-based advertisers and their agencies seeking to communicate with national market segments have still preferred to utilise domestic television. Their argument has been that just as audiences relate best to local programmes, they comprehend local television commercials better for cultural reasons, as has been argued by some academics. However local commercials, like local programmes, adopt and sometimes adapt the creative strategies, appeals, values and so on of foreign commercials, but clothe them in local personages, settings and idiom. There seem also to have been virtually no television commercials created solely for pan-Asian use as a result of transnational television, and commercials used were either global imports or the identical commercials used for domestic markets.

Research on cross-cultural advertising has not always addressed the right questions or offered much critical commentary on the consequences for cultural globalisation by advertising. It tends to test predictable hypotheses about differences in advertising creativity in contrasting cultures as typified by Ramaprasad and Hasegawa (1992) and Cheng and Sweitzer (1996). Among the few exceptions is an earlier study by Belk and Pollay (1985) which found over the period 1953–83 that Japanese print advertisements used status appeals more frequently, instrumentally materialistic themes were emphasised more in US advertisements, and that luxury appeals featured in both. As they reason, the rapid economic growth in Japan has led to a stress in advertising on status and materialism even if adapted as group rather than individualistic phenomena. Less quantitative and more critical in his analysis of Japanese and US advertising, Kline (1988) discussed the Japanese genius of incorporating foreign cultures, historically of China and Korea and later of Germany and the US, while perpetuating local traditions with some re-definition. Looking at decisions made by both US and non-US subsidiaries in non-domestic markets, Kanso and Nelson (2002) found that the vast majority of them considered localised advertising imperative. Revisiting the three-decade-old debate on standardisation of advertising, Onkvisit and Shaw (1999) decried the lack of conclusive evidence from academic research as well as the difficulties of controlling for confounding variables. It would appear then that the implications for globalisation in developing and developed countries then is not homogenisation to a western industrialised norm.

The creative styles of commercials observed on StarTV and other trans-national television in Asia suggest that advertising and marketing are indeed catalysts of cultural hybridisation.

Critical Mesh

It took StarTV a number of years to come to grips with the fact that the pan-Asian elite segment, though homogeneous on some socio-economic dimensions and generally affluent, was not large enough to support global or even continentwide advertising. Asia has either a small number of wealthy people in a large country or a large number of wealthy in a small country but StarTV was looking either for large markets (ethnic/geographic) to use mass programming and to sell advertising for, or for small segments across countries. Furthermore there is probably a far greater difference in income and lifestyle be-tween rural and urban populations in Asia, than in the West. Another view is that a pan-Asian elite market existed which coincided with frequent travellers in the region, and though small that they were the prime market for transnational television in its early global form. But this elite segment has probably little time for mass media generally and possibly prefers the more portable print medium. In any case, it was thought that pan-Asian television would not work at attracting such audiences except possibly with specialist programming, for ex-ample the all-news CNN or all-documentary Discovery channels, though not for channels like Prime Sports and ESPN because sports was culture-specific. Thus advertising on StarTV and most of the pioneering transnationals in their early years at least was largely confined to corporate image, financial services, business travel and the like.

While the business world is acutely aware of the role of advertising in the survival, character and development of any media, this relation-ship has not always been addressed adequately in academic research. Observing how advertising has had to underwrite the multichannel environment in the US, Baldwin et al. (1996: 231–57) believed it would take three main forms: of product-awareness advertising similar to that of 30-second commercials, of information-offer advertising embedded in the programming or commercial which could be stored by the viewer to future use, and direct-selling advertising similar to that of television shopping channels though more interactive. Likewise Bush and Bush (2000) addressed how the growth of the Internet has also raised questions not only about its economic viability as an advertising medium, but also significant differences between the agencies and advertisers in the decisions on whether to utilise it and whose responsibility it was. While cable and satellite channels in Asia may offer improved targeting by specialist consumer interests and geographic location, they have relatively low ratings. This requires advertisers to purchase spots across many channels which is administratively expensive for agencies even though the total media costs are no higher than on terrestrial television. Despite having benefits for the consumer, there are as many challenges ahead in Asia as globally for advertisers and media owners with an increasingly hyper-commercial and multi-channel environment where it is difficult to differentiate between media and advertising.

Cashing-in Culture

Regardless of whether its content is news, politics, education, religion or whatever, increasingly television entertains rather than informs in any depth. Updating the McLuhaneque critique, even if he did not overtly acknowledge this, Postman (1985) proposed that the message of the medium of television is entertainment. The problem is not what people watched but the fact that they did watch. In its search for larger national audiences, transnational television may be simply playing its role as a postmodern medium in reconstituting a new entertainment culture out of the fragments of traditional–local and modern–global cultures. Smythe (1981: 66–90) analysed the clear dependence of the invention of various mass media in the First World on advertising, and alleges that this is at the core of the problem there as in the Third World. Jhally (1987) argued instead that no simple relationship exists between people, things and messages in advertising, but that it depends on the psychological, physical and social context. Despite acknowledging its complexity, he championed the view that advertising is structured—by media owners and advertising agencies on behalf of their primary clients, the marketers—to reach particular audience segments more effectively than others. Perhaps there are lessons in this approach for developing countries as television, whether domestic or transnational, comes to dominate their contemporary culture.

That the majority of transnational corporations control media content and thus social consciousness in developing countries indirectly through their advertising, is an allegation long made by social commentators. Documenting comprehensively the extensive criticism of advertising's cultural impact in the academic literature of various disciplines, Pollay (1986) chides business academics for ignoring these in their research concentration of how to make marketing and advertising more effective. He portrayed advertising as a "distorted mirror" that is highly selective of the values it promotes for commercial ends, neglecting and often undermining values of greater social importance. Drawing a parallel with socialist art, Schudson (1984: 219–22) similarly stressed that advertising does not invent social values so much as it usurps and exploits prevailing ones in the service of products in the capitalist marketplace. Designating advertising as the art form of capitalism, Williams (1980: 184) argued that it influences cultural life even if it does not succeed in influencing product purchase, and vice versa. Taking it further, Cross (1996) alleged that advertising was a form of linguistic vandalism seeking to motivate the consumer without regard to truth. Television advertising in particular makes visual not logical claims that are difficult to challenge and thus is powerful in influencing culture. Thus the cultural and economic effects of transnational advertising in Asia might be quite inseparable, and their power enhanced by the globalised programming context—whether on satellite, cable or terrestrial television.

CROSS-CULTURAL/INTER-CULTURAL

The availability of various media and their use by consumers varies between nations, and these together with public ownership of television, low literacy and newspaper use, and relatively high costs of limited domestic media may have limited the use of global advertising campaigns. In any case, a common defence of advertising was that it merely reflected the symbols and values of a culture in order to be able to communicate with its people. But the advent of a new transnational medium in Asia should have meant a vital tool for the creating of new markets and better communication with potential buyers for international marketers in the developing countries of the continent. Advertisers' use of StarTV in its early days illustrates some of the distinctive features of transnational television especially when it was being positioned as a pan-Asian medium.

Target Practice

Initially StarTV adopted that strategy of targeting the socio-economic elite of Asia but discovered over its first three years that the segment was not large enough, even across this most populous continent, to attract an adequate advertising revenue stream. Despite the novelty of StarTV's largely western programming initially and its apparent popularity among this segment in a number of Asian countries, there were sizeable audiences in the footprint unresponsive to it. Early on, StarTV never disclosed its advertising revenues but its executives not-so-privately admitted to running losses and hoping to break even by the late 1990s. So when News Corporation took control of StarTV it began using split beams and differentiated programming thought to be more appropriate to audiences and advertisers alike. With its migration to the digital AsiaSat2, StarTV became ever more country-specific in its programming. Yet while adjacent nations as a whole in a region may be treated as quite distinct markets, for example India and Pakistan, minorities within each may actually be of the same ethnicity. In some other cases, minorities in nations quite geographically distant may be quite similar, as is the case with the diasporic Chinese and Indians resident virtually worldwide. Although transnational communications may have reduced the significance of geographical and political borders for advertising, the social and cultural boundaries within and across state-based nationalities are far more nuanced.

As it happened in Asia of the early 1990s, the earlier introduction of satellite television in Europe prompted speculation over whether it would revolutionise the media, foster globalised marketing strategies, further cultural homogenisation and affect advertising. Though, as De Mooij and Keegan (1991) cautioned, such consolidation of advertising on a regional basis will depend largely on the extent of organisational centralisation instituted by the marketers. Reviewing research on cable viewership in the US over the 1980s, Garay (1988) discerned a trend over several years of rejection of the pay-TV product and attributed it to disillusionment with cable programming's promise of diversity, changes in viewing patterns and the growth of VCR use over that same period. While previous research on the impact of cable television on broadcast television has been inconclusive, Glascock (1993) found that in the US the new medium actually increased advertising spending overall over the 1980s rather than eroding the share of advertising of other media. Examining the experience of the UK, Farall and Whitelock (1999) discerned no difference between the advertising on terrestrial and satellite television in terms of products advertised and regional versus global brands. Superficially this may imply that satellite television has not contributed to the global standardisation of advertising across borders in Europe. Rather more significantly it suggests though that as in Asia local and regional advertising has subtly globalised its local idiom or contextualised the global so as to be not discernibly distinct.

Branding Identity

As demonstrated earlier, the majority of commercials on a StarTV showreel in the early 1990s were of corporate image or business-to-business advertising, even when the founding owner of the broadcaster was offering advertising discounts to local business associates. Upmarket fashion/accessories were a close second and included a number of global brands, followed by consumer electronics, vehicles, banks and airlines. It was only in the food/beverage as well as cosmetics/toiletries categories that local brands were commonplace and targeted at domestic markets, while the soft drink category was dominated by the global brands of Coca-Cola and Pepsi, and regional in market focus. While some brands are categorised as global, they may actually have been manufactured locally in the region, for example Nike shoes. Furthermore the advertising might have been created in Asia as well, even if it adopted a global theme or format, western models and locations. In our postmodern age with post-Fordist flexible manufacturing systems, not to mention almost ethereal global financing, it is not quite possible to designate any products or services as global, regional or local with much accuracy any longer. Country-of-origin effects on consumption seem to have been effectively superseded by and large by brand equity, fed not just by advertising but also by integrated marketing communications that incorporates television programme sponsorships, event management, public relations, publicity, websites, m-commerce and a host of other tools.

Research by Kaynak (1989) had confirmed that consumers in developing countries are more readily affected by promotional messages than those in developed countries. But he also contended that as a country develops economically its potential market size increases but with greater exposure to advertising, receptiveness by audiences declines sharply. This appears to not yet characterise Asian markets which have had considerable experience of advertising, for Ewing (2000) found that among Generation-Xers in Singapore, Malaysia and Hong Kong over 85 per cent had a positive attitude towards advertising, regarding it as essential and important. This might help explain the Viswanath and Zeng (2002) contention that through advertising and imported programmes in India, the "glamour-communication industry" has stimulated a boom in beauty products, fitness and cosmetic surgery, and even altered concepts of body image in recent years. There appears to be little concern by the burgeoning middle class in Asia about the sweat-shop production, cultural vandalism, unfair trade and other corporate abuses in their own backyard by marketers and advertisers of the sort documented by Klein (2001) and McQueen (2001). On the other hand, Kemper (2001) has documented ethnographically that while the lower middle classes might also be exposed to the globalising power of media and advertising, their consumption response is less straightforward and predictable. Quite evidently the assumptions and ideas of marketing academics and practitioners from the developed world on globalisation and postmodernity need to be tested in and adapted to the quite different milieu of developing countries.

Style and Substance

Global marketers like Coca-Cola, for instance, were believed to be keen on StarTV's initial boast of being pan-Asian elite English-language medium, as evidenced by its extensive image advertising especially on MTV/Channel V. Transnational advertising may have some appeal to a globalised elite segment in Asia, the products targeted at them being those commonly seen on early broadcasters such as StarTV, namely airlines, hotels, resorts, upmarket cars, luxury goods, investments and so on, rather than food and clothing appealing to the larger segments. There was no formal investigation conducted for this book about creative styles in transnational and domestic television since it was not possible to obtain showreels of TVCs in the three countries from the same year for comparison. However, based on systematic watching of domestic and transnational television in Indonesia, India and Greater China, there seem to be four types of advertising creative styles discernible: traditional–domestic, cosmopolitan–domestic, cosmopolitan–regional, and western–global. The latter two types tend to predominate on the transnational channels, each coming in at least two languages: a world language, usually English, and a national or subnational–ethnic language such as Hindi, Tamil, Indonesian, Mandarin or Cantonese. The former two types predominate on the domestic channels, but there is evidence of a trickle-down effect of advertising creativity as well as product promotion from transnational advertising to domestic advertising. While transnational television has made redundant government strictures about local content in advertising, it afforded new opportunities for portraying quasi-foreignness or hybrid-globality in promoting products within the national or regional context.

Although Firat and Venkatesh (1993) cited transnational corporations as societal change agents par excellence, given their resources and expertise, they surmise that the sociocultural impact of marketing, especially advertising, and the postmodernisation of societies are simply co-dependent processes. Alternatively, Pollay (1986) submitted that thoughtful regulation has not dampened advertising and commercial growth in many developing countries, whose citizens will over time become more discerning of advertising tactics. His survey of advertising regulation worldwide implied that concern about the erosion of traditional values and culture has resulted in rather uniform controls among countries of quite different levels of economic development, colonial experience and ideological persuasion, even if they are not equally enforced. Using outdoor advertising in the special test case of post–Cold War Russia, Ciochetto (2001) observed that it promotes the consumption culture of western capitalism, even though it is dominated for the moment by cheap non-durable products from some Asian and European countries, given the low disposable income. While there may be a necessary trade-off between economic development and cultural stability, Wernick (1991: 181–97) expressed concern over the pervasive commercialisation of all contemporary culture and made a plea for the return to substantial public sponsorship of the media. Boddewyn (1988) was much more pro-business and positive about the rise of deregulation and transnational media, while advising caution in the interim in the use of global advertising campaigns. In Asia, the cultural realities of marketing rather than political regulation seem to have been more influential on the direction of advertising on transnational television.

Global-plus, Local-minus

There is considerable debate still over whether promotion should be done on a national or global basis, though most multinational corporations would subscribe to the view that a consistent international image needs to be maintained whichever approach is taken. A common compromise involves choosing to use global commercials for image purposes on television but allowing local print and radio for tactical advertising under strict guidelines imposed and an approval process controlled by corporate headquarters. This is reflected in the practice observed in Asia of using the same global or regional commercials on both transnational and domestic television. With the advent of transnational broadcasting, though, a critical issue is the transferability of television advertising cross-culturally within the geographic region covered by the satellite footprint. Some advertising appeals such as case histories, productivity, novelty and service might be more adaptable globally than other appeals such as humour, morality, lifestyles and aesthetics that are more culture-bound. But the present research was not able to investigate these issues fully within its scope, important though they may be.

In their own search for market share, domestic broadcasters in Asia all aimed at middle-of-the-road programming, which resulted in the fragmenting of their loyal mass audiences. Now transnational satellite and cable channels needing advertisers are doing the same and further fragmenting the audience, compelling all channels operating in a national market to segment aggressively. Yet quite like major networks in the US, researched by Chan-Olmsted and Kim (2001), there is some recognition of branding as critical in a competitive environment but some resistance to proceeding beyond superficial forms of graphics and promotions. All media corporations, both transnational and domestic, tend to believe in the globalisation myths that "big is better" for them and that "more is better" for their consumers (Ferguson 1993), but need to realise that in the Asian context of cultural contrasts they might be undermining themselves. Transnational television exists and grows not only when it is itself commercially viable, but because it is also lucrative to broadcasters, marketers, advertising agencies, programming producers, technology suppliers and other players in the media industries of the region. Perhaps, a strategic alternative may lie in what Alden et al. (1999) conceptualised as "global consumer culture positioning" which involves neither a foreign nor a local consumer culture, and one that need not be standardised globally. While the economic impact of transnational television is fairly evident, its cultural consequences in Asia are still tentative and perhaps too contentious a matter to determine just yet.

The responses of the advertising industry in the three key Asian markets to StarTV as an exemplar of transnational satellite broadcasters over the 1990s are in one sense studies in contrast and in another sense share a number of underlying similarities. While the Jakarta attitude towards this new transnational television medium might be characterised as disinterested avoidance, the Mumbai attitude seems to have been one of enthusiastic embrace, and the Hong Kong one was arguably of thoughtful consideration. Indonesia's advertisers saw little response to the transnational medium by audiences satiated with multiple commercial channels domestically and so largely ignored it. Indian advertisers chose to use StarTV and other domesticated satellite channels which followed as a means of circumventing some local restrictions on advertising, as well as reaching expatriate and diasporic Indians elsewhere. Hong Kong domestic advertisers likewise had little use for the medium locally but did see some potential for targeting other constituents of Greater China, while its multinational advertisers were keen to dabble in this new regional medium on an Asiawide basis. All of them saw limited scope for truly globally standardised advertising across the whole of the StarTV footprint in Asia, except perhaps in the limited cases of corporate advertising and upmarket brands. Yet as StarTV and other transnational broadcasters regionalised, even nationalised and subnationalised their programming offerings, they have come to be perceived paradoxically as just another option for domestic advertising albeit to different degrees by each market. The ultimate impact of transnational television and advertising in Asia must surely be the ongoing blurring of the boundaries between the national, regional and global strategies that the final chapter of this book will evaluate critically.

As this book and its companion volume have been largely historical and analytical, this concluding chapter attempts to be reflective and prognostic by addressing such questions as: Is the phenomenon of media globalisation good, bad or indifferent? Can or should transnational television be moderated? The broader issue must surely be: how then should governments, civil societies, broadcasters and advertising agencies in Asia act in relation to transnational media and marketing communications? The problem of ethics, always difficult without a common reference point such as Judaeo–Christian thought once was in the West, is even more problematic due to the relativism enshrined in postmodern thought, as well as in the philosophic pluralism of the East. If this book has sought to incorporate the views of diverse thinkers and practitioners in media and advertising, its final chapter constitutes rather a personal statement. Through it this author aims to grapple with some of the socio-ethical issues presented by the advent of transnational television in Asia, which should prove applicable or at least insightful elsewhere in the Third World.

ELECTRONIC MARKETPLACES

The convergence of media, telecommunications and computing technologies, the end of spectrum capacity constraints through digitisation, and the proliferation of television providers via free-to-air, satellite, broadband cable, pay-TV, interactive services, e-commerce and video-on-demand, afford the television industry many unanticipated commercial opportunities. These developments also make television less of a scarce national resource, but more of an industry like any other. Thus it is argued by proponents of free-market capitalism that it would be unfair of governments to single this industry out for special attention. Yet there are wide-ranging politico-economic as well as sociocultural implications of transnational television, worthy of some reflection by governments and civil society groups faced with myriad policy alternatives.

Media Hegemony versus Media Poverty

Mega-theories of development like dependency theory or world-systems theory may be deficient because they tend to concentrate on the relationship between nation states or groups of them such as First World versus Third World, without recognising the diversity and changeability of dependency relationships within each nation or group of nations. One major amendment needed in the world-systems model is which countries constitute the core, semi-periphery and periphery. For it is debatable today whether the US is solely at the core of the "world system" or shares it with other G8 and OECD countries. Another issue is whether the semi-periphery is now comprised primarily of some former communist states considered transitional economies (TEs) in the capitalist system, the newly-industrialising countries (NICs) and/or the big emerging economies (BEMs). Semi-periphery countries in the regions of Asia researched for this book seem to be adept at exploiting their less-developed neighbours, as for instance through privatised communications firms acting as surrogates for their countries, as Shinawatra does for Thailand, Indosat for Indonesia and Apstar for China. The old Cold War rivalry in the space race is now being played out in the bidding for contracts by the US, Europe, China and Russia to build and launch satellites for such developing countries. The periphery or Least Developed Countries (LDCs) in Asia seem pawns in the game of accepting allocated orbital slots which they can ill afford to utilise, only to then lease them to multinational corporations from the core or semi-periphery countries and on whom they become dependent for their communications infrastructure. Meanwhile, the poorer nations in Africa, Latin America, Oceania and Asia seem at risk of remaining information-poor, bypassed by the Information Superhighway while still being exploited as secondary consumer markets by global or regional media such as television via satellite and cable.

The economic downturn in a number of the Asian NICs in the late 1990s to early 2000s does not negate but actually confirms their status as relatively dependent on the economies of the core countries. Though they may still be considered semi-periphery because their rapid growth is still relatively dependent on investments by the core countries, some NICs. TEs and BEMs may soon even exceed individual "core" countries in the share of their GDP generated by industry. The next stage, one set in motion since the 1990s, is some reversal of the trade in services, including that of entertainment, information and other output of the cultural industries. This is reflected in cultural product-flows from the developing to the developed countries and exchanges among developing countries, such as those of ethnic-based television programming via satellite and/or cable. Closer examination reveals that in Asia transnational television has not only eroded government control over the broadcast media but drawn domestic commercial and even public broadcasters into the competitive arena of the global media industry. It has even engaged them, not only economically as joint venture and strategic alliance partners, but also culturally as buyers, providers and users of "glocalised" programming. The trend towards the globalisation is clearly demonstrated in the alliances and conglomerates formed in recent years in the converging television, music, advertising and news media industries, in Asia as well as worldwide.

Counter-cultures, Fragmenting Societies

The concept of cultural imperialism presupposes the primacy of the nation-state and nationalism. But if nation states are themselves "imagined communities" comprising multiple ethnic groups dominated by one such group or social class, then there might be just as much cultural imperialism from within the nation state than from without. Cultural imperialism is also neither a new phenomenon, dating only from the European colonial era, nor only unidirectional from the West towards the East, for it has existed at virtually any time societies have had contact whether through political or military interventions, or through commerce and trade. There has always been hybridisation of the colonisers' and colonised's cultures, and much more cross-pollination of cultures than admitted especially by the colonisers. Post-colonial nations may be said to be proto-globalised societies given their cultural syncretism and cosmopolitanness, particularly in their urban metropolises. As such transnational television may be a means of giving voice to such hybridised minorities—cultural, economic or both—some spanning various countries, which are ignored by their nationalistic domestic media, whether public or commercial, under the control of a dominant socio-economic group.

If the invention of printing led to the formation of dominant languages out of regional dialects, and that in turn led to the rise of nationalism, then the McLuhanesque aurality and orality of the newer electronic media such as transnational satellite television might portend a reverse process. That might signify an impending fragmentation of nation states, especially larger ones, perhaps more than we saw at the turn of the twenty-first century. Might the alarm of national governments at global media then just be a smokescreen for feared loss of cultural dominion over their latently multicultural societies? To some extent this may explain the considerable collusion between national governments in Asia and domestic commercial media often in the hands of a politico-economic elite, against the twin threats of globalised–diasporic broadcast media as well as local–ethnic narrowcast media. Thus, might overtly Asian commercial television channels be merely surrogates for western global media corporations or even just domestic or regional clones in the same capitalist cultural game? If such media hybridity is re-defined also as yet another form of cultural imperialism, then the latter may be a process far more insidious under the guise of economic globalisation than previously imagined.

Hybrid Media for Global Markets

Increasingly apparent is the phenomenon of developing countries having their cultures co-opted, in much the same way as western radical subcultures have been, and hybridised in the process of converting them into markets for global products. There has always been vocal social criticism about the alleged role that advertising plays in raising false expectations and creating artificial demands in the developing world. This has been underscored in Asia with the growth of transnational television, though tolerated as the price of global economic integration and the attendant prospect of personal wealth. Arguably the medium may also provide consumers information on alternative ecologically-sound lifestyles which may be not much different from what they have known historically or are at least aware of in their geographical area. But it is a weak argument that access to transnational television need not necessarily spell greater consumerism for developing countries because people excessively exposed may develop a reaction against materialistic modernity. The reality is rather that images of plenty beamed to those in want can only serve to heighten their sense of deprivation. The persistent migration of peoples from the Third World to the First, or from rural to urban areas within developing countries, might be just one symptom of that disenchantment with the lack of material wherewithal for what is being promoted as "the good life" via the media.

It was noteworthy that in Asia the liberalisation of media content via the availability of transnational media has not resulted in an avalanche of strictly global commercials on the domestic media. More often than not, international advertising agencies have appropriated local cultural symbols in their successful promotion of global, regional or multi-domestic products via their television commercials on domestically accessible media. Certainly the debate over localisation versus standardisation of transnational advertising appears far more complex than was envisaged by its initiators in the 1960s and 1970s in North America and Europe. Perhaps further research may even prove this debate to be irrelevant to the sociocultural and economic–technological environment of Asia in the postmodern 1990s and 2000s. Cultural imperialism theories have simply not recognised the legitimate economic aspirations of social groups, regardless of how the latter have been defined. Instead of cultural hegemony imposed from without by a medium such as transnational television, many Asian societies, especially the post-colonial ones, seem to manifest symptoms of the cultural eclecticism of postmodern cultures which was thought to be more prevalent in western countries and largely attributed to the impact of television media and advertising there.

MEDIA ETHNOSCAPES

Countries which choose to develop and modernise in a capitalist-dominated world invariably globalise, both economically and culturally. As such they have little immunity against newer media like transnational television, except to seek to domesticate it by subtitling or dubbing, and even cloning its programming. As transnational television ceases being an elite medium in many countries of Asia, a much larger proportion of the population cannot help but have their lives touched by the globalised hybrid culture which that medium is propagating, along with the new products and services available locally, and the lifestyles that their own social elite exemplify. No longer is the printed or spoken word the primary persuader of cultural change, but the tele-visual image warranting no logical arguments for or against, while persistently invites imitation. Thus transnational television could have significant cultural impact in Asia despite the best efforts of national governments to resist cultural globalisation.

Policy Circumvention amidst Hyper-capitalism

As the opponents of the NWICO had predicted in decades past, the countries in Asia that reacted most forcefully to transnational television were those which had authoritarian governments and therefore felt most under threat. The mistake that such governments seem to have made with their initial media policies towards transnational television is that of assuming that it was simply a more powerful form of domestic television. In other words, transnational television is clearly not an unchallenged mass medium aiming to acculturate the national population in the same way that domestic television, whether public or commercial under licence, was designed to. Furthermore governments have had only limited success with their regulatory policies because of popular demand, which has always found ways to circumvent the restrictions. Domestic media businesses have been only too willing to collude with transnational ones, officially or unofficially, to meet this demand. There have also been political and economic imperatives for the governments to abandon or at least not enforce their policies, such as their desire to achieve integration of their economies into the capitalist world system.

This research affirms that the impact of transnational television on domestic broadcasting and advertising industries may not be moderated by regulatory policies alone. Instead the impact of transnational television on each country under its footprint varies considerably depending on the domestic media scene, government policy, cultural heritage, political ideology, economic affluence and a host of other factors. Thus there might be various sociocultural and political–economic impacts upon television from the society in which it operates, which are less discussed as issues and so less researched than vice versa. There could well be a paradox between the perceived power of the transnational medium in bringing about social change, and the evidence of selective use and dissenting interpretation of transnational television by audiences throughout Asia. Thussu (1998) was quietly confident that despite the risk of "Murdochisation", the newer electronic media might facilitate local cultural resistance against both state control and global corporate imperialism. The real question might not be whether transnational television will swamp national cultures, but whether its growth renders the populace either disinterested in domestic political discourse while motivated to personal material affluence, or actively pursuing ethnic cultural renaissance and even agitating for subnational political autonomy. Future research on transnational television ought to address such issues at subnational, national and transnational levels, however challenging to frame.

Quasi-identities in Postmodernity

Postmodernism may be thought of sceptically as the aftermath of the optimistic humanism and technological utopianism of the modern industrialised era. In the postmodern era, the process of production has been superseded by that of consumption as the determinant of social relations and an inevitable next stage of capitalism. Thus politico-economic production relations are being overtaken by cultural consumerist identities, while social-class membership is being superseded by ethnic or subcultural affiliation. Naturally, then, governments are concerned about controlling access to cultural identity-generating technologies such as the media, whether domestic or transnational. Consequently, as we have seen, consumers in many countries are getting not direct access to but a nationally-filtered version of transnational television. But the question remains as to who should control the filter: the consumers individually or collectively, civil society groups, national or state governments, local cultural industry, global media corporations keen not to be shut out or some coalition of these entities?

Should the renaissance of enduring cultural contours subregionally and rise of newer diasporic pockets be curtailed by national governments or promoted by transnational marketers?

Characteristically, the media pervades our postmodern societies, structuring our social experience of reality while expressing politico-economic relations, reflecting cultural values and helping to define personal and national identity. Therefore a case has been made strongly from time to time, for domestic broadcasting to be supported as a cultural or civic resource and not be left to commercial interests or government dominance. This is usually accompanied by a somewhat patronising appeal that its programming not cater to the lowest common denominator but aim to educate tastes. Such a plea makes little sense if directed at transnational television, usually commercial in nature, which seems to fragment and co-opt contemporary popular culture in various countries it broadcasts to and then reformulate it in varying forms of hybridised global culture. The global pervasiveness of electronic media, presently, might shift societies from being literate to being post-literate in a generation or less, making their people more comfortable communicating via images or music rather than via reading, speaking or writing. Perhaps viewers of transnational television feel increasingly part of a global pseudo-community, capable of political participation on a global scale, assisted by interpersonal communication via the Internet, while somewhat alienated from their national societies or local communities.

Media Monoliths or Networks

Satellite television in Asia is scarcely global in compass any longer, and increasingly multi-domestic in the strict definition of the term. It is arguably transnational in the sense that it offers a synergistic model or format that forms the basis for symbiotic relationships, even strategic alliances with domestic broadcasters, cable operators or multi-service operators in different countries. Cable television especially may be seen as an expression in the broadcasting industry of the business trend of "mass customisation" by which globalised products are capable of rapid reproduction in numerous permutations of specifications to cater for regional, local, even individual preferences. Thus transnational channels today do not resemble the mass media for captive nation-wide audiences that terrestrial television was alleged to be in decades past. Instead they serve rather as virtual programming libraries digitally domiciled on satellites, cable head-ends, computer servers and the like, accessible selectively by "active audiences" faced today with numerous other alternatives in electronic information and entertainment. Summing up diverse contributions on global media from around the world, Sreberny-Mohammadi et al. (1997) had noted that vertical integration of media industry nationally was matched by globalising or horizontal networks of media production and consumption, with complex and subtle impacts on culture and society. Transnational television may be partly responsible for a global trend towards quasi-individualistic assemblage of cultural identity, seemingly done unconsciously out of all the alternatives presented on the media, rather than collective assimilation to a dominant culture, regardless of whether imposed deliberately or adopted incidentally.

Those who subscribe to the view that an economically-dominant medium imposes a globalised culture could be failing to realise the power of discernment and discretion of audiences, even in developing countries with relatively recent experience of electronic media. This mistaken assumption of docile audiences can and has been made both by transnational television broadcasters in their marketing strategies, as well as by the governments in Asia seeking to regulate access to them. As television becomes plentiful through various technologies and in all likelihood repetitive in content, it should become more like books and magazines indulged in intermittently and at leisure, rather than something demanding attention by its previous characteristic of being a one-time performance. Blanketing a continent or even the globe with television simply cannot mean that people will watch everything on offer. Nonetheless most viewers will watch something virtually everyday, and so the question remains: what they will watch most commonly? Since monopolistic national broadcasters are giving way to multi-channel television and multi-mode infotainment, will there be space for new community-based or civil society–run television? Will the ubiquity of globalised cultural products drive a collective desire for distinctly local options or for some regional subcultural niche offerings? It is still an open question how individuals and social groups might re-order their own cultural consumption out of the myriad media offerings available in Asia at the start of the twenty-first century.

ADVERTISING CULTURES

As the competition between transnational television in Asia intensifies and the market fragments, the targeting of the audiences becomes essential for channel survival. Transnational television broadcasters face the dilemma of selling advertisers on the efficiency and effectiveness of the new media, while reassuring governments of only limited social and cultural effects. While satellite, cable and other new electronic technologies can potentially break down political borders to reaching consumers in diverse countries, in reality only certain programming genre such as news, sports and music seem to cross cultural barriers effectively. If domestic public television—whether via terrestrial or satellite transmission—was a tool of nationalism and modernisation in the hands of the nation state, then transnational commercial television via satellite and cable might well be an instrument in the hands of the multinational corporation for the globalisation of markets and postmodernisation of consumption in their favour.

Citizens Deemed Consumers

The overwhelming choice in television channels, among electronic media surrogates or substitutes, may not represent real choice between distinct alternatives, because most promote the same overarching message of material and cultural consumption. Commercial media is invariably inundated by advertising that tends to convey images and feelings triggering consumption, rather than facts and opinions in support of civil society participation. Transnational and domestic television under the control of multinational or regional corporations and devoted to promoting consumerist messages might actually be inhibiting a society's ability to debate public issues via the forum of the electronic media. The electronic media is arguably more powerful a medium of socialisation than the family, community, school or any other social institution, and may be undermining the ability of citizens to cope with complex discourses.

In a sense, hyper-capitalism or rampant world marketisation, of which the pervasive commercialised electronic media is symptomatic, might

be no less totalitarian than state socialism. With the demise of communism in Eastern Europe and the former Soviet Union, there is
little hope of an alternative politico-economic world system to rival
the capitalist world system as some social philosophers envisaged.
The market socialism of some countries like China and Vietnam appears inconsistent, while social democracy in Western Europe and
Australasia is being progressively eroded. Since the aim of capitalism
is not to educate but to market, its media—notably transnational television programming and advertising—might actually undermine the
realisation of the liberal-democratic ideals of modern urban society
by promoting instead the status quo of economic inequities and cultural hegemony. Secondary centres of geo-linguistic cultural production,
such as those in Asia investigated, could be taken as fulfilling the role
of semi-periphery countries to stabilise the capitalist world system.
Cultural eclecticism in a postmodern world is evident in the cosmopolitan lifestyles and consumption habits of the developed world as
well as among the rising urban middle class of developing countries.
Despite having alternative identities by virtue of consumption patterns, most people seem to retain primary cultural identities in terms
of birth-place, citizenship, ethnic cultures, even social class, albeit to
varying degrees. So, does postmodern culture represent the threat of
a form of moral bankruptcy and an excuse for lack of activism over
the direction of social and political change, by privatising the notion
of cultural identity and associating it closely with materialistic
lifestyle?

Inter-cultural Osmosis

Almost too complex to define, cultures are certainly not static but
permeable and changeable over time, a fact which advertisers and
marketers have been quick to realise and to exploit. Cultures may be
changed by any innovation of product or service, though the extent
of change could range from the gradual and evolutionary to the dramatic and revolutionary. They are not as distinct and immutable as
Huntington (1998) suggests in prophesying a "clash of civilisations",
convenient as it may seem in explaining cultural conflicts in a globalising world. The process is less novel than believed via our national
cultural myths, but what is new must be the rapid pace at which it is

being achieved through multiple new communication technologies, with the growth of transnational television being just one. But might hybridisation of culture be really homogenisation in another guise, or a preliminary stage of the latter? If identity is a sociocultural construct, then the natural question must be who constructs it or stands to benefit from that construction—governments, socio-political movements, ethnic groups, or marketers and advertisers? Heightened awareness of this issue through education holds hope that there will be greater social engagement with the shape of our media environment. The notion of cultural rights for all human beings needs to be reasserted with dignity in a world where it has been marginalised by globalising political and economic agenda.

Distinctions between cultures are often stereotypical since there is a human fascination with the exotic otherness of cultures. There is also a tendency to claim moral superiority, if not geographical sovereignty, with cultures; hence often the desire to contrast western and eastern cultures in Asia. In reality these are mere labels which mask an incredibly rich cultural diversity, which ironically the expansion of media alternatives and their subsequent differentiation in recent years has highlighted. There has been more borrowing of cultures in Asia—whether in proximity or at a distance—over the centuries than is it often considered politically correct to acknowledge. The historic interpenetration of culture and religion between South Asia and Northeast Asia, most cogently seen in Southeast Asia, is a case in point. Such osmosis of culture has proven especially true contemporarily with the plethora of transnational channels across Asia which have been developed to target the ethnic minorities of a region previously unrecognised or not catered for by the domestic public broadcaster carrying out its national integration agenda. Globalisation is reflected in both the import of foreign cultural products and the export of domestic ones and which represents, in essence, a de-territorialisation of culture on an incremental basis.

Commercial Propaganda

The growth of media and the advertising industry is symptomatic of an increasingly capitalist world economy, particularly following the demise of the USSR and its hegemony over other satellite communist nations. Is globalisation then just another form of colonialism? Or is it, as implied in the precise definition of a transnational business, about adapting from any national market what is best, most appropriate or especially saleable for use anywhere else in the world or in the markets covered? Might targeting by multinational marketers of the urban–cosmopolitan elite in the megacities of Asia, such as Mumbai, Jakarta and Hong Kong as well as others be the thin end of the wedge through which their wider national and regional hinterlands are gradually being brought into the global economy? In other words, is hybridisation of media and thus culture the key to homogenising consumer markets? Cultural change progressively towards "western" norms as means of promoting socio-economic development is proposed by Harrison (2000), but this may be easier said than done by political fiat. Perhaps advertisers, marketers and broadcasters today are covertly or unwittingly achieving the sustainable economic and cultural hegemony that political and military strategists through the ages have long found elusive. Could there someday be a new social-class hierarchy worldwide, defined by media use: with the global-media users at the top and domestic-media users at the bottom with regional-media users in the middle?

If history be any guide, modernisation and technological change tend to be adjuncts or catalysts, rather than radical replacements for traditional culture and practice. They are often the very means by which a traditional culture previously in decline is resuscitated, as seems to be the case via transnational television in parts of Asia. In all probability, only surface culture, such as dress, music and forms of speech, changes rapidly with globalisation, while deep culture, such as values, attitudes and social habits, metamorphoses at a much slower pace. So while urban metropolitan or cosmopolitan cultures across the world may seem rather similar, this phenomenon may be simply an illusion or at least a deceptive veneer. Given the accelerated commodification of culture via television, consumer markets might be growing increasingly integrated on a global or regional basis, while nation states seem increasingly split by ethnic, religious and political differences. Cultures are generally not adopted in toto but adapted selectively and given unique interpretations in foreign contexts, a phenomenon reflected in domestication of television programme genre which originated in the West such as soap operas and talk shows, and sometimes their re-export to the original countries. Hopefully this book has been helpful

in underscoring the importance of recognising that transnational
television has subtly influenced cultures in Asia, much as that medium
has been transformed by them in turn.

Global Media Governance

Convergence of media and communications technologies into the
Information Superhighway has been too sudden for planned response
by nation-states, but not for effective use by social groups and business.
By virtue of trends in deregulation, there is increasing vertical integration and horizontal conglomerisation, leading to business oligopolies,
if not monopolies, in the field of communications. Such media corporations are beholden to marketers and consumers for advertising and
their owners and shareholders for profits, and not to the wider nations
and societies in which they operate. Perhaps because they operate across
borders in a number of nations, these corporations feel less constrained
to acknowledge the jurisdiction of any one of them. Globalisation
seems therefore the password for exemption from social governance
of business activity for MNCs. Since global media corporations have
no inter-government organisations that can effectively regulate their
activities, they enjoy the freedom to communicate as they choose to.

One response might be to create checks-and-balances on an equally
global scale through inter-governmental organisations (IGOs) such
as UNESCO, even though these have been anathema since the collapse
of the NWICO lobby. But the deeper issues are how does such an IGO
arrive at a global standard of communication ethics in a postmodern
age and how does it monitor, let alone enforce, the same in a world
dominated by MNCs. What are the ethics of denying access to transnational television to some sectors of society or even whole countries
due to their lack of economic resources to participate in an increasingly commercialised media and communications system? What are
the consequences for local political participation by the masses if the
media agenda is set by a global socio-economic elite? Yet without
global regulation, these corporations will be tempted to favour the
lowest ethical standards as being the most suitable for profitability in
the short-to-medium term. The only accountability tolerated within
a capitalist system seems to be towards financial shareholders and
funding institutions. Hence corporate social responsibility is often a

veneer to assuage critics or at best a minimalist acknowledgement of longer-term profitability. There is certainly a place for activism by individuals, communities and concerned citizen groups for a say in the development of our shared media ecology or global media "commons". If IGOs are not up to the task or responsive enough, perhaps it might be left to multiple non-governmental organisations (NGOs) and activist movements working synergistically in characteristic postmodern fashion to exercise influence, if not globally, at least in significant centres of cultural production and markets of media consumption.

RE-VISIONING GLOBALISATION

Globalisation is doubtless characterised by that sense of belonging to one world, through the experience of time-and-space compression made possible via electronic media and communications, as illustrated in this book. Together with its companion volume *Imagi-Nations and Borderless Television* it has highlighted also the interdependence of nations and economies in a capitalist world system. The globalisation of television operates at several levels: in the increase of foreign commercial broadcasts available in a country or region, in the imports of programming or cloning of various programme genre, in the foreign equity, strategic alliances and consultancy relationships in domestic cultural industries, and so on. The globalisation of advertising is discernible in the dominance of international advertising agencies and their affiliates in national markets, in the adoption or adaptation of global-format television commercials, the growth in the number of imported brands and product categories advertised, the buying of regional media or domestic media on a regional basis, and so on. The globalisation of the economy and polity is all too evident in the integration of world markets for capital, commodities, labour, products and services, and the interdependence of nation states in the capitalistic world system which is documented daily in our news media. The globalisation of society and culture via hybridisation is more subtle and controversial, but no less real to the more discerning participants in, and observant critics of, media, for instance. Thus the process of globalisation taking place across these fields and arenas is holistic in effect and multi-directional in causal links, and hence well-nigh impossible to operationalise for micro-analysis via quantitative–reductionist research.

The phenomenon of globalisation represents both the antecedence and consequence of the spread of marketing and advertising practices, and the convergence of urban elite lifestyles and consumption patterns, all of which is enhanced via communication technologies and the ubiquity of television worldwide. If domestic television may be seen to assist in the fashioning of national cultures out of various taste cultures within the country, then subcultures might be said to find their expression in both smaller, community media as well as in global–regional media. The narrowcasting made feasible through cable might represent in future one of the alternative media favoured by subcultures within a country or reaching across borders. To extend this reasoning on an international scale: while domestic terrestrial television gives expression to national cultures, however artificial, perhaps transnational television furthers the development of globalised cultures, whether hybrid or diasporic or both. Yet, globalisation via transnational television need not spell the relative homogenisation of cultures or subcultures worldwide into a westernised culture, but the renaissance of ethnic cultures often geographically dispersed or the hybridisation of local ethnic subcultures with foreign neo-colonial cultures. Will diversified transnational television programming and advertising, rather than ideological treatises and literary narratives, be the nascent basis of cultural identity and political formation in a postmodern world? Or will ethnic cultures and religious practice given new lease by electronic media and communications replace political ideology as the basis of international or intra-national conflict, even wars, in the post-Cold War era? Our understanding of the cultural economy within a globalised world is still embryonic despite much conjecture and so deserving of further attention.

A recurrent theme underscoring this and the preceding book, lest it still be insufficiently explicit, has been that globalisation of media takes place via a process of local contextualisation, "glocalisation" or hybridisation. More often than not, transnational television in Asia represents a form of synergistic blend of the West and East. Invariably, some dysfunctional mutations may result occasionally from the peculiar melange of economic, political, social and cultural processes within a particular country. When not managed with sensitivity, the cumulative outcome of such processes could well be a form of globalised banality through the extensive cloning of the ordinary in media from abroad. Doubtless the local cultures in Asia are being gradually co-opted to serve the global capitalist imperative, in much the same way that subcultures in the West get drawn into mainstream media, fashion, language and music. Benign remote neo-colonialisation by the pervasive media and advertising industries and their multinational corporate sponsors may do more to globalise societies and cultures around the world than more interventionist forms of economic imperialism and political subjugation. The preoccupation of media firms, like all corporations in our hyper-capitalist world, with shareholder value and financial appeal rather than with government policy and civil society advocacy is unwisely myopic. Yet there is scant need to think of dichotomies in terms of public versus commercial, or of transnational versus national television, if subject to appropriate social governance both might co-exist and challenge one another to programming innovation, cultural renaissance and creative excellence, thereby producing hybrids that represent the best of all media pedigrees.

Appendix A Industry Sources/Secondary Data

A&M India [1994]. "The Press Fight Back", *Advertising and Marketing* (India), 31 August.

AC Nielsen [2001]. *Indonesia CabSat & Netwatch Report*. Hong Kong: AC Nielsen.

Advertising Age [2000]. "At Agencies, a Growth Year for the Ages: 56th Annual Agency Report", *Advertising Age*, 24 April.

AMCB [1996]. "Indian Regional Channels Enjoying Best of Broadcast Boom", *Asian Mass Communications Bulletin*, 26 (5), September–October.

——— [2001]. "First Foreign TV Network Allowed to Broadcast Legally in China", *Asian Mass Communications Bulletin*, 31 (6), November–December.

APT-C [1995]. *Asia Pacific Television Channels*. Thousand Oaks, CA: Baskerville Communications Corporation.

Arenstein, Seth [1999]. "Programmer of the Year: StarTV", *International Cable*, 10 (12): December.

Asia-Pacific Broadcasting [1993]. "StarTV Still on Rocky Road", *Asia-Pacific Broadcasting*, December.

ASIAcom [1999]. "Cronyism Adds to Existing Broadcasters Woes", *ASIAcom*, 5 (6), 23 March.

Asian A&M [1993]. "Satellite Television in Asia: Facts and Figures", *Asian Advertising and Marketing*, 7 (3), 21 May. Hong Kong: Zindra Ltd.

——— [1994]. "Top Ten", *Asian Advertising & Marketing*, 22 April.

——— [1995]. "New Program Helps to Build Sports Culture in China", *Asian Advertising and Marketing*, 1 December.

——— [1996a]. "Digital Roll Out for Indian TV", *Asian Advertising and Marketing*, 1 November.

——— [1996b]. "StarTV Claims a Slice of Hindi TV", *Asian Advertising and Marketing*, 29 November.

——— [1996c]. "Profile of Hong Kong", *Asian Advertising and Marketing*, 6 March.

——— [1997a]. "Phoenix Rises" and "Cablers Bury the Hatchet", *Asian Advertising and Marketing*, 7 March [asianad.com/issues].

——— [1997b]. "Indovision Service Grows", *Asian Advertising and Marketing*, 21 March. Hong Kong: Zindra Ltd.

——— [1997c]. "Broadcast Laws Face Re-jig", *Asian Advertising and Marketing*, 16 May. [asianad.com/issues/970516/n-law2.html]

Asian A&M [1997d]. "New Research Project for India", *Asian Advertising and Marketing*, 16 May.

Asian Media Access [1997]. *Pan Asia X Media Survey (www.asianmediaaccess. com.au/lmm/regional/rmbr-research.htm* accessed in June 2000).

Bailes, Andrew and Neil Hollister [1996]. *Asian Cable and Satellite: Unrivalled Growth Opportunities*. London: Financial Times Telecoms & Media Publishing.

Balfour, Frederick [1993]. "Rock around the Clock", *Far East Economic Review*, 25 February.

BBC [1994]. *BBC Worldwide Magazine*, September. London: BBC World Service.

Boulestreau, Emmanuelle [1996]. "Pacific Rim Watch: India", *International Cable*, November.

——— [1997]. "Pacific Rim Watch", *International Cable*, February.

Broadcasting Authority [1993]. *Satellite Television Code of Practice on Advertising Standards* [Revised edn, May]. Hong Kong: Broadcasting Authority.

Brown, Gerald [2000]. "Stations/networks", *e-broadcastnewsasia*, 3 (5), 22 November.

——— [2001]. "Regulatory matters", *e-broadcastnewsasia*, 7 (2), 4 July.

Chaitra Leo Burnett [1994]. "In-house Documents", Bombay: Chaitra Leo Burnett.

Ciotti, Paul [1994]. "Why Satellites will Prevail over Censorship", *Asia, Inc.*, March.

Conlon, F. [1994]. "Your Wish, Saheb, is my Command". (Working paper published on the Internet <conlon@u.washington.edu>).

Couto, Vivek [1999]. "Murdoch is Back in Favor", *Asia Cable & Satellite World*, May.

——— [2000]. "Murdoch Remains on the Prowl: News Corp Unlocks Value", *Asia Cable & Satellite World*, 3 (2), March.

DD-ARU [1994]. *Doordarshan 1994 Facts and Figures*. New Delhi: Doordarshan Audience Research Unit.

——— [1999]. *Annual Report*. New Delhi: Doordarshan Audience Research Unit.

Department of Information [2000]. *Indonesia 2000: An Official Handbook*. Jakarta: Department of Information/National Communication and Information Board.

Dua, M.R. [1991]. "Cable TV—The Coming Thing", *Communication 2000 AD*. Commemorative Publication by the Indian Institute of Mass Communications.

Equitymaster.com [2004]. "Media: 'Ad'ing Growth". (http://equitymaster. com/detail.asp?date=4/20/2004&story=3, accessed 1July 2005)

Expression [1992–93]. "Star Wars", *Expression*, December–January.

FEER [1993a]. "Realigning the Stars", *Far East Economic Review*, 1 July.

FICCI [2000]. *The Indian Entertainment Industry*. New Delhi: Federation of Indian Chambers of Commerce and Industry.

Grafik McCann-Erickson [1994]. *Media Monitor*, March. Jakarta: Grafik McCann-Erickson.

Haeems, Anita [1994]. "The Great Indian Diaspora—II", *The Sunday Times of India*, 4 September.

Hong Kong Government [1994a]. *Hong Kong 1994*. Hong Kong: Government Information Services.

———— [1994b]. "Television Broadcasting in Hong Kong", Hong Kong Information Note, Chief Secretary's Office, March.

HTA [1994]. "Television Advertising Review—1993", *Media Update*, April. Hindustan Thompson Advertising, Bombay office.

Hughes, Owen [1996]. "StarTV's Phoenix Rises from the Ashes", *Television Asia*, May.

Indian MIB [1993]. *Mass Media in India, 1993*. New Delhi: Government of India, Ministry of Information and Broadcasting, Research and Reference Division.

Indiantelevision.com [2000]. "The Numero Uno Shows in C$S and All TV Homes". (www.indiantelevision.com/tvr, accessed 7 September 2002).

International Cable [1999a]. "Murdoch courts China", *International Cable*, 10 (2): 18 February.

———— [1999b]. "Asia: Taiwan Opens Market", *International Cable*, 10 (4), April.

Jacob, Paul [1994]. "TV Stations Reminded to Reduce Foreign Content", *Straits Times*, 26 August.

Jifri, Farah [1998]. "Deep impact? The Broadcasting Bill Unravelled", *Middle East Broadcast & Satellite*, September.

Johnstone, Patrick and Jason Mandryk [2001]. *Operation World*. Gaynesboro, GA: Paterrnoster.

Kang, B. [1993]. "DD Lures Metro Channel Ads", *The Pioneer*, 21 December.

Khar, Rakesh [1994]. "StarTV Plans 50 per cent Rise in India Programming", *The Economic Times*, 30 May.

King, Thomas [1996]. "A Golden Era for Pakistan TV", *Asia-Pacific Broadcasting*, October.

Kohei, Shinsaku and Naswil Idris [1990]. *The Audience Needs Survey on Radio and Television Programmes in Indonesia*. Jakarta: Department of Information/Japan International Cooperation Agency.

Kwang, Mary [1996]. "Pacific Rim Watch", *International Cable*, July.

Lahiri, Indrajit [1995a]. "Uplink Monopoly Broken", *Television Asia*, March.

———— [1995b]. "India Braces itself for Cable Blitz", *Television Asia*, May.

———— [1995c]. "Viewing Researchers Fail to Come to a Consensus", *Television Asia*, December.

Leung, W.H. [2000a]. "Newsbytes: Cable", *Communications Technology International*, November.

——— [2000b]. "Newsbytes: Satellite", *International Cable*, October.

——— [2001]. "China's Liberalizing Cable Markets", *Communications Technology International*, February.

Menon, G. [1994]. "DD: Graduating from Reactive to Pro-active Planning", *Hindu Business Line*, 24 February.

Mitra, Ananda [1993]. "Cable Operators against ZeeTV", *The Hindustan Times*, 15 December.

Nadkarni, Sirish [1994]. "Rupert Murdoch: Star Gazing in India", *Asia-Pacific Broadcasting*, 11 (6).

Nag, Madhumita [1993]. "StarTV, Others Force Shelving of Order", *Observer*, 15 June.

Ong, Catherine [1993]. "Why is Li Ka-Shing Reducing Stake Just When StarTV is Getting its Act Together?", *Business Times*, 28 July.

Pardosi, Karidun [1999]. "StarTV to Offer Programmes to Metra", *Television Asia*, January–February.

PPPI [1994]. *Media Scene Indonesia, 1993–1994*. Jakarta: Persatuan Perusahaan Periklanan Indonesia.

——— [1996]. *Media Scene Indonesia, 1995–1996*. Jakarta: Persatuan Perusahaan Periklanan Indonesia.

——— [2000]. *Media Scene Indonesia, 1999–2000*. Jakarta: Persatuan Perusahaan Periklanan Indonesia.

Rayner, Caroline (ed.) [1992]. *Philip s Encyclopedic World Atlas*. London: George Philip Ltd.

Saggar, R.L. [1993]. "Advertising: A Vehicle of Communication", *Mass Media in India 1992*. New Delhi: Government of India, Ministry of Information and Broadcasting, Research and Reference Division.

Samudera, Luas and Owen Hughes [1999]. "Indovision to Sue StarTV for Termination of Services", *Television Asia*, January–February.

Singhal, Arvind and Nandini Ghoshal [2002]. "Demystifying the Indian Market", *Strategic Marketing*. (www.etstrategicmarketing.com/Smnov-dec04/art1.html)

SRI [1994]. "Top Programmes by Name", *Multi Market Telescope*, 12–25 December 1993 and 1–7 May 1994. Jakarta: Survey Research Indonesia.

StarTV [1992]. "Star Chinese" (publicity brochure). Hong Kong: StarTV.

——— [1993]. *Media Pack*. Hong Kong: StarTV.

——— [1994]. *Media Pack*. Hong Kong: StarTV.

——— [1995]. *Media Pack*. Hong Kong: StarTV.

——— [1996]. *Media Pack*. Hong Kong: StarTV.

——— [1997]. *Media Pack*. Hong Kong: StarTV.

——— [1998]. *Media Pack*. Hong Kong: StarTV.

——— [2000]. *Media Pack*. Hong Kong: StarTV.

——— [2001]. *Media Pack*. Hong Kong: StarTV.

Stine, Stephen [1994]. "TV Entertainment: Opiate of the Masses", *Asia Inc.*, March.

Straits Times [1992]. "Satellite TV Blamed for Communal Riots in India", *Straits Times*, 12 December.

——— [1993]. "Satellite TV Plans not for the Faint-hearted", *Straits Times*, 19 December.

——— [1994]. "How Li Ran StarTV", *The Straits Times*, 21 January.

Suara Pembaruan [1994]. Various advertisements for satellite dishes on the back page of *Suara Pembaruan*, 14 January.

Television Asia [1996a]. "Packer Agrees Programme Deal with CCTV", *Television Asia*, March.

——— [1996b]. "Hong Kong Government Shelves Broadcasting Bill but Telecom Defers Launch", *Television Asia*, March.

——— [1996c]. "RFT's Hardline Moves Reflect Central Directives", *Television Asia*, November.

——— [1997]. "Indonesian Government Begins to Re-evaluate Broadcasting Bill", *Television Asia*, March.

Tharp, Marye (ed.) [1997]. "Advertising Agencies in Hong Kong"; "Advertising Agencies in India" and "Advertising Agencies in Indonesia", *International Advertising Resources*. (www.ou.edu/class/jmc3333)

Wanvari, Anil [1996]. "Post No Bills", *Cable & Satellite Asia*, November–December.

Yeap, Soon Beng [1993]. "Invading Asian Skies: The Fourth Stage of Imperialism", *Business Times*, 25–26 September.

A s they were keenly aware of the issues surrounding transnational television, key decision makers in the media sector of each Asian region were interviewed as sources of primary data for this book. Most of the advertising industry representatives were drawn from among chief executives or media managers of international agencies or large domestic agencies with international affiliations. For the broadcasting industry, interviews were obtained with executives of leading domestic and transnational television broadcasters in each country and they tended to be audience research, public relations, or operations managers. The researchers were sought in market research firms, social research institutes and universities, while the policy makers/opinion leaders approached were either government officials or members of broadcasting regulatory/advisory bodies.

Table B.1
Distribution of Expert Interviewees

	Indian Subcontinent	Malay Archipelago	Greater China	Total
Advertising Agencies/Marketers:				
Account	6	6	4	16
Media	9	7	5	21
Creative	2	1	–	3
Sub-total	17	14	9	40
Media Owners/Programme Producers:				
Domestic	16	17	7	40
Transnational	5	6	5	16
Sub-total	21	23	12	56
Market/Media Researchers:				
Market/Media	9	8	6	23
Academic/Social	6	8	5	19
Sub-total	15	16	11	42
Policymakers/Opinion Leaders:				
Government Officials	4	6	5	15
Community Leaders	4	5	1	10
Sub-total	8	11	6	25
Total	**61**	**64**	**38**	**163**

INDIAN SUBCONTINENT

Advertising Agencies/Marketers [Ind01.01–Ind01.17]

Everest Advertising, Mumbai (Saatchi & Saatchi affiliate)
Chaitra Leo Burnett, Mumbai (Leo Burnett affiliate)
J. Walter Thompson, Chennai
Hindustan Thompson Advertising, Mumbai (J. Walter Thompson affiliate)
Mudra Communications, Mumbai
Ammirati Puris Lintas, Bangalore
Lowe Lintas, Mumbai
Sobhagya Advertising, Mumbai
Euro-RSCG, Mumbai
Radeus Advertising, Mumbai
ImageAds & Communications, Mumbai
Anugrah Madison DMB&B, Chennai
TBWA/Anthem, Delhi
Ogilvy & Mather, Mumbai
Advertising Agencies Association of India, Mumbai
Hindustan Lever, Mumbai
FCB-Ulka Advertising, Bangalore

Media Owners/Programme Producers [Ind02.01–Ind02.21]

Doordarshan (DD), Delhi
ZeeTV, Mumbai
Sun TV, Chennai
United Television, Mumbai
Tara Channel, Mumbai
Nimbus Communications, Delhi
Siticable, Delhi
StarTV, Mumbai
Eenadu Television
JainTV, Delhi
Discovery Channel, Delhi
Final Take Films, Mumbai
Channel 9 Gold, Mumbai
Cable Operators Federation of India, Delhi
CNN, Delhi
NDTV, Bangalore

Market/Social Researchers [Ind03.01–Ind03.15]

Indian Institute for Mass Communication, Delhi
Indian Institute of Management, Bangalore
Centre for Media Studies, Delhi

University of Poona, Dept of Communication and Journalism, Pune
Tata Institute of Social Research, Delhi
Times of India Response, Mumbai
TAM Media Research, Mumbai
A&M (Advertising & Marketing) magazine, Delhi
Resource Centre for Media Education & Research, Pune
IMRB (Indian Market Research Bureau), Mumbai
IMRB (Indian Market Research Bureau), Chennai
ORG-MARG [Marketing and Research Group], Mumbai
Indian Newspaper Society, Delhi

Policy Makers/Opinion Leaders [Ind04.01–Ind04.08]

Indian Reserve Bank, Mumbai
Indian Space Research Agency, Ahmedabad
Frederich Egbert Stiftung (FES), Delhi
Consortium for Education Television, Delhi
Board of Censors, Delhi
Ministry of Information and Broadcasting, Delhi
DD Audience Research Unit, Delhi

MALAY ARCHIPELAGO

Advertising Agencies/Marketers [Mly01.01–Mly01.14]

Grafik McCann, Jakarta (McCann-Erickson affiliate)
Cabe Rawit Advertising, Jakarta
Leo Burnett, Kuala Lumpur
Perwanal Advertising, Jakarta (D'Arcy affiliate)
Matari Advertising, Jakarta (BBDO affiliate)
Ogilvy & Mather, Jakarta
Citra Lintas Indonesia, Jakarta (Lintas affiliate)
Lowe Lintas, Jakarta (re-branded Lintas affiliate)
Inter-Admark, Jakarta (Dentsu affiliate)
B&B Advertising, Jakarta
Sil-Ad, Jakarta and Singapore
Saatchi & Saatchi, Singapore
JWT Advertising, Kuala Lumpur

Media Owners/Programme Producers [Mly02.01–Mly02.23]

Astro/Measat, Kuala Lumpur
RCTI, Jakarta
Anteve, Jakarta
SCTV, Jakarta
TV3, Kuala Lumpur

Indosiar Visual Mandiri, Jakarta
NTV-7, Shah Alam/Kuala Lumpur
TPI, Jakarta
Malicak/Indovision, Jakarta
Cableview/MegaTV, Kuala Lumpur
Indosat, Jakarta
Kabelvision, Jakarta
Multivisions Plus, Jakarta
Indostar, Jakarta
Prambors Radio, Jakarta
Asian Business News, Singapore
TransTV, Jakarta
StarTV South East Asia office, Singapore
Dunia Visitama Produksi, Jakarta (Pearsons affiliate)

Market/Social Researchers [Mly03.01–Mly03.16]

Survey Research Indonesia, Jakarta (AC Nielsen affiliate)
Survey Research Group, Singapore
AC Nielsen, Kuala Lumpur
Inmar Infos Sarana, Jakarta (media research firm)
Institut Technologi Mara, Kuala Lumpur
Department of Mass Communication, University of Gajah Mada, Jogjakarta
Faculty of Communication Science, University of Padjajaran, Bandung
University of Indonesia, Depok
University of Malaya, Kuala Lumpur
Open University, Ciputat
MASTEL (Telecommunications Society)
Institute of Mass Communication Research and Development, Jakarta
Media Information Centre, Department of Information, Jakarta

Policy Makers/Opinion Leaders [Mly04.01–Mly04.11]

Department of Posts, Telecoms and Tourism, Jakarta
Bureau of Information and Communication, Jakarta
Bappenas, Jakarta
Radio-Television Malaysia
Dept of Information, Jakarta
Universitas Terbuka (Open University), Ciputat
Asia-Pacific Broadcasting Union (ABU), Kuala Lumpur

GREATER CHINA

Advertising Agencies/Marketers [Chn01.01–Chn01.09]

Ogilvy Media Asia, Hong Kong
McCann-Erickson Hong Kong

J. Walter Thompson China
D'Arcy Masius Benton & Bowles HK
DDB Needham Worldwide, Hong Kong
Leo Burnett, Hong Kong
Grey Advertising, Hong Kong
United Advertising, Taipei

Media Owners/Programme Producers [Chn02.01–Chn02.12]

TVB International head office, Hong Kong
Po-Hsin Multimedia, Taipei
Turner International/CNNI Far East regional office, Hong Kong
ATV head office, Hong Kong
TTV, Taipei
StarTV head office, Hong Kong
Wharf Cable head office, Hong Kong
Oriental TV, Shanghai, PRC

Market/Social Researchers [Chn03.01–Chn03.11]

Survey Research Group, Hong Kong
AC Nielsen, Hong Kong
Chinese University of Hong Kong
Research Asia, Hong Kong
Frank Small and Associates, Hong Kong
Survey Research Taiwan, Taipei (Nielson SRG affiliate)
World College of Journalism and Communication, Taipei
Rainmaker Industrial, Taipei (media research firm)
National Chengchih University, Taipei

Policy Makers/Opinion Leaders [Chn04.01–Chn04.06]

Television and Entertainment Licensing Authority, Hong Kong
Hong Kong Broadcasting Authority
Government Information Office, Taipei
Broadcast Development Fund, Taipei

APPENDIX C MONITORING NEWER MEDIA

G iven the multidisciplinary nature of media and communications, there were many alternatives in research design available to this exploration of their globalisation. Beginning with an overview of the diverse theoretical perspectives on social and economic impact within media and communications studies, we will examine the various research paradigms to which they lead as well as the relative merits and biases of each. The rationale for the multi-method approach adopted for researching the development of transnational television and advertising in Asia is thus explained retrospectively. The sources of data collection and process of data analysis are evaluated, along with challenges encountered and caveats about the information conveyed and conclusions drawn. Thus this appendix serves as a backdrop for the case studies on the impact of one transnational broadcaster, StarTV, on the globalisation of television and advertising in three Asian regions, which form the empirical crux of this book and its companion volume.

THEORETICAL PERSPECTIVES

In spite of considerable research over decades, a common lament about the field of media and communications has been its lack of a grand theory or of clearly defined disciplinary borders. There is an ongoing striving for hegemony over the emergent field of media and communications in teaching departments and research fora from the more established disciplines such as sociology, literature, journalism, film/television studies, political science and marketing. Even the various interdisciplinary schools of thought within the field of media reflect these disciplinary biases. For instance, while the political economy school in media theory examines the control of the media by the financial and thus political elite of a society, the cultural studies school is concerned with how popular culture is created and integrates subgroups in society. This current research project draws largely on an innovative media strategy approach, a middle path which needs to be explained since this seems most pertinent to analysis of developments in transnational television in Asia. However, the related theoretical perspectives of political economy, social effects, cultural studies and active audiences are taken cognisance of and discussed, as and when deemed relevant.

Social Effects

Just as there are social and political concerns in Asia over the introduction of transnational media, similar concerns in the US over the then new media of cinema and radio saw research funded in the 1930s to assess possible social effects. While the prevailing ideas in communication theory were still of individuals being vulnerable to the all-powerful mass media, Katz and Lazarsfeld (1955) propounded a more sophisticated theory of limited effects. Their "two-step flow" model of communication highlighted the selective exposure of audiences to media and the influential role of "opinion leaders". It demonstrated that the effect of media messages was greater when it was relayed inter-personally than when communicated directly by the medium. Nonetheless the mediated-flow research tradition was subjected to criticism from Adorno (1969) of the European critical theory school that it was "administrative research", sponsored by and supportive of the cultural industry and tending towards short-term effects. Subsequently Katz (1987) responded to these criticisms by stating that the findings of mediated-flow research actually debunk assumptions about all-powerful media effects. But this misses the point since the primary thesis of the critical theorists was that such effects could not be comprehensively measured at the level of individual consumption, not that social effects could never be described by quantitative research.

Long associated with Gerbner (1970) and his studies on television violence, cultivation theory described the way the media fosters certain values and attitudes in its audiences in particular and society in general, over time. Through conducting surveys of audience media habits, attitudes and behaviour, he found that heavy viewers of television were more susceptible to cultivating a fear of violence. One way that Gerbner et al. (1980) explained this cultivation was through a process termed "mainstreaming" by which heavy viewing of television created a convergence of attitudes amongst its disparate viewers into the societal mainstream as defined by television. When replication of Gerbner's US research on cultivation effects of heavy-viewing versus light-viewing of television violence did not lead to similar findings in the UK, Wober and Gunter (1988) accounted for this by citing the difficulties of cross-cultural comparisons in research, even between developed countries. Cultivation theory has been criticised for demonstrating a weak relationship, measuring only time watched not motivation for watching, failing to control for other factors, directionality of cause and effect and so on. Still, the conventional wisdom has remained that a heavy diet of violent programming must have some effect on its viewers (Griffin 1991: 307–9). Certainly this conviction is often cited by governments in Asia wishing to regulate transnational television because of its high content of foreign, mainly US, programming. At the same time, their officials often seem blinkered towards programming of similar or identical content and origin available on their domestic television stations, both commercial and public.

These early media theorists have tended to emphasise how the new electronic media has superseded older media, and created new social effects. But they could be criticised rightly for ignoring the fact that the new media has co-existed with the old and furthermore created new contexts for the latter's use. In contrast, Severin and Tankard (1992: 12) believed that newer communications technologies spelt a shift from the study of media effects on audiences towards how the media interact with each other and how audiences use the various media. Besides, late last century the media was becoming increasingly "de-massified" through new communication technologies, narrowcasting and audience segmentation, and there was greater recognition that even with mass audiences, meanings generated differed greatly among its constituent individuals and subcultures. In the case of VCR ownership, Straubhaar (1990) argued that its diffusion was related to economic growth of a country, and that in developing countries this diffusion revealed cleavages of social class and ethnicity along the lines of their economic and cultural integration with the world capitalist economy. If television could no longer be assumed to be monolithic and uniform with the introduction of VCRs, satellite, cable, pay-TV and the like, then there were implications for the applicability of "social effects" media theories in developing and developed countries alike. Yet this viewpoint still has currency in public opinion, in the popular media and among many government policy makers, as evidenced in their reactions to the advent of transnational television in Asia.

Active Audiences

Criticism of mediated-flow theory spurred research on the social dimensions of the media and led to two further, if somewhat divergent, directions in mass communication research namely uses-and-gratifications research (Blumler and Katz 1974) and diffusion research (Rogers 1962). Since mediated-flow theory emphasised how individuals could be empowered against the media there was a research paradigm shift from what effects the media had, to what active use individuals put the media to and what gratifications they gained from it. On the basis of in-depth interviews and survey questionnaires, its researchers sought therefore to define broad categories of uses audiences have for various media. For instance, McQuail et al. (1972)

identified the major uses or needs met by the media as diversion or escape from routine and problems, relationships or companionship, personal identity or reference with reality, and surveillance or information-gathering. However, the uses-and-gratifications theory could be criticised for imprecision because a viewer's needs could be met by a variety of television content, while a single programme could meet the multiple needs of any individual viewer or group of viewers. Even early proponents have admitted that uses-and-gratifications research relied too much on self-reports, defined social needs ambiguously, ignored textual constraints and neglected dysfunctional satisfaction (Kubey and Csikszentmihalyi 1990: 28–31). It was also a psychological rather than sociological explanation of media use, focusing on individual instead of social behaviour that is beyond the scope of this book.

Defending the uses-and-gratifications theory of media, McQuail (1987: 233–37) pointed out that it emphasised the non-passive role of audiences and sought to measure why they watched and what benefits were sought. So he believed that uses-and-gratification theory simply needed reformulation to emphasise factors identified as critical by research such as the audience's social background, prior use of media, expected satisfactions and evaluations for consequent use. Wilson (2000) argued that global talk shows such as *Oprah* were a gendered programme genre emphasising egalitarian discussion along with the dissemination of information, and prefigure the informal interactivity of Internet usage. The present research was not able to adopt a uses-and-gratifications approach because of the breadth of its scope across three regions and multiple countries in each. Furthermore there was limited access possible to audiences by a foreign researcher, without the approval of certain national governments, because of the perceived politically sensitive nature of media research. Yet since these factors could prove helpful in understanding the uses to which audiences in Asia put transnational television, questions on what gratifications were sought from such media by audiences and whether they were found in the various countries under the satellite footprints, were put to the key informants.

Another perspective on audience research has been provided by media system dependency theory as described by Ball-Rokeach (1982). This stressed the interdependence of mass media and society, particularly its political and economic systems, and argued therefore that the effects of media may not be studied in isolation from the society in which it functioned. For example, the dependence of the audience on the media for information increased with the degree of social change experienced and the availability of alternative information channels. In the case of transnational television, of course, this posed the issue of quite different impact in various societies of the same medium, such as those observable under the footprint of StarTV. Since the media effects on individuals were three-fold: cognitive, affective and behavioural, any research on effects must specify which of these was to be measured (Ball-Rokeach 1982: 232–55). This could not be attempted in this research due to constraints of time and access to the widely spread Asian audiences. However, decision makers occupying various key roles in the cultural industries of each country were interviewed for their perceptions of social and economic changes effected since the advent of transnational television.

Cultural Studies

A relatively recent school of thought, cultural studies has been described as the critical study of contemporary culture characterised by an engagement with such issues as social inequality or cultural imperialism, and thus differentiated from the objective–scientific and macro perspective that sociology adopts (During 1993). Critical scholars of the Frankfurt School such as Adorno, Horkheimer and Marcuse had alleged that quantitative research methods failed to explicate the more insidious effects of the media, but did not offer an empirical alternative. The Birmingham School in the UK, from which much of cultural studies traces its roots, melded theory and empirical research in the analysis of contemporary media, culture and society. One of its leading lights, Hall (1986) theorised that various manifestations of each culture needed to be understood in terms of the wider social, economic and political structure. He also demonstrated that encoding and decoding of cultural texts were quite distinct and complex processes, and the relationship of the viewers to the dominant ideology encoded would invariably result in dominant, oppositional or negotiated decodings by them. Thus the textual or semiotic analysis commonly used in cultural studies measured more than the content of messages because it aimed to provide insights into their significance in terms of its wider political and cultural context (Hall 1990). But any such analysis run the considerable risk of the researcher reading into the text his or her own biases without sufficient external controls on the range of valid interpretations. As such, cultural studies methodologies are highly interpretative and their theories still have elements of the quite deterministic mass-culture presuppositions that characterised the early critical theories of the Frankfurt School that they would wish to distance themselves from.

Another major objection raised to this approach is that it fails to give due credence to the capacity of individuals and groups to generate their own, varied meanings from the text. Fiske (1987: 62–67) objected to the assumption often made that effects of the text were those of the ideologically preferred encoding, especially when the decoding process has not been empirically ascertained. Neither was the oppositional reading to the ideologically encoded one necessarily the only other one decoded by the audience of the text as some cultural studies exponents take it to be, because it fitted their theoretical framework which over-emphasises social class as a factor. Besides, television was multi-layered in content and meaning, and so its effects could be studied best through a range of methods apart from textual analysis. In a landmark audience study, Morley (1980) demonstrated that receiving socio-economic subcultures re-defined media in terms of their own values, regardless of how hard the producers try to limit the ambiguity of their messages. Rather than alleging cultural change caused by media content, cultural studies emphasises the reproduction of societal relations which could then be critically demonstrated through textual analysis. Thus cultural studies has furthered this tradition of the critical theory school of recognising culture as a site of struggle between dominant and subordinate groups in society, but is more confident of subtle resistance by the latter.

Audience-centred research represented a shift from a strict effects-of-message approach to the interpretative activity of the audiences as individuals and the constraints they faced as members of an interpretative community. Thus it was concerned with the construction of meaning as audiences engage with a media text, and the strategies they use to decode it. Quite aptly Lewis (1991) described as an "ideological octopus" the elusive and complex relationship between viewer and the television medium. Potentially any text could lead to a number of interpretations and it was argued that the chosen interpretation was one that reinforced opinions, values, attitudes and motivations of the audience rather than one that effected any major change. As Liebes and Katz (1990) demonstrated, cultural groups brought to an imported television programme, such as *Dallas*, their own life experiences and expectations of the genre. This resulted in readings of the text that actually resisted homogenisation by the imported culture and allowed the viewers the pleasure of making sense of it from their own perspectives. There can be little doubt that a similar paradoxical experience explains the popularity of satellite and cable programming in Asia, and would be a fruitful avenue of audience research and textual analysis in future.

Political Economy

The political economy tradition in media research adopts a Marxist analysis of how economic control of the cultural industry determines its message production. In reality, the relationship is much more complex and controversial than theorists make it out to be. In any case, the cultural industry was seen as an integral part of the political and economic systems by Golding and Murdock (1991), with close links of ownership and influence to both, and therefore its message content was an ideological reflection of those national or global systems even without political coercion. Economic forces were said to conspire to further the interests of media and other industries, to the detriment of social forces which might lack financial and political clout. As Boyd-Barrett (1995) pointed out, the political economy approach to media theory made claims about the functioning of media as an industry in society that were empirically verifiable or at least supportable by critical observation and analysis. This revealed its origin as yet another reaction to the emphasis of the social effects approach in early media research that was concerned only with simplistic measurement of stimuli–response at an individual or small group level.

The roots of the relationship of media and the political structure may be traced to the seventeenth and eighteenth centuries when belief in freedom of speech and rational public discussion in opposition to feudal and absolute political power led to the emergence of the bourgeois public sphere. But as Habermas (1989) explained, from the mid-nineteenth century onwards public discourse had been gradually manipulated and effectively muzzled by political bureaucrats and commercial media interests, even though ostensibly there remained freedom of the press in society. Extending this thesis to the late twentieth century, Herman and Chomsky (1988) took the radical view that there was a propaganda system in capitalist societies because the so-called free press served the interests of the political and economic elite through, among other things, ownership concentration, advertising revenue and sourcing of information. Though primarily an institutional critique, these authors used secondary data, content analysis and textual analysis to bolster their case that news in the developed world was selectively filtered in the process of production. On the other hand, Altheide (1984: 476–90) found that the journalists' views did not necessarily coincide with that of the politico-economic elite and claimed that news might shape society rather than the other way around, as with the Vietnam War and Watergate Crisis. It is doubtful if that still holds true of journalism in the post-Gulf War, Balkan Conflict and post–September 11 era as exemplified by the practices of transnational broadcasters like CNN.

Any media corporation has also to balance the demands of its stakeholders: owners, advertisers/marketers, software and hardware suppliers, audiences, employees (especially journalists and programme creators), governments, as well as other sociocultural and political–economic institutions of the countries in which it operates. This raises also the issue of which of these social entities a media corporation such as a transnational television broadcaster serves primarily and what its mission is economically and socially. As media businesses enter the mainstream of a capitalist economy, the greater the likelihood, Murdock (1982) claimed, that their content would increasingly reflect, even support, capitalist values or at least not seek to undermine them. But empirical research seemed neither to confirm nor deny the media hegemony thesis at least in relation to news reportage. Berwanger (1987) reminded us that while research on the social effects of television has made little progress since the 1930s, political and commercial expediency has meant media policy decisions continue to be made on the basis of popularly-held views concerning the power of the modern mass media. He was of the extreme opinion that television undermined the status quo by inevitably revealing more than political leaders would prefer, but this might be so largely because it served commercial interests of attracting a wider audience for advertisers. Yet all of these factors affect the locus of control over the media and their content in any nation state, and are even more complex in the case of global and regional corporations such as those that dominate the transnational television industry in Asia.

Both Marxist and capitalist economists seem to concur that late capitalism is characterised by global capital accumulation, surplus capital in search of new investments, and growth in the services sector, all of which have implications for the global media industry. With some validity, Garnham (1990: 43–44) criticised research focus on the content of the media to the detriment of understanding the role of mass media within the political economy and resisting the capitalist logic of cultural production. Nonetheless, content and control might be quite inseparable as two sides of the same coin. For commercial television has become the prime medium within the cultural industry, and is characterised by its dependence on advertising income, which in turn virtually dictates its programming offerings and target markets in order to attract the right advertiser clients away from their current media. More than programming, the media produced audiences as marketable commodities as primed consumers for advertisers' products, as Smythe (1977) demonstrated. Thus a new media entrant such as transnational television was not interested in the geographical reach per se of their satellite footprints, but in attracting audiences with sufficient buying power and inculcated with the right consumer behaviour attitudes through its programming in order to interest advertisers. If the media is believed to have considerable impact on society, then where the source of its power resides and how it is managed is a valid arena of analysis. It ought to be no less a part of systematic research on the impact in Asia of the introduction of a new medium such as transnational television.

Media Strategy

Contrary to the expectations of their early proponents, social effects, political economy and cultural studies approaches appear to be converging through an increasing emphasis on producers, regulators and consumers as mutually active participants in the social process of the media, both nationally and globally. Contemporary cultural studies theorists would argue that cultural production, while controlled and manipulated by societal elite, is not deterministic but actually invites oppositional readings. Similarly, later social-effects approaches temper ideas of powerful media effects with recognition that the media serves to reinforce existing attitudes and behaviours through personal decoding of their message, even when the range of meanings possible are limited. The political economy approach has also been increasingly cognisant of the active role of individuals and groups within the power structures in the media institution, industry, government and wider society. The criticisms of each school of thought might well be answered by another, because they analyse different facets of the same media phenomenon and are able to compensate for excesses or loopholes of the other. Speculating that the contrasts between political economy and cultural studies approaches may not be irreconcilable, Curran and Park (2000) advocated a broadening of media theory through comparative studies of non-western countries, as indeed this book seeks to do.

In his call for renewal of the political economy paradigm, Mosco (1996) surveyed the extensive contributions of its exponents historically and internationally, and reminded us of its affinity with cultural studies against positivism. He was cognisant of the challenges of new arenas such as links between production and reception, structural changes in communications industries, and relationships between private and public media. Yet Mosco took the rather conservative stance that there was still a place for analysis of communications within the wider social, economic and political totality. But in the light of the unprecedented globalisation of television via satellite and cable, Comor (1994) made a case for the micro-level analysis of political economy of communications complementing the macro-level concerns of what he terms a "global political economy of communication" approach. Drawing on a number of authors on international political economy, he argued that neither a realist perspective which majors on inter-state relations in a stable world order nor a liberal perspective which majors on the global market of multinational corporations is adequate for analysing the interdependent state–corporate world system. A thorough-going "political economy of communication" approach was one which investigated the power relationships between audiences, producers and distributors all the way from the local level of analysis to the global. This was something which Comor advocated as invaluable for understanding the complex processes of globalisation, though he was rather vague on the details of how this might be operationalised for research. Still this is something the present book aspires, and even attempts, to achieve.

Signalling the need to re-define cultural imperialism concerns, McAnany and Wilkinson (1992) had advocated more emphasis in media research on the economics of cultural production, in particular national, international or inter-corporate contexts. Taking up that theme, Sinclair (1994) argued that in our post-Marxist, postmodern age the search for a meta-theory of mass communication might be misplaced. Instead media analysts would find it more fruitful to theorise at mid-range levels such as the structure of the media industry or to adopt a "cultural industries" approach. Likewise Tunstall (1991) advocated a "media industry" perspective that analysed media organisations, their occupational structures, entrepreneurs and barons, comparative media systems and content. On the other hand, Flew and Cunningham (2000) cautioned against "strong globalisation" theories such as those from the political economy perspective that have overemphasised the power of global media corporations. Such theories tend to ignore the persistence of the nation state as a regulator as well as the role of audiences in selective appropriation and interpretation of media, in a way that industry-level perspectives may not.

As a framework for analysis of the media industry and its constituent corporations, such as the present research warrants, Wilson (1988) suggested six relevant aspects: ownership, production, technology, distribution, consumption and the role of the state. Since the structure of the global media industry is especially complex, Dimmick and Coit (1982) stipulated nine levels at which the media could be analysed including supra-national, society, industry, supra-organisational, intra-organisational and individual. Galtung (1999) was quite clear in defining international media monitoring as involving representative media in different parts of the world, their organisation, form and content. Its purpose was to provide data for differential analysis of media or countries, or both, which could lead to theorising. Nordenstreng (1999) went further to promote the role of professionals and academics to hold the powerful players in society accountable through content analysis and consequent media criticism. As evident in the preceding chapters of this book, a number of these dimensions were included in this study that proffers a comparative approach focusing on the various players involved in transnational television in Asia. After reporting the findings, the final and penultimate chapters of this book endeavour to provide such a critique and through which this author hopes to encourage further research and reflection on the phenomenon of transnational television, particularly in developing regions around the world.

RETROSPECT AND PROSPECTS

This book has sought to document systematically the globalising impact of transnational television on the broadcasting and advertising industries in Asia, even if it does not address all the issues raised. Previous discussions on the topic have tended to depend on anecdotal evidence and speculative projections, in large part because of the complexity of the phenomenon. Furthermore, measuring impact is still a controversial theoretical and methodology issue given the many other intervening variables such as penetration, access cost, service quality, competitive offerings, cultural preferences, political–legal constraints and economic affluence, to name but a few. From the vantage point of hindsight, this section will review some of the methodological issues raised by research into transnational television impact in Asia, review the limitations of the present study and seek to chart some possible courses for future exploration on this topic.

Reflections on Method

The inherent difficulty in any research attempted on media impact, is separating the effect of one factor such as transnational television or pop music or movies or any particular consumer good from that of other concurrent factors such as affluence, government policies, education and so on. No culture is static now or has ever been, for while what we now call Chinese, Indian or Indonesian may have roots in the historic past, these cultures over the last decade would not be identical to what they were two centuries ago. But perhaps it is more important these cultures thus labelled as national are artificial constructs, for cultures in any geographical region are far from homogeneous. Han Chinese culture has its roots in the dynasty by that name, so-called Indian culture is an amalgam of cultures of various kingdoms that predated the British colonial establishment of a single empire, and Indonesian culture is a post-colonial creation to meld the quite distinct cultures of the numerous islands of the archipelago. If anything, what is held up as national is predominantly that of one subcultural or ethnic group, perhaps the majority though sometimes a minority, which holds political and economic power. At best it is a composite culture attempting to represent some of the diversity within the nation, though this is often of a character that does not inspire any of the constituents particularly.

Much current global media research is often lacking in rigour because, influenced by some variant of the cultural imperialism viewpoint, it tends to seek to demonstrate some sociocultural impact of "western" media on "eastern" cultures. However, such change is difficult to demonstrate, let alone to isolate from other contributory factors of modernisation such as other media, marketing efforts, economic affluence, immigration and so on. Hence, for a more realistic portrayal of international television programme flows, Sepstrup (1990) insisted on a two-stage analysis, the first referring to the transnationalisation of supply and consumption of television within a country, and the second referring to cultural and economic effects of that transnationalisation. If, instead of anecdote and conjecture, some measurement of the impact over time of transnational satellite television were to be attempted, it would have to take one of four basic forms: first, content analysis of programmes and advertising; second, textual analysis of the meanings conveyed by them; third, surveys of values of audiences exposed to such broadcasting in differing degrees; and fourth, monitoring of actual economic, social and political behaviours.

Yet the first research form, involving content analysis, may be considered inadequate to the task of explaining media impact because it fails even to take into account audience perception, especially cross-culturally, let alone resultant behaviour. As Chapman et al. (1997) pointed out, based on their cross-national research experience, there are segments of Indian society that are decidedly of "developed world" standards and segments of the UK society that live in "developing world" standards. Thus the context in which a mass medium is received, has implications for how even similar content is perceived. While the second form, involving textual analysis, attempts to incorporate perception, it is prone to subjectivity of interpretation by the researcher. The difficulty that the latter two forms of measurement encounter is that of demonstrating causality when there are, quite self-evidently, numerous intervening variables in the wider social context. Besides, the logistics of conducting surveys or monitoring behaviours in multiple Third World countries are too cumbersome for any single researcher, not to mention the insurmountable difficulties of obtaining government permission for access to audiences in many of them.

Interviews used in the present research were invaluable in filling in the gaps in published secondary data and for gaining access to proprietary data. They were also crucial when, in the case of some countries, relatively little research had been done, let alone published, at least in English. The preliminary interviews in 1992–94 in two locations served as a pilot study for the later interviews in eight countries in Asia, some visited more than once, between the late 1990s and early 2000s. The process of interviewing multiple respondents from the media industry might be considered similar to that of a focus group in that the researcher did seek comment from each respondent on the views of others, except that the respondents were not in the same room at the same time, a physically proximate situation being not feasible given their job constraints. In any case, the respondents were probably freer with their comments in the privacy of their offices than they would be at a focus group and in the presence of their competitors or regulatory overseers.

By conducting multiple interviews within each profession, it was possible during the data analysis to counteract extremes of perception and achieve a consensus of opinion at least within each sector. Furthermore the qualitative interviews, which comprised a major part of this research, were a form of ethnographic study of the broadcasting and advertising industries of the countries concerned. Respondents were asked about their perspectives on developments in their industry, the fruits of which were readily observable on the television broadcasts. Survey research of such key decision makers would not have been effective since the respondents were likely not to return their questionnaires, as evidenced by non-response for subsequent requests for feedback. This was probably due to their work priorities and also because they might have felt that whatever answer options they were given in a questionnaire did not plumb the depths of the issue's complexity. Besides a mail questionnaire or even a structured interview would have failed to reveal the richness of data on Asia that has been possible through the multiple sourcing used in this research.

As an example of qualitative research, this book would argue for a revision of the technical criteria for evaluation of rigour. It is entirely inappropriate to apply the rules of quantitative research such as validity and reliability, even if they could be stretched to fit. Because qualitative research involves gathering a great amount of data about a small range of cases, this research has endeavoured instead to meet alternative criteria as credibility, integrity and dependability. For instance, the methodology used in this research was credible because it would have been impossible to use quantitative methods such as surveys when the phenomenon of transnational television was complex and the variables unclear, not to mention the impossibility of achieving a reasonable response rate, as explained above. The integrity of the research is demonstrated in the commitment to an empathic understanding of the media industry and of the political, economic, social and cultural contexts of countries researched, as well as the approach of in-country face-to-face interviews.

The dependability of the findings is underscored by the triangulation of primary data sources such as the interviews and videotaped commercials, secondary data sources such as news-clippings and reports, as well as observation such as systematic viewing of prime time programming. In any case, media practitioners in particular and business executives as a whole have little problem with using qualitative research by itself or in conjunction with quantitative, often secondary data in their decision making. Yet social scientists, especially in the business field, tend to be insistent on quantitative primary data in support of almost simplistic hypotheses, in order to feel justified in making generalised conclusions. Put quite simply, qualitative research is primarily about quality or richness of information inasmuch as quantitative research is largely about quantity or wide sampling. The case-study approach used in this book is particularly suited to deal with the complexities of structure, context and audiences combined, and to provide insights on media globalisation from multiple national contexts in Asia.

Assets and Caveats

The author's own nationality and ethnicity was a factor in the fieldwork, especially given its qualitative nature. Being ethnically Asian was an advantage in inter-personal relations, for it was possible for the interviewees mostly of similar heritage to identify with me and feel that I would understand their points of view. Having worked in the First World and with expatriates in Asia, and being effectively bi-cultural made it possible to interact equally well with the western executives interviewed. Although the interviews were conducted in English, my minimal knowledge of local languages or accents and diction was invaluable in communicating with the interviewees as well as secretaries, receptionists and such in order to establish contact with the interviewees. As someone of South Asian extraction I was able to establish rapport particularly with interviewees in India, certainly after I had satisfied their curiosity (after expecting a Welshman from Australia) about my complicated ancestry. It was also helpful in Indonesia that I was a fellow-citizen of ASEAN and Malay-speaking, able to make small talk in their language. In Hong Kong, China and Taiwan, my knowledge of Chinese culture and a smattering of the language from having been born and bred in Singapore, was probably of some value in opening doors. Though, all these were perhaps not as much critical as my career experience in advertising in the Asia region that gave me personal "connections" within some parts of the media industry and thus an entrée into other parts as a former fellow media professional.

While my cultural background was beneficial in interviewing the decision makers, it would not have been as valuable for a survey or ethnographic study of audiences. For one thing, any audience research in Indonesia then and China still would have required official permission. This would have meant submitting the questionnaire for official approval, translation and back-translation, collaborating with a local public institution, and having a government official accompany me on field trips or even having the government official select the respondents. All of which would have delayed the research and changed its design, if not significantly biased the findings. Besides my experience with community surveys in Asia has been that there is a strong tendency to provide socially-desirable answers as well as expressing politically-expedient opinions. Furthermore, being resident abroad and working as an academic full-time outside Asia precluded being able to spend lengthy periods in-country for data gathering. Besides, the research project had evolved from one concerned with generalised media-induced socio-cultural change to one interested primarily in understanding the impact of transnational satellites on the globalisation of television and advertising industry in Asia.

One disadvantage of any qualitative method, obviously, is the volume and disparate types of data which are time-consuming to collect, complex to analyse and awkward to summarise. This proved to be the case with this research project and is reflected in the fact that it has taken two books to incorporate all of the interview responses. Despite collecting more data than was actually needed or used, there still were some gaps in knowledge for some country case studies which could not be filled easily later from a distance. The researcher had to be content with updating parts of the book up to late 2002 from published sources including from the Internet and information garnered on incidental travels in Asia. In addition it was seldom possible to find strictly comparable data, due to differing availability, methodologies, language constraints and so on. The challenges that Dogan and Pelassy (1990) cite in selecting nations to use in comparative politics, hold relevance to comparing media systems as well. Even though there is a shared signifying system within the media and advertising industries spawned by capitalism, the data analysis in this research on transnational television has had to be somewhat tentative given the slight possibility of cross-cultural misinterpretations.

The present study involved researching not one but seven countries in depth plus others in each region superficially, each with somewhat different politico-economic and sociocultural backgrounds. This was done not at just one point in time but over a decade of considerable change in their media and advertising environments. There was considerable difficulty of keeping track of developments in a rapidly adapting industry across a large continent, as there is invariably a time lag between announcement and event, and an even greater one between sighting the former and the publishing of this book. There was also the challenge of verifying the reliability of data from secondary sources such as trade magazines but generally one has to accept these sources as the very same ones that those in the broadcasting and advertising industry were dependent upon for their strategic business decisions. While secondary data on domestic and transnational television in Asia may be subject to some scepticism about unreliability, such data as was made available to this researcher has been cited and analysed in this research with appropriate caveats. Depth of detail might only have been possible with a single-country case study, but then any one country would be far less representative of the diversity of responses to the new transnational medium across the region or continent. What this researcher has chosen to do in this book therefore is trade depth of information for the more critical insights possible only through breadth of analysis across Asian regions.

For this book, considerable and varied data collected on the field had to be sifted through later in order to discover and describe the complex contexts and consequences of the phenomenon of transnational satellite television in Asia. Having returned to Australia after each field trip it was not easy to clarify responses or seek additional information during the data analysis stage. While fax, phone and email may theoretically lessen the tyranny of distance, the likelihood of receiving a timely and accurate response was found to be quite minimal in the cases where it was actively sought. Furthermore, the process of data analysis after each trip took over a year each that in terms of the rate of change in the advertising and broadcast industries was quite long. The respondents would not have remembered what they said then, and their opinions could have changed since given new circumstances. The few interviewees who asked for copies of academic papers based on the fieldwork, made little response to the papers sent subsequently despite a specific request for feedback. Besides the interviewees themselves were likely to be preoccupied with the practical concerns of having to anticipate the market developments years in advance rather than reflecting on events of years past. Given the nature of the advertising industry particularly and the broadcasting industry to a lesser degree, by the time any follow-up interviews could be conducted the original interviewees were often no longer in the same professional positions they held or even in the same organisations when the fieldwork was first conducted.

SIGNPOSTS FOR THE FUTURE

If this research has had to trade breadth for depth, then there remains much scope for future researchers to delve further into the impact of transnational television in Asia. For a start, given the nature of the industry there would be significant developments in the three major regions studied by the time this book is published, and it could be about time for a follow-up field study to the last one in 2001, in one or more of them. It would be instructive to chart over time how StarTV has fared with its regionalisation programme and how domestic broadcasters have responded since. The regulatory situation in Indonesia, India and China, for instance, has shifted further over early 2000s, albeit slower that in the previous decade, and this has implications for the transnational broadcasters as well as the domestic cable and terrestrial networks. Even though some countries like India and China were less affected by the economic downturn of the late 1990s and early 2000s than others, like Indonesia, how this affected transnational broadcasters' ongoing expansion plans based on previous projections of rapid economic growth in the region is worth following up on.

Media Strategy Approach

The present study could be replicated with other secondary television markets from the three regions, perhaps Philippines and Thailand for Southeast Asia, Sri Lanka and Nepal for South Asia, and Japan and South Korea for Northeast Asia. Alternatively a similar media strategy study could be extended to the Asian regions not covered by the present one, namely the satellite-saturated West Asia, the embryonic commercial television market of Central

Asia, the Australasian-media-dominated South Pacific and US-media-dominated North Pacific nations. Through such extensions of the present research design, it would be instructive to discover whether the findings of the present research are as generalisable as the concluding three chapters suggest. Future research could concentrate instead on the strategic alliances of global–commercial broadcasters such as AOL Time Warner, CNBC Asia, TNT/Cartoon Network and Discovery Channel in the same key markets in the Indian subcontinent, Malay archipelago and Greater China. Perry (2002: 113), for one, speculated that convergence in media ownership result in programming synergies and thus overall decline in content diversity. Studies could also done of regional commercial broadcasters such as TVB, Phoenix and ZeeTV and their relative impact on domestic broadcasters in comparison with other transnationals.

The expansion of domestic–public channels such as DD1, CCTV-4 and TCSI (Television Corporation of Singapore International) into Asiawide, even global, broadcasts in response to the continuing competition from transnational commercial broadcasters, makes for an interesting case study of strategic re-orientation. Now that some of the key variables in the globalisation of television in Asia via transnational satellites have been identified, it might be possible to conduct extensive surveys of decision makers in the broadcasting industries in a number of countries in the region. This could be done via mailed questionnaires, though, based on this researcher's experience of organisational cultures in Asia, it would be more productive to conduct administered questionnaires or, better yet, face-to-face highly structured interviews. Through the use of more quantitative methodologies it might be possible to establish statistically significant relationships between some of the factors identified in the analytical framework proposed in the preceding book *Imagi-Nations and Borderless Television* and revisited in Chapter 7 in the present book. There is scope, of course, for the application of other theoretical perspectives to the analysis of transnational television in Asia.

Audience-research Approaches

One area that the present research did not focus on for lack of resources was on the audiences for transnational television. An "active audience" approach could seek to analyse viewing habits and motivations perhaps by convening focus groups. There have been only the beginnings of such a shift in research on transnational television in Asia to looking at what uses-and-gratifications audiences have gained from it as compared to domestic television and other media. Research on transnational television should ideally include ethnographic observation at other social sites such as the workplace, school, shops and clubs at which audiences process their television viewing through discourse. Moores (2000: 95–104) quite rightly suggested that there was fruitful research to be done on the human geography of television, that encompasses both industry practices as well as audience reception. Perhaps television is unlike any other product or service because there is something addictive, almost mesmerising, about seeing reality played back selectively and sensationally as news, information, documentary, or seeing pseudo-reality created as soap operas and sitcoms which provide escapism. Ethnography may be gaining popularity in advertising and marketing circles as a means of providing in-depth psychological insights into consumers, but ought rather, as Sunderland and Denny (2003) argue, to concentrate on its traditional social anthropological strengths in discerning underlying shared meanings in cultural contexts.

Greater diversity of choice in television entertainment made possible via satellite, cable, VCRs, video-on-demand, computer games, even the internet, may mean that consumer-citizens exercise greater selectivity in watching only what interests them. Apart from issues of privacy involved in media-based systems of audience measurement, it has become evident that the greater the content options, such as satellite and cable channels measured, the less reliable the quantitative data (Napoli 2001), a problem that is compounded in developing countries. Invariably the growth of television channels and other electronic media has been accompanied by higher number of hours devoted to them, but the opportunity cost of this in terms of other personal and community activities has seldom been explored qualitatively. Are television soap operas and sitcoms taking the place of local community, talk show hosts or news anchors superseding social and political leaders, or televised sports substituting for religious gatherings? There might be much globalisation of programme genre, formats, plots and production effort, but not necessarily of consumption of such creative content by audiences. The kind of holistic explorations by anthropologist on media by contributors to Ginsburg et al. (2002), hold much promise in the arena of transnational television consumption. On the other hand since the qualitative research of the present book has demarcated the broader issues, it may be feasible to conduct extensive surveys of the urban populations or postmodern cities in the region effects on viewership patterns in a multi-media, multi-channel entertainment environment.

Cultural Studies Approaches

By adopting a cultural-studies approach the popularity of some transnational television programmes in Asia and the non-acceptance of others could be understood in terms of their wider social and political context, such as the relative exposure to other cultures or subcultures within and across national borders. Textual analysis is identified particularly with the cultural studies school of media theory and has been referred to variously as a naturalistic, interpretative, even postmodern paradigm. Audience studies have demonstrated amply that there can be no pre-judged dominant reading, but simply points of departure for alternative readings to be generated by different socio-cultural groups, thus making cross-cultural textual analysis of a medium such as transnational television a challenge. A cultural-studies approach could be utilised to show how the new transnational medium is used by the masses in Asia to give voice to their lives, rather than how they have been co-opted to serve the capitalist system. This may be simply in terms of seeking entertainment alternatives which reflect their aspirations, or a way of quiet assertion, perhaps even rebellion against the predominant nationalistic cultural straitjacket. Even if there were universal availability of and access to transnational television in Asia, it is not necessarily or certainly seldom that there is a homogeneous interpretation of it as a cultural text. Thus the need to move beyond an aesthetic critique of transnational television from an elitist perspective could be highlighted by research studies adopting a cultural studies approach.

Political Economy Approaches

Researchers favouring a strict political economy approach could be interested in investigating further the utilisation of present and to-be-launched satellites which would be indicative of the formal or informal alliances between satellite owners and channel providers, global, regional and national, while there might even be globalisation of programme genre, formats and plots, but not of production source or actual creative content. Content analysis of programming schedules or videotaped programmes for country-of-origin, genre types and programme flows would provide further insights into the complex relationships of global capital in the cultural industries. But political economists may need to look also at the demand side of global television, not just its supply, as the source of the phenomenon of globalisation. The growth of the transnational and domestic broadcasting industries would also be a barometer of business confidence in the economic recovery of the newly-industrialising countries (NICs) and big emerging markets (BEMs) in Asia. But business researchers, in particular, need to go beyond theorising of the development of international businesses such as the media conglomerates, to critically evaluating their role and contribution to national societies and the world economy. Less of the micro-positivist approach is needed, for there is ample such research produced in the service of economic interests, and instead more of the macro-critical approach for there is little of that in the service of the wider political economy.

Whatever might be the shortcomings of its research approach, this book has sought to provide vital independent feedback to transnational and domestic broadcasters in Asia on the long-term implications for their investments, in terms of the likelihood of attracting audiences and thus advertisers, given particular satellite footprints and programming. The findings reported may also assist marketers and advertising agencies in the rest of the developing world in assessing qualitatively the effectiveness of and corporate social responsibilities in their utilisation of this new medium versus domestic media, given the experience and perceptions of their counterparts in Asia. Finally the comparative analysis of national markets and regions may help guide governments, inter-government agencies and non-governmental organisations on cultural policy formulation and on the consequent regulation of terrestrial, cable and satellite broadcasting. Learning from the experiences of Asia might save developing countries in other parts of the world from ineffectual attempts at control, but instead encourage the exploration of ways to moderate, compete or collaborate with transnational commercial television which increasingly inhabits the globalised societies we live in.

Satellite Platforms

Apstar/Galaxy:	www.apstar.com/
AsiaSat:	www.asiasat.com.hk
Astra:	www.astra.lu
Inmarsat:	www.inmarsat.org
Intelsat:	www.intelsat.int
Measat/Binariang:	www.measat.com.my
Optus Communications:	www.optus.net
PanAmSat:	www.panamsat.com
SingTel:	www.singtel.com
Shinawatra/Thaicom:	www.thaicom.net

Footprint Maps

Geo-Orbit:	www.geo-orbit.org/easthemipgs/fcrackp.html
Measat2:	www.measat.com.my/footprint2.html
SatcoDX:	www.satcodx-op.com/
SeaTel:	www.seatel.com/footprints/
ISatAsia:	www.isatasia.com/cmeng.html

Transnational Broadcasters

ABC Asia Pacific:	www.abcasiapacific.com
BBC World Asia:	www.webhk.com/bbc
China Entertainment TV:	www.cetv.com
CNBC Asia:	www.cnbcasia.com.sg
CNN International:	www.turner-asia.com
Channel News Asia:	www.channelnewsasia.com
Channel V:	www.channelv.com
Chinese Television Network:	www.ctn.net
Deutsche Welle:	www.dwelle.de
Discovery Channel Asia:	www.discovery.com
ESPN Star Sports:	www.espnstar.com
MTV Network Asia:	www.mtvasia.com

NHK International: www.nhk.org.jp
Phoenix Satellite Channel: www.phoenixtv.com
Star TV: www.startv.com
Sony Entertainment TV: www.setindia.com
ZeeTV Network: www.zeetelevision.com

Domestic Broadcasters

Asia Television (ATV):   www.atv.com.hk
China Central TV (CCTV):   www.cctv.com
Doordarshan India (DD):   www.ddindia.net
Formosa TV (Taiwan):   www.ftv.com.tw
Indosiar (Indonesia):   www.indosiar.com
Media Corporation of   www.mediacorp.com.sg
    Singapore:
MetroTV (Indonesia):   www.metrotvnews.com
Munhwa Broadcasting   www.mbc.co.kr
    Corporation (Korea):
Oriental TV (China):   www.orientaltv.com
Radio TV Hong Kong: www.rthk.org.hk
Radio Television Malaysia: www.asiaconnect.com.my/rtm.net
RCTI (Indonesia):   www.rcti.co.id
SCTV (Indonesia):   www.sctv.co.id
Shanghai TV (China):   www.stv.sh.cn
TPI (Indonesia):   www.tpi.co.id
Taiwan TV Enterprise: www.ttv.com.tw
Television Corporation   www.tcs.com.sg
    of Singapore:
TV3 (Malaysia):   www.tv3.com.my
TVB (Hong Kong):   www.tvb.com.hk
TV New Zealand: www.tvnz.co.nz

Cable/Pay-TV Networks

ABS-CBN (Philippines):   www.abs-cbn.com
Asian Television (Canada):   www.aci.on.ca/AsianTvnet
Astro (Malaysia):   www.astro.com.my
Chinese TV Service (Taiwan):   www.cts.com.tw
Hong Kong Cable/Wharf: www.cabletv.com.hk
Indovision (Indonesia):   www.indovision.co.id
ITV (Thailand):   www.itv.co.th
JET TV (Japan):   www.jettv.com
Kabelvision (Indonesia):   www.onklik.com/ontv

MegaTV (Malaysia):	www.megatv.com.my
Optus Vision (Australia)	www.optus.net.au
Philippines Cable:	www.geocities.com/televisioncity/ studio/2608
Singapore Cablevision:	www.scv.com.sg

Advertising Agencies

Euro RSCG Advertising:	www.eurorscg.com
J. Walter Thompson:	www.jwtworld.com
Leo Burnett:	www.leoburnett.com
Lowe Lintas Indonesia:	www.lowelintas.co.id/
McCann Erickson:	www.mccann.com
Mudra Advertising:	www.mudra.com
Ogilvy & Mather:	www.ogilvy.com
Saatchi & Saatchi:	www.saatchi-saatchi.com

Regulatory/Policy Bodies

Government Information Office (Taiwan):	www.gio.gov.tw
Ministry of Information & Broadcasting (India):	http://mib.nic.in/
State Administration of Radio Film and Television (China):	www.chinaonline.com/refer/ministry_ profiles
Television and Entertainment Licencing Authority (Hong Kong):	www.info.gov.hk/tela

Industry Resources

AC Nielsen:	asiapacific.acnielsen.com.au/home.asp
Broadcast & Broadband Asia:	http://web.singnet.com.sg/~meson/ aboutus.html
Cable Quest:	www.cable-quest.com/
China Marketers' Guide:	www.shanghai-ed.com/j-market.htm
Communications Technology:	www.cabletoday.com
The Economic Times, India:	http://economictimes.indiatimes.com/
Indiantelevision.com/Ambez:	www.indiantelevision.com
Television Asia:	www.tvasia.com.sg/homepage.html
Transnational Broadcasting Studies:	www.tbsjournal.com
Via Satellite:	www.omeda.com/vs/

Academic Resources

Asian Media, Information and Communication Centre	www.amic.org.sg
Asian J. of Communications:	www.amic.org.sg/ajcv11n2.html
Centre for Media Studies:	www.cmsindia.org
Continuum:	www.cowan.edu.au/pa/continuum/
Journal of International Communications:	www.mucic.mq.edu.au/JIC/
Media, Culture and Society:	http://mcs.sagepub.com
Media Development:	www.wacc.org.uk/wacc/publications/media_development
Institute for Media and Communications Management	www.mcm.unisg.ch

ABN:	Asian Business News, the first Asiawide, satellite business news service, owned by a consortium of foreign and regional news corporations; merged with CNBC.
AC Nielsen:	Global market research company which monitors television ratings and advertising expenditure, formerly known as Survey Research Group in Asia.
Adspend:	Expenditure by marketers on various advertising media, which is a major constituent of "billings" which includes creative development and production charges.
Advertising agency:	A firm specialising in advertising services such as creative production of television and print advertisements, selecting and buying media time and space, which works on behalf of a number of marketing organisations.
AMIC:	Asian Media, Information and Communications Centre, a non-governmental research and consultancy organisation based in Singapore.
AMCB:	Monthly media industry news bulletin produced by AMIC for its members.
APTC and APTC&S:	*Asia Pacific Television: Channels* and *Asia Pacific Television: Cable and Satellite*, annual reference guides to the media industry in the region.
ASEAN:	Association of South East Asian Nations comprising initially the non-communist countries of Malaysia, Indonesia, Thailand, Singapore, Philippines and Brunei, and later expanding to include the countries of IndoChina such as Vietnam, Myanmar (Burma), Cambodia and Laos; proposing in future to act as a free trade area, Asean FTA or AFTA.
Asian A&M:	*Asian Advertising and Marketing*, leading regional bi-monthly magazine for practitioners, which later became *Adweek Asia*.

Asianet:	A commercial television service via satellite in Malayalam serving the dominant ethnic group of the southern Indian state of Kerala as well as expatriates from there in West Asia.
ATV:	Asia Television, a Hong Kong–based commercial television station.
ATVI:	Australia Television International, the original name of the satellite television channel of the ABC broadcasting to Southeast Asia, which now prefers to be known simply as Australia Television to differentiate it from the Hong Kong broadcaster immediately above. Now known as ABC Asia Pacific.
AWSJ:	*Asian Wall Street Journal*, regional edition of the finance/business newspaper.
Beam:	Signals from a satellite aimed at a particular area on the earth; broad beams covering almost a third of the earth's surface and spot beams focusing on a small area. See also "footprint".
BEMs:	Big emerging markets, a term used to characterise countries such as India, Brazil, China, Poland, etc. which have belatedly adopted free-market policies and are anticipated to be significant engines of economic growth in their regions.
Bollywood:	Colloquialism for the prodigious Indian movie industry based in Mumbai. The term is a condensation of "Bombay–Hollywood".
BPS:	Acronym in Bahasa Indonesia for the Central Bureau of Statistics (Biro Pusat Statistik), which conducts census.
Broadband cable:	Usually in the form of fiber optics technology which can carry multiple communications and high speed, including television, telephony, video-on-demand, e-commerce and the Internet, and thus enabling bi-directionality and interactivity between service provider and consumer.
Cable television:	A system of delivering television channels from a number of terrestrial or satellite sources via underground or overhead cable to subscriber homes.
Canto-pop:	Popular or rock music composed in or translated into Cantonese from English, though often used generically of pop music in other Chinese dialects.

CATV:	Traditionally standing for "community access television" but currently used to refer to any cable-delivered television.
C-band:	A frequency band, around 4–6 Ghz, allocated for the transmission of satellite signals, but prone to interference from other terrestrial services using microwave transmission.
CCTV:	China Central Television, the central government-owned network in PRChina which broadcasts nationwide and increasingly regionally.
CEO:	Chief executive officer of an organisation or corporation, though in Asia variously called managing director, president-director, general manager or president.
CETV:	China Entertainment Television, a commercial satellite broadcaster based in Hong Kong noted for its "no sex, no violence, no news" programming policy to gain acceptance with authorities in the People's Republic of China.
Channel providers:	Often cable systems which compile channels for their subscribers out of other terrestrial and satellite channels, domestic or transnational, and from programme providers.
CNN:	Cable News Network, a global news network established by the US-based Turner Broadcasting Network which has since merged with the AOL (America Online) Time Warner media conglomerate.
Critical theory:	Political economy perspective exemplified by the thinkers of the "Frankfurt School" pre-World War II.
Crore:	Ten million (or one hundred lakhs), often used in India, usually to quantify money in rupees without having to string together numerous zeros.
CTN:	An all-Chinese all-news satellite service headquartered in Hong Kong, owned by interests there and in Taiwan, and serving the whole Greater China region.
CTS:	China Television Service, a Taiwanese terrestrial broadcaster owned by the Taiwan ROC army.
CTV:	China Television Company, a Taiwanese terrestrial broadcaster owned by the ruling KMT party.

Cultural imperialism:	Often subtle imposition of a culture by a dominant economic and political power on other nations in support of its interests.
DBS, DTH or DTU:	Direct broadcast satellites, direct-to-home or direct-to-you satellite transmissions for which homes need use only a small satellite dish to receive the television signal and not have to go through a cable/MMDS service.
DD:	Doordarshan, the Indian public television broadcaster which accepts advertising.
DD-ARU:	Audience Research Unit of Doordarshan, which monitors broadcasting and advertising in India.
Developed countries/ economies:	*See* First World
Developing countries/ economies:	*See* Third World
Digital cable:	Often an optional service by broadcasters that encodes transmission to produce better reception of sound and pictures, arguably of "CD quality" or "cinema quality".
Digital compression:	Technology using binary numbers to convey information; in satellite television it enables transmission of multiple channels from a single transponder with improved sound and picture quality and interactive services.
Downlink:	Process of obtaining television signals transmitted from a satellite transponder via its beam.
DPI:	Acronym in Bahasa Indonesia for the Ministry of Information (Departemen Penerangan Indonesia), which regulates broadcasting.
E-commerce:	The marketing and sales of products and services via the World Wide Web or Internet either as a supplementary channel to a "bricks-and-mortar" business or solely as a "clicks-and-views" one.
Encryption:	Scrambling of television signals to allow reception only by paying subscribers using a decoder.
EL-TV:	An Indian pay-TV channel available via satellite, a joint venture of ZeeTV and its affiliate StarTV.
ESPN:	Entertainment and Sports Program Network, a US-based satellite channel now in strategic alliance with StarTV in Asia.
EU:	European Union, a regional economic and political union comprising countries of Western

Europe and increasingly some of the transitional economies of Eastern Europe; previously known as the European Community (EC) and European Common Market (ECM).

FEER: *Far East Economic Review*, a leading political and business newsmagazine in East Asia, comparable to *The Economist*.

First World: Refers to the industrialised economies or developed countries of North America, Western Europe, Australasia and often Japan; sometimes collectively, if inaccurately, referred to as the "North" or "West".

Footprint: The area on the earth's surface covered by signals from one or more beams from the satellite's transponder.

Fibre optic cable: A fine glass fibre through which digitally-encoded laser light is passed, capable for carrying about 10 times the capacity of the older coaxial cable.

G8: Group of Eight comprising the US, Canada, the UK, France, Germany, Italy, Japan and more recently Russia, which represents two-thirds of the world economy.

GATT: General Agreement on Tariffs and Trade, which governed international trade through rounds of negotiation; superseded by the World Trade Organisation (WTO).

Geostationary orbit: A satellite placed at 35,800 km about the equator, a region known as the Clarke Belt, would have an orbital speed equal to that of the world's rotation. Hence it is also known as geosynchronous orbit, though satellites need occasional assistance from rocket propulsion to remain perfectly stationary.

GIO: Government Information Office in Taiwan/ROC, which regulates broadcasting.

HBO: Home Box Office, a US-owned channel offering largely Hollywood movies on satellite/cable television via subscription.

HDTV: High-definition television using digital technology to provide better resolution and picture clarity.

Head-end: A central facility where television signals from diverse sources are received, processed, often encrypted and even converted into new channels for re-transmission by local cable networks.

HK:	Common acronym for Hong Kong, the British colony returned to China's sovereignty in 1997 and now a Special Administrative Region (SAR) of the PRC under the "one country, two systems" political–economic policy.
HK$:	The Hong Kong dollar; pegged at about HK$8 to the US$, and hence relatively stable.
Homes passed:	All the homes in the community that are passed by the cable network and could conceivably connect to it on subscription.
HTA:	Hindustan Thompson Advertising, the Indian affiliate of the international advertisement agency J Walter Thompson (JWT). In the early 2000s, after five decades, it reverted to using the latter name reflecting the greater acceptability of MNCs in India currently.
Hybridity:	Characteristic of new composite cultures formed out of the fusion of two different cultures, often one "Western/Occidental" and the other "Eastern/Oriental".
IGOs:	Intergovernmental organisations, which include Intelsat, the UN and its agencies, WTO, NATO, ASEAN and so on.
IMF:	International Monetary Fund, closely affiliated to the World Bank, and both funded largely by the US and to a lesser extent other western governments.
IMRB:	Indian Media Research Bureau, which compiles television ratings in India, now affiliated with the global media/market research firm AC Nielsen.
Intelsat:	International Telecommunication Satellite Organisation, a consortium of governments to share satellite technology, which makes transponders on its own satellites available to developing countries on concessionary terms.
Interactive services:	Enables subscribers to use the television to shop, bank, make travel arrangements, play games, etc., independently or in conjunction with television programmes.
ITU:	International Telecommunications Union, regulatory body for transborder telecommunications, whether terrestrial or satellite, which seeks to allocate orbital slots on a national basis equitably without regard to each nation's ability to utilise the slots immediately.

JSkyB:	It all started when British Satellite Broadcasting (BSB) got taken over by Sky Television (of Rupert Murdoch's News Corporation) and was christened BSkyB. Ever since, any of its operations abroad follow the same nomenclature, i.e., J for Japan, I for India.
JWT:	A major US-based international advertising agency operating in Asia, now part of the British-owned mega-agency group WPP (originally standing for Wire and Paper Products, which was its original business—including making supermarket carts—long before it started acquiring prestigious advertising firms. So you can see why they never spell it out!).
Ku-band:	A frequency band, around 11–15 Ghz, allocated for the transmission of satellite signals potentially direct-to-home, and free of interference from microwave transmissions but reception is affected by weather such as rain.
Lakh:	One hundred thousand, often used in India to quantify currency in rupees.
LDCs:	Less/Least Developed Countries, sometimes used as a synonym for developing or Third World countries in general, but usually to refer to a subset of them which have been even slower at achieving social and economic development.
MIB:	Ministry of Information and Broadcasting, India which regulates telecommunications and broadcasting, including cable and satellite television.
Microwave transmission:	High-capacity signals utilised for terrestrial re-transmission of television broadcasts.
MMDS:	Multichannel Multipoint Distribution System, a cable or microwave system transmitting TV channels to households within a limited area.
MNCs:	Multinational corporations or businesses whose operations span a number of countries; sometimes referred to by the UN as transnational corporations (TNCs) or by others as global corporations though these terms are not strictly synonymous.
MRFT:	Ministry of Radio, Film and Television in China, which regulates broadcasting, subsequently renamed SARFT.
MSO:	Multiple System Operator, a company owning more than one cable system and providing hardware,

channels, programme production, internet services, VOD, etc. (Also multi-service operators—see http://www.auditmypc.com/acronym/MSO.asp.)

NAM:

Non-Aligned Movement, a group of Third World nations which sought to be independent of the parties in the Cold War, particularly the US and USSR; not to be confused with American colloquial abbreviation of Vietnam.

News Corporation:

One of the leading global media conglomerates, controlled by the family of Rupert Murdoch; Australian-based but involved in the media industry on most continents.

NGOs:

Non-governmental organisations, which include worldwide bodies such as Greenpeace, International Red Cross, Amnesty International, Medecins Sans Frontieres, Intermediate Technology Group, World Wide Fund for Nature and the like.

NICs:

Newly-industrialising Countries or a subset of developing/Third World countries that have been successful at achieving rapid economic development, those in East Asia also referred to as "Tiger Economies".

NICAM:

Near Instantaneously Compounded Audio Multiplex, an innovation allowing television viewers choice of multi-lingual sound tracks in digital stereo.

NIEO:

New International Economic Order, proposed by Third World countries under the auspices of UNCTAD and the UN, and largely ignored by the First World in favour of GATT and the WTO.

NT:

New Taiwan dollar; at the time of the research fieldwork in the 1990s worth about NT27 to the US$.

NTSC:

The US colour transmission standard used in a number of countries, disparaging called "Never The Same Colour" by those who prefer the technically superior European PAL standard.

NWICO:

New World Information and Communication Order, proposed by Third World countries under the auspices of UNESCO and the UN in the 1970s and 1980s.

O&M:	Ogilvy & Mather, a leading MNC advertising agency with offices throughout Asia, now part of the mega-agency group WPP.
OECD:	Organisation for Economic Cooperation and Development, comprised mostly of developed countries and some transitional economies that are committed to democratic government and free-market economics.
Orbits:	Satellites may be placed in equatorial, polar or inclined paths around the earth, and their orbits could also be either circular or elliptical
Orbital slot:	Point in the Clarke Belt above the equator where geostationary satellites are "parked" and designated by geographical coordinates relative to the earth.
PAL:	A superior colour transmission system developed in Germany and the standard for television in most of Western Europe, Latin America and Asia.
Pay-TV:	Cable or satellite channels offered to households or businesses for a subscription fee; usually providing superior programming to that available free-to-air and without interruptions by ad breaks.
Political economy:	Theoretical stance that is a critique of the ownership and organisation of the economy, including the media-communications industry, drawing from its Marxist roots.
Postmodernity:	The fluid, fragmented social condition currently in the developed world characterised by lack of objective standards and overarching structures, affecting all forms of culture from art, literature, music, architecture and media.
Programme providers:	Often film/video production houses and sometimes media brokers who trade programming to television channels in return for advertising time.
PRC:	People's Republic of China, communist-led nation of mainland China.
PPPI:	Acronym in Bahasa Indonesia for the Indonesian Association of Advertising Agencies, which produces comprehensive data on advertising and media.
Region:	Used in this book to refer to parts of the continent of Asia, such as South Asia, Greater China, West Asia and Malay Archipelago.

Rmb: Renminbi, the PRC currency; at the time of research fieldwork in the 1990s worth about Rmb 8 to the US$.

RCTI: Rajawali Citra Televisi Indonesia, a dominant Indonesian commercial domestic broadcaster.

ROC: Republic of China, the anti-communist government of China pre-1947; and then in exile, based in Taiwan, though claiming sovereignty over mainland China as well till the 1980s.

Rp.:   Rupiah, the Indonesian currency; at the time of the research fieldwork in the mid-1990s worth about Rp. 2,200 to the US$, but by the early 2000s, worth about Rp. 8,000 and fluctuating.

Rs: Rupees, the Indian currency; at the time of the research fieldwork in the 1990s worth about Rs 35–40 to the US$.

RTM: Radio Television Malaysia, the Malaysian public broadcaster of radio and television, which accepts advertising.

SARFT: State Administration of Radio, Film and Television in China (PRC), which regulates broadcasting, formerly MRFT.

Satellite: An artificial object placed in space and moving in orbit around a planet relaying telecommunications and television signals.

Satellite dishes: Dish-shaped antennae which can receive television signals from satellites but not transmit them; known variously as satellite dishes, TVRO (TV receive-only) antennae, parabolic antennae, and simply parabolas (in Indonesia).

Satellite television: Transmission of television programming via the use of satellites which may be directed either primarily at a domestic market or a transnational one.

SCMP: *South China Morning Post*, a respected English-language newspaper published in Hong Kong.

SCTV: Surya Citra TeleVisi, the second Indonesian commercial television domestic broadcaster to be established, possibly still the second or third largest.

SECAM: French improvement on the NTSC colour broadcasting system, used largely in Eastern Europe, Francophone Africa and the CIS (ex-USSR).

Second World: Usually refers to the former planned economies of the USSR and Eastern Europe and often included their satellites such as Cuba, Angola and Vietnam. Previously collectively referred to as the "Eastern Bloc" or "East" in contrast to the "West". See also Transitional Economies.

SMATV:
Satellite master antennae television systems, where one TVRO dish feeds a number of television sets inside an apartment block, office building or hotel.

Smart card:
A key that allows only authorised subscribers to unscramble encrypted pay-TV television signals.

SonyET:
Sony Entertainment Television, a joint venture between Sony Corporation and Indian interests to provide satellite television, mainly for South Asia though also for diasporic and expatriate Indians abroad.

SRG:
Survey Research Group, a leading research company in Asia subsequently taken over by ACNielsen, which specialised in media and marketing research, known then in each country as SRI (Indonesia), SRH (Hong Kong) and SRT (Taiwan).

StarTV:
Strictly an acronym for Satellite Television Asia Region but used as a brand name for the pioneering transnational satellite television broadcaster in Asia.

Subregion:
Used in this book to refer to parts of a country such as southern India, the Cantonese-speaking areas of China, and peninsular Malaysia, i.e. subnational regions.

SunTV:
A commercial television service via satellite in Tamil serving the dominant ethnic group of the southern Indian state of Tamil Nadu as well as migrants from there in Southeast Asia. (Confusingly, there is a more recent broadcaster of identical name in Northeast Asia but it is not featured in this book.)

TELA:
Television and Entertainment Licensing Authority, which regulates domestic and transnational broadcasts originating in the territory of Hong Kong.

Third World:
Usually refers to developing countries/economies which were former colonies of European powers in Asia, Africa and Latin America; sometimes col-

	lectively, if inaccurately (geographically) referred to as the "South".
TPI:	Television Pendidikan Indonesia, or Indonesian Educational Television, a quasi-commercial station.
Transnational or trans-border television:	Television signals which deliberately cross national tional boundaries, usually through the use of satellite technology.
Transitional countries/ economies:	Formerly communist/socialist planned economies, mostly in Eastern Europe, now seeking full membership in the capitalist world economy and regional organisations like the EU through marketisation/privatisation. See also Second World.
Transponder:	Equipment on a satellite which receives and transmits a television or other telecommunication signal (made up from the words "transmitter" and "responder").
TTV:	Taiwan Television, a terrestrial broadcaster owned by the Taiwan provincial government.
TV3:	The dominant commercial television broadcaster in Malaysia, known locally in the Malay-Indonesian language as "TV Tiga".
TVB:	Television Broadcasters Ltd, a major Hong Kong–based television broadcaster and programme producer, operating internationally as TVBI.
TVBS:	TVB's Superchannel, a transnational satellite television service in Mandarin to Greater China and more recently to diasporic communities of ethnic Chinese elsewhere.
TVRI:	The Indonesian public broadcaster, which does not accept advertising but "taxes" advertising income of the commercial broadcasters.
TVRs:	Television Rating points, sometimes referred to by the acronym TRPs.
TVRO:	TV Receive-Only, describing satellite dishes which can receive television signals but not transmit them; a.k.a. parabolic antennae.
TVNZ:	Television New Zealand, previously a public broadcaster, now privatised and active in Pacific Islands television markets.
UNESCO:	United Nations Educational, Scientific and Cultural Organisation, an intergovernment body responsible for issues of culture and media, among other social, scientific and educational matters.

It has a general mandate to enhance global communication flows among nations, and funds "communications development" projects to increase the communications capacity of developing countries.

Uplink: Process of transmitting television signals from earth to a satellite, usually through large uplink centres though increasingly possible from small mobile equipment.

UTV: An Indian programme production house, subsequently part-owned by News Corporation and since then expanding operations to other Asian countries.

VoD: Video-on-demand, a cable television system which allows subscribers to select programming to watch at their own time on a pay-per-view basis; also known as interactive cable.

WTO: World Trade Organisation, successor organisation to the GATT, following the successful completion of its final Uruguay Round; headquartered in Singapore.

WWW or World Wide Web: Often used synonymously with "Internet" of or which it is the part that allows communication via text, graphics, audio and video.

ZeeTV: A pioneer transnational satellite broadcaster in Hindi, first targeted at India and subsequently diversified into other South Asian dialects/languages and diasporic/expatriate markets.

BIBLIOGRAPHY

Adorno, Theodor W. (1969). "Scientific Experiences of a European Scholar in America", in P.F. Lazarsfeld and F.N. Stanton (eds), *The Intellectual Migration: Europe and America, 1930–1960*. Cambridge, MA: Harvard University Press.

Albarran, Alan B. and Sylvia M. Chan-Olmsted (1998). *Global Media Economics*. Ames: Iowa State University Press.

Alden, Dana L., Jan-Benedict E.M. Steenkamp and Rajeev Batra (1999). "Brand Positioning through Advertising in Asia, North America and Europe: The Role of Global Consumer Culture", *Journal of Marketing*, 63, January.

Ali, Owais Aslam and Shelton A. Gunaratne (2000). "Pakistan", in Shelton A. Gunaratne (ed.), *Handbook of the Media in Asia*. New Delhi: Sage Publications.

Altheide, David (1984). "Media Hegemony: A Failure of Perspective", *Public Opinion Quarterly*, 48.

Anderson, Michael H. (1984). *Madison Avenue in Asia: Politics and Transnational Advertising*. Cranbury, NJ: Associated University Presses.

Ayish, Muhammad (1992). "International Communication in the 1990s: Implications for the Third World", *International Affairs*, 68 (3).

Bagdikian, Ben H. (2000). *The Media Monopoly*. Boston: Beacon Press.

Baldwin, Thomas F., D. Stevens McVoy and Charles Steinfeld (1996). *Convergence: Integrating Media, Information, and Communication*. Thousand Oaks: Sage Publications.

Ball-Rokeach, Sandra (1982). "Toward an Integrated Model of Mass Media Effects", in Melvin de Fleur and Sandra Ball-Rokeach (eds), *Theories of Mass Communication* (4th edn). New York: Longman.

Barker, Chris (1997). *Global Television: An Introduction*. Oxford: Blackwell.

Baudrillard, Jean (1988). "The Masses: The Implosion of the Social in the Media", in Mark Poster (ed.), *Selected Writings*. Stanford: Stanford University Press.

Belk, Russell and Richard Pollay (1985). "Materialism and Status Appeals in Japanese and US Print Advertising", *International Marketing Review*, 2 (12), Winter.

Berwanger, Dietrich (1987). *Television in the Third World: New Technologies and Social Change*. Bonn: Friedrich-Ebert-Stiftung.

Bhatt, S.C. (1994). *Satellite Invasion of India*. New Delhi: Gyan Publishing House.

Bhuiyan, Serajul I. and Shelton A. Gunaratne (2000). "Bangladesh", in Shelton A. Gunaratne (ed.), *Handbook of the Media in Asia*. New Delhi: Sage Publications.

Bishop, Robert L. (1989). *Qi Lai! Mobilising One Billion Chinese: The Chinese Communication System*. Ames: Iowa State University Press.

Blumler, J.G. and Elihu Katz (eds) (1974). *The Uses of Mass Communications*. Beverly Hills and London: Sage Publications.

Boddewyn, Jean J. (1998). "The One and Many Worlds of Advertising: Regulatory Obstacles and Opportunities", *International Journal of Advertising*, 7.

Bourgery, Marc and George Guimaraes (1993). "Global ads", *The Journal of European Business*, May/June.

Boyd-Barrett, Oliver (1995). "The Political Economy Approach", in Oliver Boyd-Barrett and Chris Newbold (eds), *Approaches to Media: A Reader*. London: Arnold.

Brierley, Sean (1995). *The Advertising Handbook* (Media Practice Series: James Curran, ed.). London and New York: Routledge.

Brosius, Christiane and Melissa Butcher (1999). *Image Journeys: Audio-Visual Media and Cultural Change in India*. New Delhi: Sage Publications.

Browne, Donald (1999). *Electronic Media and Industrialized Nations: A Comparative Study*. Ames: Iowa State University Press.

Bush, Alan J. and Victoria D. Bush (2000). "Potential Challenges the Internet Brings to the Agency–Advertiser Relationship", *Journal of Advertising Research*, 40 (4).

Butcher, Melissa (2003). *Transnational Television, Cultural Identity and Change: When STAR Came to India*. New Delhi: Sage Publications.

Callahan, Francis (1985). "Advertising and Economic Development", *Media Asia*, 12 (3): 151–56.

Chan, Joseph Man (1994). "National Responses and Accessibility to StarTV in Asia", *Journal of Communication*, 44 (3), Summer.

Chan-Olmsted, Sylvia M. and Yungwook Kim (2001). "Perceptions of Branding among Television Station Managers: An Exploratory Analysis", *Journal of Broadcasting and Electronic Media*, 45 (1).

Chang, Chin-Hwa Flora (2000). "Multiculturalism and Television in Taiwan", in David French and Michael Richards (eds), *Television in Contemporary Asia*. New Delhi: Sage Publications.

Chang, Won-Ho (1989). *Mass Media in China: The History and the Future*. Ames: Iowa State University Press.

Chapman, Graham, Keval Kumar, Caroline Fraser and Ivor Gaber (1997). *Environmentalism and the Mass Media: The North–South Divide*. London: Routledge.

Chen, Ping-Hung (2004). "Transnational Cable Channels in the Taiwanese Market", *Gazette*, 66 (2).

Cheng, Hong and John C. Sweitzer (1996). "Cultural Values Reflected in Chinese and US Television Commercials", *Journal of Advertising Research*, May–June.

Ciochetto, Lynne (2001). "Outdoor Advertising and Social Change in Contemporary Russia", *Media International Australia*, 101, November.

Collins, Richard (1992). *Satellite Television in Western Europe* (Academia Research Monograph 1). London and Paris: John Libbey.

Collins, Richard, Nicolas Garnham and Gareth Locksley (1988). *The Economics of Television: The UK Case*. London: Sage Publications.

Comor, Edward A. (1994). "Introduction: The Global Political Economy of Communication and IPE", in Edward A. Comor (ed.), *The Global Political Economy of Communication: Hegemony, Telecommunication and the Information Economy*. London: MacMillan Press and NewYork: St Martin's Press.

Costa, Janeen Arnold and Gary J. Bamossy (eds) (1995). *Marketing in a Multicultural World: Ethnicity, Nationalism, and Cultural Identity*. Thousand Oaks: Sage Publications.

Cross, Mary (1996). "Reading Television Texts: The Postmodern Language of Advertising", in Mary Cross (ed.), *Advertising and Culture: Theoretical Perspectives*. Westport, CT: Praeger Publishers.

Cunningham, Stuart (1992). *Framing Culture: Criticism and Policy in Australia*. North Sydney: Allen and Unwin.

Cunningham, Stuart and Elizabeth Jacka (1996). *Australian Television and International Mediascapes*. Cambridge: Cambridge University Press.

Curran, James and Myung-Jin Park (2000). "Beyond Globalization Theory", in James Curran and Myung-Jin Park (eds), *De-Westernizing Media Studies*. London and New York: Routledge.

Daniel, Kate (ed.) (2003). *The SBS World Guide* (11th edn). Melbourne: Hardie Grant Books.

De Mooij, Marieke K. (1998). *Global Marketing and Advertising: Understanding Cultural Paradoxes*. Thousand Oaks: Sage Publications.

——— (2004). *Consumer Behavior and Culture: Consequences for Global Marketing and Advertising*. Thousand Oaks: Sage Publications.

De Mooij, Marieke K. and Warren Keegan (1991). *Advertising Worldwide*. London: Prentice-Hall.

Dimmick, J. and P. Coit (1982). "Levels of Analysis in Mass Media Decision-Making", *Communications Research*, 9 (1).

Dogan, Mattei and Dominique Pelassy (1990). *How to Compare Nations: Strategies in Comparative Politics* (2nd edn). Chatham, NJ: Chatham House Publishers.

Domzal, Teresa J. and Jerome B. Kernan (1993). "Mirror, Mirror: Some Postmodern Reflections on Global Advertising", *Journal of Advertising*, 22 (4).

During, Simon (1993). *The Cultural Studies Reader*. London and New York: Routledge.

Ellis, John (1990). "Broadcast TV as Cultural Form", in Tony Bennett (ed.), *Popular Fiction*. London: Routledge.

Ewing, Michael (2000). "The Asia Pacific Tigers", in John Philip Jones (ed.), *International Advertising: Realities and Myths*. Thousand Oaks: Sage Publications.

Farall, Niall and Jeryl Whitelock (1999). "Global and Satellite versus Local and Terrestrial: An Exploratory Study of Advertising within the UK", *International Journal of Advertising*, 18.

Ferguson, Douglas A. and Elizabeth M. Perse (2000). "The World Wide Web as a Functional Alternative to Television", *Journal of Broadcasting and Electronic Media*, 44: 155–74.

Ferguson, Marjorie (1993). "Globalisation of Cultural Industries: Myths and Realities", in Marcus Breen (ed.), *Cultural Industries: National Policies and Global Market* (Proceedings of a CIRCIT conference, 10 December 1992). Melbourne: Centre for International Research on Communications and Information Technologies.

Firat, A. Fuat and Alladi Venkatesh (1993). "Postmodernity: The Age of Marketing", *International Journal of Research in Marketing*, 10.

Fiske, John (1987). *Television Culture*. London and New York: Routledge.

Flew, Terry and Stuart Cunningham (2000). "Thank You Very Much and Good Luck: Media", in Christopher Sheil (ed.), *Globalisation: Australian Impacts*. Sydney: University of New South Wales Press.

Frederick, Howard H. (1993). *Global Communication and International Relations*. Belmont, CA: Wadsworth Publishing.

Frith, Katherine Toland (ed.) (1996). *Advertising in Asia: Communication, Culture and Consumption*. Ames: Iowa State University Press.

Frith, Katherine Toland and Barbara Mueller (2004). *Advertising and Society: Global Issues*. New York: Peter Lang.

Galtung, Johan (1999). "Prospects for Media Monitoring: Much Overdue, but Never too Late", in Kaarle Nordenstreng and Michel Griffin (eds), *International Media Monitoring*. Cresskill, NJ: Hampton Press.

Garay, Ronald (1988). *Cable Television: A Reference Guide to Information*. Westport: Greenwood Press.

Garnham, Nicholas (1990). *Capitalism and Communication: Global Culture and the Economics of Information*. London: Sage Publications.

Gerbner, George (1970). "Cultural Indicators: The Case of Violence in Television Drama", *Annals of the American Association of Political and Social Science*, 338.

Gerbner, George, Larry Gross, Michael Morgan and Nancy Signorelli (1980). "The 'Mainstreaming' of America: Violence Profile No. 11", *Journal of Communication*, 30 (3), Summer.

Ginsburg, Faye, Lila Abu-Lughod and Brian Larin (eds) (2002). *Media Worlds: Anthropology on New Terrain*. Berkeley, Los Angeles and London: University of California Press.

Glascock, Jack (1993). "Effect of Cable Television on Advertiser and Consumer Spending on Mass Media, 1978–1990", *Journalism Quarterly*, 70 (3).

Golding, Peter (1977). "Media Professionalism in the Third World: The Transfer of an Ideology", in James Curran, Michael Gurevitch and Janet Woollacott (eds), *Mass Communication and Society*. London: Edward Arnold (Publishers) Ltd./Open University Press.

Golding, Peter and Graham Murdock (1991). "Culture, Communications, and Political Economy", in James Curran and Michael Gurevitch (eds), *Mass Media and Society*. London: Edward Arnold.

Goldman, Robert (1992). *Reading Ads Socially*. London: Routledge.

Goonasekera, Anura and Duncan Holaday (eds) (1993). *Asian Communications Handbook*. Singapore: Asian Mass Media Information and Research Centre.

Goonasekera, Anura, Lee Chun Wah and S. Venkataraman (eds) (2003). *Asian Communications Handbook*. Singapore: Asian Mass Media Information and Research Centre, and Nanyang Technological University.

Goonasekera, Anura and Paul S.N. Lee (eds) (1998). *TV without Borders: Asia Speaks Out*. Singapore: Asian Mass Media Information and Research Centre.

Gould, Stephen J., Dawn B. Lerman and Andreas F. Grein (1999). "Agency Perceptions and Practices on Global IMC", *Journal of Advertising Research*, 39 (1).

Green, Robert T., William H. Cunningham and Isabella C.M. Cunningham (1978). "The Effectiveness of Standardised Global Advertising", *Journal of Advertising*, 4 (3).

Griffin, Em (1991). *A First Look at Communication Theory*. New York: McGraw-Hill.

Gunaratne, Shelton A. (ed.) (2000). *Handbook of the Media in Asia*. New Delhi: Sage Publications.

Gupta, Dipankar (2000). *Mistaken Modernity: India between Worlds*. Delhi: HarperCollins.

Gupta, Nilanjana (1998). *Switching Channels: Ideologies of Television in India*. Delhi: Oxford University Press.

Ha, Louisa (1997). "Limitations and Strengths of Pan-Asian Media: A Review for International Advertisers", *International Journal of Advertising*, 16.

Habermas, Jürgen (1989). *The Structural Transformation of the Public Sphere*. Cambridge, MA: Massachusetts Institute of Technology Press.

Hall, Stuart (1986). "Cultural Studies: Two Paradigms", in Richard Collins, James Curran, Nicholas Garnham, Paddy Scannell, Philip Schlesinger and Colin Sparks (eds), *Media, Culture and Society: A Critical Reader*. London: Sage Publications.

——— (1990). "Encoding, Decoding", in *Culture, Media and Language*. London: Unwin Hyman.

Hamelink, Cees (1983). *Cultural Autonomy in Global Communications*. New York: Longmans.

Hao, Xiaoming and Yu Huang (1996). "The Commercialization of China's Broadcasting Media: Causes and Consequences". Paper Presented at the Asian Media Information and Communication Conference, Singapore, July.

Harding, Harry (1993). "The Concept of 'Greater China': Themes, Variations and Reservations", *The China Quarterly*, 136.

Harrison, Lawrence E. (2000). "Promoting Progressive Cultural Change", in Lawrence E. Harrison and Samuel P. Harrington (eds), *Culture Matters: How Values Shape Human Progress*. New York: Basic Books.

Hashim, Rahmah (1997). "At the Crossroads of Terrestrial and ET: Whither Malaysian TV Broadcasting?", *Asian Journal of Communication*, 7 (2).

Hebdige, Dick (1989). "After the Masses", in Stuart Hall and Martin Jacques (eds), *New Times: The Changing Face of Politics in the 1990s*. London: Lawrence and Wishart in Association with Marxism Today.

Herman, Edward S. and Noam Chomsky (1988). *Manufacturing Consent: The Political Economy of the Mass Media*. New York: Pantheon Books.

Herman, Edward S. and Robert W. McChesney (1998). *The Global Media: The New Missionaries of Corporate Capitalism*. London and Washington: Cassell.

Hill, Charles (2003). *International Business: Competing in the Global Marketplace* (4th edn). Burr Ridge, IL: Irwin.

Hill, John and William James (1991). "Product and Promotion Transfers in Consumer Goods Multinationals", *International Marketing Review*, 8 (2).

Hoskins, Colin, Stuart McFadyen and Adam Finn (1997). *Global Television and Film: An Introduction to the Economics of the Business*. Oxford: Clarendon Press.

Howard, Donald and John Ryans (1988–89). "The Probable Effect of Satellite TV on Agency/Client Relationships", *Journal of Advertising Research*, 28 (6), December/January.

Huntington, Samuel (1998). "The Coming Clash of Civilizations or, the West against the Rest", *The Global Agenda: Issues and Perspectives*. Boston: McGraw-Hill.

Initiative Media Indonesia (1999). *Media Facts Indonesia 1999*. Jakarta: Initiative Media Indonesia/Lowe Lintas.

Jain, Subhash C. (1989). "Standardization of International Marketing Strategy: Some Research Hypotheses", *Journal of Marketing*, 53, January.

James, Jeffrey (1983). *Consumer Choice in the Third World*. London and Basingstoke: MacMillan Press.

Janus, Noreene (1981). "Advertising and the Mass Media in the Era of Global Corporation", in Emile McAnany, Noreene Janus and Jorge Schnitman (eds), *Communication and Social Structure: Critical Studies in Mass Media Research*. New York: Praeger Publishers.

Jhally, Sut (1987). *The Codes of Advertising: Fetishism and the Political Economy of Meaning in the Consumer Society*. New York and London: Routledge.

Johnson, Kirk (2000). *Television and Social Change in Rural India*. New Delhi: Sage Publications.

Joy, Annamma and Christopher A. Ross (1989). "Marketing and Development in Third World Contexts: An Evaluation and Future Directions", *Journal of Macromarketing*, 18, Fall.

Jun, Young-Woo and Hyun Kim (1995). "Direct Broadcast Satellite in Asia and Advertising Opportunity for International Marketers", *Media Asia*, 22 (1).

Kale, Sudhir H. (1991). "Culture-specific Marketing Communications: An Analytic Approach", *International Marketing Review*, 8 (2).

Kanso, Ali (1992). "International Advertising Strategies: Global Commitment to Local Vision", *Journal of Advertising Research*, January/February.

Kanso, Ali and Richard Alan Nelson (2002). "Advertising Localization Overshadows Standardization", *Journal of Advertising Research*, January/February.

Kaplan, E. Ann (1987). *Rocking around the Clock: Music Television, Postmodernism, and Consumer Culture*. New York and London: Methuen.

Karthigesu, R. (1994). "Broadcasting Deregulation in Developing Asian Nations: An Examination of Nascent Tendencies Using Malaysia as a Case Study", *Media, Culture and Society*, 16.

Katz, Elihu (1987). "Communications Research since Lazarsfeld", *Public Opinion Quarterly*, 51.

Katz, Elihu and Paul F. Lazarsfeld (1955). *Personal Influence: The Part Played by People in the Flow of Mass Communications*. New York: Free Press.

Kaynak, Erdener (1989). *The Management of International Advertising: A Handbook and Guide for Professionals*. New York, Westport CN and London: Quorum Books.

Kaynak, Erdener and Pervez Ghauri (1986). "A Comparative Analysis of Advertising Practices in Unlike Environments: A Study of Agency–Client Relationships", *International Journal of Advertising*, 5: 121–46.

Keane, Michael (2003). "Civil Society, Regulatory Space and Cultural Authority in China's Television Industry", in Philip Kitley (ed.), *Television, Regulation and Civil Society in Asia*. London and New York: RoutledgeCurzon.

Kelly, Sean (1979). "UNESCO, Mexico and the Third World Complaint", in Dante Fascell and David M. Abshire (eds), *International News: Freedom under Attack*. Beverly Hills: Sage Publications.

Kemper, Steven (2001). *Buying and Believing: Sri Lankan Advertising and Consumers in a Transnational World*. Chicago and London: University of Chicago Press.

Kim, Kwangi Ko (1995). "Spreading the Net: The Consolidation Process of Large Transnational Advertising Agencies in the 1980s and Early 1990s", *International Journal of Advertising*, 14.

Kinnear, Thomas C. and James R. Taylor (1996). *Marketing Research: An Applied Approach* (5th edn). New York: McGraw-Hill.

Kitley, Philip (1994). "Fine-tuning Control: Commercial Television in Indonesia", *Continuum: Australian Journal of Media and Culture*, 8 (2).

———(2003). "Civil Society in Charge?: Television and the Public Sphere in Indonesia after Reformasi", in Philip Kitley (ed.), *Television, Regulation and Civil Society in Asia*. London and New York: RoutledgeCurzon.

Klein, Naomi (2001). *No Logo*. London: HarperCollins/Flamingo.

Kleinwachter, Wolfgang (1993). "Three Waves of the Debate", in George Gerbner, Hamid Mowlana and Kaarle Nordenstreng (eds), *The Global Media Debate: Its Rise, Fall and Renewal*. Norwood, NJ: Ablex Publishing.

Kline, Stephen (1988). "The Theatre of Consumption: On Comparing American and Japanese Advertising", *Canadian Journal of Political and Social Theory*, 12 (3), Fall.

Kohli, Vanita (2003). *The Indian Media Business*. New Delhi: Response Books.

Kottak, Conrad (1991). "Television's Impact on Values and Local Life in Brazil", *Journal of Communication*, 41 (1).

Kubey, Robert and Mihaly Csikszentmihalyi (1990). *Television and the Quality of Life: How Viewing Shapes Everyday Experience*. Hillsdale, NJ: Lawrence Erlbaum.

Kumar, Keval J. (1989). *Mass Communication in India*. Bombay: Jaico Publishing House.

Lee Chin-Chuan (1980). *Media Imperialism Reconsidered: The Homogenising of Television Culture*. Beverly Hills: Sage Publications.

Lee, Wei-Chin (ed.) (1990). *Taiwan* (World Bibliographical Series, 13). Oxford: Clio Press.

Levitt, Theodore (1983). "The Globalization of Markets", *Harvard Business Review*, May–June; and in *The Marketing Imagination*. New York: MacMillan.

Lewis, Justin (1991). *The Ideological Octopus: An Exploration of Television and its Audience*. New York and London: Routledge.

Liebes, Tamar and Elihu Katz (1990). *The Export of Meaning: Cross Cultural Readings of "Dallas"*. New York: Oxford University Press.

Liu, Jeanne (2001). "Advertising in Taiwan", in Ingomar Kloss (ed.), *Advertising Worldwide: Advertising Conditions in Selected Countries*. Berlin/Heidelberg: Springer.

Lo Ven Hwei, Chen Jei-Cheng and Lee Chin-Chuan (1994). "Television News in Government News in Taiwan: Patterns of Television News Sources Selection and Presentation", *Asian Journal of Communication*, 4 (1).

Lovelock, Peter and Charles Goddard (1999). "Hong Kong's Television Policy in an Age of Convergence", in Venkat Iyer (ed.), *Media Regulations for the New Times*. Singapore: Asian Media Information and Communication Centre.

Lowe, Vincent and Jaafar Kamin (1982). *TV Programme Management in a Plural Society*. Singapore: Asian Mass Communication Research and Information Centre.

MacBride, Sean and Colleen Roach (1993). "The New International Information Order", in George Gerbner, Hamid Mowlana and Kaarle Nordenstreng (eds), *The Global Media Debate: Its Rise, Fall and Renewal*. Norwood, NJ: Ablex Publishing.

Mattelart, Armand (1983). *Transnationals and the Third World: The Struggle for Culture*. Massachusetts: Bergin & Garvey Publishers, Inc.

——— (1991). *Advertising International: The Privatisation of Public Space*. London: Routledge.

Maxwell, Richard (1997). "International Communication: The Control of Difference and the Global Market", in Ali Mohammadi (ed.), *International Communication and Globalization: A Critical Introduction*. Thousand Oaks: Sage Publications.

Mazzarella, William (2003). *Shovelling Smoke: Advertising and Globalization in Contemporary India*. Durham and London: Duke University Press.

McAllister, Matthew P. (1996). *The Commercialization of American Culture: New Advertising, Control, and Democracy*. Thousand Oaks: Sage Publications.

McAllister, Mathew P. and Joseph Turow (2002). "New Media and the Commercial Sphere: Two Intersecting Trends, Five Categories of Concern", *Journal of Broadcasting & Electronic Media*, 46 (2).

McAnany, Emile G. and Kenton T. Wilkinson (1992). "From Cultural Imperialists to Takeover Victims? Questions on Hollywood's Buyouts from the Critical Tradition", *Communications Research*, 19 (6).

McChesney, Robert (1999). *Rich Media, Poor Democracy: Communication Politics in Dubious Times.* Urbana and Chicago: University of Illinois Press.

McGregor, James (2005). *One Billion Customers: Lessons from the Front Lines of Doing Business in China.* New York: Wall Street Journal Books/Free Press.

McQuail, Denis (1987). *Mass Communications Theory: An Introduction.* London: Sage Publications.

McQuail, Denis, Jay G. Blumler and J.R. Brown (1972). "The Television Audience: A Revised Perspective", in Denis McQuail (ed.), *Sociology of Mass Communication.* Harmondsworth: Penguin.

McQueen, Humphry (2001). *The Essence of Capitalism: The Origins of our Future.* Sydney: Sceptre/Hodder Headline.

Mehta, Arun and Venkat Iyer (1999). "Regulation in the New Media Environment: The Indian Experience", in Venkat Iyer (ed.), *Media Regulations for the New Times.* Singapore: Asian Media Information and Communications Centre.

Moores, Shaun (2000). *Media and Everyday Life in Modern Society.* Edinburgh: Edinburgh University Press.

Moran, Albert (1996). *Copycat TV: Globalisation, Program Formats and Cultural Identity.* Luton: University of Luton Press.

Moran, Albert and Michael Keane (2003). *Television across Asia: Television Industries, Programme Formats and Globalization.* London and New York: RoutledgeCurzon.

Morley, David (1980). *The "Nationwide" Audience.* London: British Film Institute.

Mosco, Vincent (1996). *The Political Economy of Communications.* London: Sage Publications.

Mowlana, Hamid (1996). *Global Communication in Transition: The End of Diversity?* Thousand Oaks: Sage Publications.

Mueller, Barbara (1996). *International Advertising: Communicating across Cultures.* Belmont: Wadsworth Publishing Co.

Murdock, Graham (1982). "Large Corporations and the Control of the Communications Industry", in Michael Gurevitch, Tony Bennett, James Curran and Janet Woollacott (eds), *Culture, Society and the Media.* London and New York: Routledge.

Nain, Zaharom and Mustafa K. Anuar (2000). "Marketing to the Masses in Malaysia: Commercial Television, Religion and Nation-Building", in David French and Michael Richards (eds), *Television in Contemporary Asia.* New Delhi: Sage Publications.

Napoli, Philip (2001). "The Audience Product and the New Media Environment: Implications for the Economics of Media Industries", *Journal of Media Management,* 3 (2).

Ndumbu, Abel (1991). "Africa", in Peter Larsen (ed.), *Import/Export: International Flow of Television Fiction.* Paris: UNESCO Press.

Nordenstreng, Kaarle (1999). "Toward Global Content Analysis and Media Criticism", in Kaarle Nordenstreng and Michael Griffin (eds), *International Media Monitoring* (International Communications Series: Richard Vincent, ed.). Creskill, NJ: Hampton Press.

Nordenstreng, Kaarle and Herbert Schiller (eds) (1979). *National Sovereignty and International Communication.* Norwood: Ablex Publishing Corporation.

Nordenstreng, Kaarle and Tapio Varis (1974). *Television Traffic: A One-Way Street?*, Reports and Papers on Mass Communication, 70. Paris: UNESCO.

Onkvisit, Sak and John J. Shaw (1987). "Standardized International Advertising: A Review and Critical Evaluation of the Theoretical and Empirical Evidence", *Columbia Journal of World Business*, 22 (3).

——— (1999). "Standardized International Advertising: Some Research Issues and Implications", *Journal of Advertising*, 39 (6).

Page, David and William Crawley (2001). *Satellites over South Asia: Broadcasting, Culture and the Public Interest*. New Delhi: Sage Publications.

Panjaitan, Hinca IP (2000). "The Impact of the Dissolution of the Department of Information on the Regulation of Broadcasting Media in Indonesia". Paper presented at the International Association of Mass Communication Research Conference, Singapore, July.

Pérez de Cuéllar, Javier (1995). *Our Creative Diversity: Report of the World Commission on Culture and Development*. Paris: UNESCO Publishing.

Perry, David K. (2002). *Theory and Research in Mass Communication: Contexts and Consequences* (2nd edn). Mahwah, NJ: Lawrence Erlbaum.

Pollay, Richard (1986). "Quality of Life in the Padded Sell: Common Criticisms of Advertising's Cultural Character and International Public Policies", *Current Issues and Research in Advertising*, 9 (2): 173–250.

Postman, Neil (1985). *Amusing Ourselves to Death: Public Discourse in the Age of Show Business*. New York: Viking Penguin.

Price, Monroe (1998). "Conclusion", in Monroe Price and Stefaan Verhulst (eds), *Broadcasting Reform in India*. Delhi: Oxford University Press.

Ramaprasad, Jyotika and Kazumi Hasegawa (1992). "Creative Strategies in American and Japanese TV Commercials: A Comparison", *Journal of Advertising Research*, 32 (1), January/February.

Reeves, Geoffrey (1993). *Communications and the "Third World"*. London: Routledge.

Reis, Raul (1999). "What Prevents Cable TV from Taking Off in Brazil?", *Journal of Broadcasting and Electronic Media*, 43 (3), Summer.

Ritzer, George (1996). *The McDonaldization of Society: An Investigation into the Changing Character of Contemporary Life*. Thousand Oaks: Pine Forge Press.

Roach, Colleen (1987). "The US Position on the New World Information and Communication Order". *The Journal of Communication*, 37 (4).

Rogers, Everett M. (1962). *The Diffusion of Innovations*. New York: Free Press.

Safar, H.M. and Yussof Ladi (2000). "Brunei Darussalam", in Shelton A. Gunaratne (ed.), *Handbook of the Media in Asia*. New Delhi: Sage Publications.

Said, Edward (1994). *Culture and Imperialism*. London: Vintage Books.

Samiee, Saeed, Insik Jeong, Jae Hyeon Pae and Susan Tai (2003). "Advertising Standardization in Multinational Corporations: The Subsidiary Perspective", *Journal of Business Research*, 56.

SBS World Guide (1996). *The SBS World Guide* (5th edn). Port Melbourne: Reed Reference Australia/DW Thorpe.

Schiller, Herbert I. (1989). *Culture, Inc.: The Corporate Takeover of Public Expression*. New York: Oxford University Press.

Schiller, Herbert I. (1991). "Not Yet the Post-imperialist Era", *Critical Studies in Mass Communication*, 8.

Schudson, Michael (1984). *Advertising: The Uneasy Persuasion: Its Dubious Impact on American Society*. New York: Basic Books/HarperCollins.

Schultz, Don E. and Philip J. Kitchen (2000). *Communicating Globally: An Integrated Marketing Approach.* London: MacMillan Press and Chicago: NTC Business Books.

Sepstrup, Preben (1990). *Transnationalization of Television in Western Europe* (Acamedia Research Monograph 5). London, Paris and Rome: John Libbey & Co.

Sepstrup, Preben and Anura Goonasekera (1994). *TV Transnationalization: Europe and Asia.* Paris: UNESCO Publishing.

Severin, Werner J. and James W. Tankard (1992). *Communications Theories: Origins, Methods and Uses in the Mass Media* (3rd edn). New York and London: Longman.

Shao, Alan T. and John S. Hill (1994). "Global Television Advertising Restrictions: The Case of Socially Sensitive Products", *International Journal of Advertising*, 13.

Sinclair, John G. (1987). *Images Incorporated: Advertising as Industry and Ideology.* London: Routledge.

———— (1992). "The decentering of Cultural Imperialism: Televisa-ion and Globoization in the Latin World", in Elizabeth Jacka (ed.), *Continental Shift: Globalisation and Culture.* Double Bay: Local Consumption Publications.

———— (1994). Culture and Trade: Some Theoretical and Practical Considerations on "Cultural industries", Melbourne: Centre for International Research on Communications and Information Technologies.

Sinclair, John G., Elizabeth Jacka and Stuart Cunningham (eds) (1996). *New Patterns in Global Television: Peripheral Vision.* Oxford: Oxford University Press.

Sklair, Leslie (1991). *Sociology of the Global System.* New York: Harvester Wheatsheaf.

Skovmand, Michael and Kim Christian Schrøder (eds) (1992). *Media Cultures: Reappraising Transnational Media.* London and New York: Routledge.

Smythe, Dallas (1977). "Communications: Blindspot of Western Marxism", *Canadian Journal of Political and Social Theory*, 1 (3).

———— (1981). *Dependency Road: Communications, Capitalism, Consciousness and Canada.* Norwood, NJ: Ablex Publishing Corporation.

So, Clement, Joseph Man Chan and Chin-Chuan Lee (2000). "Hong Kong SAR (China)", in Shelton A. Gunaratne (ed.), *Handbook of the Media in Asia.* New Delhi: Sage Publications.

Speake, Jennifer (ed.) (1993). *The Hutchinson Dictionary of World History.* Oxford: Helicon Publishing.

Sreberny-Mohammadi, Annabelle, Dwayne Winseck, Jim McKenna and Oliver Boyd-Barrett (eds) (1997). *Media in Global Context: A Reader* (Foundations in Media series: Oliver Boyd-Barrett, ed.). London: Arnold.

Sriram, Ven and Pradeep Gopalakrishna (1991). "Can Advertising be Standardized among Similar Countries?: A Cluster-based Analysis". *International Journal of Advertising*, 10.

Straubhaar, Joseph D. (1990). "Context, Social Class, and VCRs: A World Comparison", in Julia R. Dobrow (ed.), *Social and Cultural Aspects of VCR Use.* Hillsdale, NJ: Lawrence Erlbaum.

Straubhaar, Joseph D. and Gloria M. Viscasillas (1991). "Class, Genre and the Regionalization of Television Programming in the Dominican Republic", *Journal of Communication*, 41 (1).

Sunderland, Patricia L. and Rita M. Denny (2003). "Psychology vs Anthropology: Where is Culture in Marketplace Ethnography?", in Timothy Dewaal Malefyt and Brian Moeran (eds), *Advertising Cultures.* Oxford and New York: Berg.

Svenkerud, Peer J., Rita L. Rahoi and Arvind Singhal (1995). "Incorporating Ambiguity and Archetypes in Entertainment-Education Programming: Lessons Learned from Oshin", *Gazette*, 55.

Tahir, S.N. (1996). "Television in Pakistan: An Overview", in David French and Michael Richards (eds), *Contemporary Television: Eastern Perspectives*. New Delhi: Sage Publications.

Tai, Susan (1997). "Advertising in Asia: Localize or Regionalize?", *International Journal of Advertising*, 16 (1).

Tharp, Marye and Linda M. Scott (1990). "The Role of Marketing Processes in Creating Cultural Meaning", *Journal of Macromarketing*, Fall.

Thomas, Amos Owen (2005). *Imagi-Nations and Borderless Television: Media, Culture and Politics Across Asia*. New Delhi: Sage Publications.

Thussu, Daya Kishan (1998). *Electronic Empires: Global Media and Local Resistance*. London: Arnold.

——— (2000). "The Hinglish Hegemony: The Impact of Western Television on Broadcasting in India", in David French and Michael Richards (eds), *Television in Contemporary Asia*. New Delhi: Sage Publications.

Tracey, Michael (1988). "Popular Culture and the Economics of Global Television", *Intermedia*, 16 (2), November.

Tunstall, Jeremy (1977). *The Media are American: Anglo-American Media in the World*. London: Constable.

——— (1991). "A Media Industry Perspective", in James A. Anderson (ed.), *Communication Yearbook*, 14. Newbury Park: Sage Publications.

Varis, Tapio (1988). "Trends in International Television Flow", in Cynthia Schneider and Brian Wallis (eds), *Global Television*. New York: Wedge Press; Cambridge, Massachusetts and London: The MIT Press.

Vasquez, Francisco J. (1983). "Media Economics in the Third World", in L. John Martin and Anju Chaudhary (eds), *Comparative Mass Media Systems*. New York: Longman.

Venkateswaran, K.S. (ed.) (1993). *Mass Media Laws and Regulations in India*. Singapore: Asian Mass Communication Research and Information Centre.

Vincent, Richard (1997). "The New World Information and Communication Order (NWICO) in the Context of the Information Superhighway", in M. Bailie and D. Winseck (eds), *Democratizing Communication? Comparative Perspectives on Information and Power*. Cresskill: Hampton Press.

Viswanath, K. and Li-Ren Benjamin Zeng (2002). "Transnational Advertising", in William B. Gudykunst and Bella Mody (eds), *Handbook of International and Intercultural Communication* (2nd edn). Thousand Oaks: Sage Publications.

Wallerstein, Immanuel (1979). *The Capitalist World Economy*. New York: Cambridge University Press.

Wang, Georgette (1993). "Satellite Television and the Future of Broadcast Television in the Asia Pacific". Paper presented at the "AMIC Conference on Communication, Technology and Development: Alternatives for Asia", Kuala Lumpur, Malaysia.

Wang, Georgette and Ven-Hwei Lo (2000). "Taiwan", in Shelton A. Gunaratne (ed.), *Handbook of the Media in Asia*. New Delhi: Sage Publications.

Waterman, David and Everett M. Rogers (1994). "The Economics of Television Program Production and Trade in Far East Asia", *Journal of Communication*, 44 (3), Summer.

Wei, Ran (2000). "China's Television in the Era of Marketisation", in David French and Michael Richards (eds), *Television in Contemporary Asia*. New Delhi: Sage Publications.

Wernick, Andrew (1991). *Promotional Culture: Advertising and Ideology in Late Capitalism.* London: Sage Publications.

West, Douglas C. (1996). "The Determinants and Consequences of Multinational Advertising Agencies", *International Journal of Advertising*, 15.

Williams, Raymond (1980). *Problems in Materialism and Culture.* London: Verso Editions and New Left Books.

Williamson, Judith (1978). *Decoding Advertisements: Ideology and Meaning in Advertising.* London: Marion Boyars.

Wilson, Helen (1988). "Communication as an Industry", in Gunther Kress (ed.), *Communication and Culture.* Kensington: New South Wales University Press.

Wilson, Tony (2000). "Media Convergence: Watching Television, Anticipating Going On-line", *Media Asia*, 27 (1).

Wind, Yorram (1986). "The Myth of Globalization", *The Journal of Consumer Marketing*, 3 (2), Spring.

Wober, Mallory and Barrie Gunter (1988). *Television and Social Control.* New York: St Martin's Press.

Yan, Li-Qun (2000). "China", in Shelton A. Gunaratne (ed.), *Handbook of the Media in Asia.* New Delhi: Sage Publications.

Yin, Jia-Fei (1999). "International Advertising Strategies in China: A Worldwide Survey of Foreign Advertisers", *Journal of Advertising Research*, November–December.

Zandpour, Fred, Veronica Campos, Joelle Catalano, Cypress Chang, Young Dae Cho, Renee Hoobyar, Shu-Fang Jiang, Man-Chi Lin, Stan Madrid, Holly Scheideler and Susan Titus Osborn (1994). "Global Reach and Local Touch: Achieving Cultural Fitness in TV Advertising", *Journal of Advertising Research*, 34 (5).

INDEX

ABN, 58
adspend: 128, 176; shift, 123, 130–33; transnational, 123–25, 132, 133, 135–36
advertising, advertisers: 15, 16–17, 18–19, 20, 21, 22, 25, 26, 27, 31, 71, 87, 103–10, 113–15, 144, 146, 147, 150, 152–55, 159–60, 163, 166, 169, 170–73, 176–77, 180, 184, 193, 197–98; business strategy, 105–106; creative execution, 136–43, 155; cultures, 191–96; expenditure, 37, 38, 123–25, 129–30; globalisation, 18–19, 22, 23, 41, 121, 136; impact, 38, 39–40, 42–43; management, 18, 110–11; —, Bombay-based, 111–15, 121; —, Hong Kong–based, 118–21; —, Jakarta-based, 115–17, 121; and marketing, 31–32; media alternatives, 154; press, 128; product categories, 153–54, 177; standardisation, 33, 36–38, 39, 41, 43; in the Third World, 39–41
advertising agencies: 22; Mumbai-based, 123–30, 136–39, 152, 155, 170; Hong Kong–based, 123, 132–36, 141–43, 153–55, 170; international, 26, 34–36, 38–39, 40, 43, 81, 121, 141, 152, 170; Jakarta-based, 123, 130–32, 139–41, 152, 154–55, 170; and market alignment, 112–13, 118–19; quasi aligned, 169–70
Africa, 19, 28, 30
All India Radio (AIR), 76
Anglo-Dutch Treaty (1824), 86

AOL Time Warner, 151, 163
ApStar, 49, 183
ASEAN, 82
Asia Television (ATV), 100
Asian Business News, 16
AsiaSat, 15, 24, 45, 51, 61, 63, 64, 67, 78, 79, 94, 175
Associated Press TV (APTV), 94
Astro, 88
ATN, 58
ATV, 69, 154
audience: 17–18, 20, 21, 24, 42, 45, 46, 70–71, 73, 114–15, 117, 129, 148, 149, 151, 163, 164, 165, 173, 175, 179, 190; active audience, 25, 190; research, 15
Australia Television, 49, 58

B4U, 54
Bangladesh: 72, 73, 115, 161; cable network, 149–50; geography and history, 79–80; local programmes, 151; spillover television, 149; television governance, 80–81
Bangladesh Awami League, 80
Bangladesh Television Corporation (BTV), 80–81
BBC World, 45, 46, 49–50, 55, 60, 68, 101, 106, 113, 138
BBDO, 35
Bengali (language), 73, 79, 81
Bhutan, 72, 73, 91
Bhutto, Benazir, 78
BMG Entertainment, 53
Bollywood, 159
Borneo, 63, 64, 82, 86, 88, 89
Boxer rebellion, 92

About the Author

Amos Owen Thomas is Associate Professor of International Business at the Maastricht School of Management. For the last 16 years, he has taught at five universities and colleges in the Netherlands, Australia, Papua New Guinea and Singapore, while researching in the Asia-Pacific region. In 14 energetic years prior to joining academia, he worked as a copywriting manager at MNC advertising agencies, a fledgling consultant to SMEs, a minion in national government and a gopher with NGOs in refugee relief and community services.

Delighted at being invited to, Dr Thomas has contributed chapters to edited works such as the *Encyclopedia of the Developing World* (2005), *Toward the Common Good: Perspectives in International Public Relations* (2004), *Television in Contemporary Asia* (Sage 2000), and *Marketing in the Third World* (1996). Much of his research has found its way into academic journals of varying pedigree including the *Journal of Global Marketing, Gazette, Journal of International Communications, Global Business Review* and *Journal of Marketing Communications*. Occasional articles have been written for policy/practitioner journals like *Media Development, Media Asia* and *InterMedia*, reaching a wider audience.

Being an internationalist, he has savoured stints as a visiting professor in France, Germany and Kazakhstan, plus at a score of campuses in Africa, South America, Europe, Asia and the Middle East affiliated with the institutions he has worked for. His critique of international business usually engenders interest from graduate students, though not always ("Will this be in the exam?"). With a longer-term dream of inaugurating an informal network of Professors Beyond Borders, Amos Owen Thomas welcomes collaboration on teaching and research—with particular relish if these should be on critical issues in developing, transitional and emerging economies.